I0640970

KEITH EARLS

FIGHT OR FLIGHT

MY LIFE, MY CHOICES

KEITH EARLS

FIGHT OR FLIGHT

MY LIFE, MY CHOICES

WITH TOMMY CONLON

Reach Sport

*This book is dedicated to all the
people in life who struggle to believe
in themselves*

Reach Sport

www.reachsport.com

Copyright © Keith Earls 2021.

The right of Keith Earls to be identified as the owner of this work has been asserted in accordance with the Copyright, Designs and Patents Act, 1988.

All Rights Reserved. No part of this publication may be reproduced, stored in a retrieval system, or transmitted in any form, or by any means, electronic, mechanical, photocopying, recording or otherwise without the prior permission in writing of the copyright holders, nor be otherwise circulated in any form of binding or cover other than in which it is published and without a similar condition being imposed on the subsequent publisher.

Published in Great Britain and Ireland in 2021 by
Reach Sport, a Reach PLC business,
5 St Paul's Square, Liverpool, L3 9SJ.

www.reachsport.com
@Reach_Sport

Reach Sport is a part of Reach PLC.
One Canada Square, Canary Wharf, London, E15 5AP.

Hardback ISBN: 9781914197093
eBook ISBN: 9781914197109

Photographic acknowledgements:
Keith Earls personal collection, Inpho, Sportsfile, Alamy.
Every effort has been made to trace the copyright.
Any oversight will be rectified in future editions.

Written with Tommy Conlon.
Design and production by Reach Sport.
Edited by Roy Gilfoyle.
Design: Rick Cooke.
With thanks to Gill Hess Ltd.

Printed and bound by CPI Group (UK) Ltd,
Croydon, CR0 4YY.

CONTENTS

Acknowledgements 1

Foreword 7

Introduction 13

1. On The Brink 19

2. Moyross 31

3. Rookie In Red 41

4. Ger And Sandra 55

5. The Lion Cub 71

6. Hank 83

7. Speed 107

8. Green 119

9. Career Guidance 137

10. Swimming 157

11. Anthony Foley RIP 167

12. The Waiting Game 175

13. Action And Suffering 199

14. Hard Labour 221

15. The Joe Show 233

16. Maldini 267

ACKNOWLEDGEMENTS

IN MY KIND OF CAREER, YOU SPEND MOST OF YOUR working life with men. No two ways about it, it's a man's world. And yet without the women in my life I don't think I'd have made it at all. They were so strong and influential for me, they helped me become a better man than I'd ever have been without their support and guidance.

I was absolutely blessed to meet the love of my life so young. We were just about into our teens when Edel and I started dating. And even at that age she was a rock of sense compared to me. In those years I was tempted more than once to go drinking and messing with my buddies. It might not have ended up well. But Edel had her principles. She wouldn't allow it, she didn't want to be with someone who was making wrong choices. So I stayed on the straight and narrow because she was more important to me – and thank God that I did. Otherwise I don't know how I'd have got through the struggles I've documented in this book. She suffered alongside me. There were times when it was probably harder on her than it was on me. She stuck with me through thick and thin, every step of the way. Edel is understated, she stays in the background, but more than anyone she is the reason I have had the career I had. I can't thank her enough for all she's done for me.

Becoming a mother brought out a whole new dimension in her. Becoming a father brought out a whole new dimension in me too. I love being a daddy to my three daughters. The girls have brought out emotions in me that I'd kept locked away before that. You can't not show your emotions when you've got three girls at home. They want their hugs and cuddles and they make no bones about wanting them! Ella May is nine now, Laurie six, Emie three. I was twenty-four when Ella was born. I copped myself on fairly quickly after that. All I really knew about life until then was rugby and sport and having the craic with the lads. The three girls gave me a far deeper appreciation of life. Providing for them became my number one priority. Every big decision we make as a couple, we make for them. When they tell you that you are their everything, it's all you need to hear. Ella, Laurie and Emie will be the light of my life for ever and a day.

A bit like Edel, my mother stayed in the background too and was also amazingly supportive to me in every way. She doesn't get half the credit she deserves for the role she played in my life and my career. When my father was away working and training and playing, it was me and my mother together. She encouraged me in my sport without ever telling me to do it. We spent hundreds of hours in the car together going to training and games and physio and school. She always made sure I was on time and that I was organised.

My mother and father took their time about giving me a sibling! But when Jenny came along she brought great joy and happiness into our family. I was delighted to have a baby sister. I even did a bit of the bottle-feeding when my parents were stuck. Having to take care of Jenny helped me grow up and

ACKNOWLEDGEMENTS

prepared me for fatherhood just a few years later. I will always look out for Jenny as she makes her way in the world.

At that time I was making my way in the world of pro rugby. I wouldn't have got to that stage without all my underage coaches at Thomond RFC who gave so much of their time to make me a better player, and to teach me the values that are part of the sport. Not just me but the thousands of other young people who they took under their wing. And all of it done voluntarily for the love of the game. The older I get, the more I appreciate how important their work was and still is.

John Broderick became an important mentor to me in my late teenage years at St Munchin's College. It was John who paved the way for me to get back to Munchin's so as I could play Munster schools senior cup rugby. In terms of preparing me for the fulltime game, those years were vital.

Winning the senior cup remains one of my favourite memories from my whole career. John looked after that team so well. He spoke to us as grown-ups. He treated us with respect and passed on to us a huge amount of his rugby knowledge.

Eddie Fraher was another person who looked out for me in those years. Eddie gave me one of my first jobs, working in his bar in Limerick to make a bit of pocket money. Then he offered me an electrician's apprenticeship with his company when I left school. I had the security of knowing that if the rugby didn't work out, I'd have a trade and a job to go back to. I am grateful to Eddie for his generous support of me in those years.

As it happened, the rugby did work out. Numerous coaches and team mates helped me get there. I thank them all for the good times we had together and the many ways in which they helped to improve me as a player and a colleague.

No one probably did more for me in that regard than Paul O'Connell. What I owe Paul I will never be able to pay back. He took me under his wing when I first joined the professional ranks and basically he has been there for me ever since, right up to this day. His advice and support went way beyond rugby. I needed someone in this environment to be my mentor, my confidante, my trusted friend. Paul has been all those things to me and more. His friendship means the world to me.

You get banged up a lot in this game. You need good people to put you back together again. I have had the best of people looking after my body over the years. Some of them were even pretty good at looking after my mind too, and that was no easy task. Many of them went beyond the call of duty in taking care of me. To all the physios, masseurs, doctors, rehab specialists, S&C staff who got me back onto the field to continue my career, I am really grateful not just for your expertise but for the compassion and patience you showed when I needed it most.

On the field, it has been a privilege to play in front of the best supporters anywhere in world rugby. Ireland fans have been kind and generous to me over the years. The Munster fans have been incredibly good to me down all the seasons. They took me to their hearts when I was starting out and never let go. It has been a fair old rollercoaster of a ride. I am eternally grateful for the amount of times they lifted me up and roared me on.

Off the field, I first met my agent John Baker as a 20-year-old when I was facing into the negotiations for my first contract. He looked after that contract and has been doing the job for me since. My sincere thanks to John for taking care of business all these years.

He sent me in the direction of Tommy Conlon when it came

ACKNOWLEDGEMENTS

to the writing of this book. I'm glad he did. Tommy has helped me put a narrative to my story. I struggled for years to put my life experiences into words. I have done that now. I couldn't be happier with how he has handled my story. My thanks also to Paul Dove at Reach Sport for giving me the opportunity to tell that story, and to Roy Gilfoyle for the great care he has taken with the text.

Finally, the man himself, my father. As I mention in the book, when I first started playing as a young fella, you'd hear people saying, "That's Ger Earls's lad". I'd be proud to hear it. He was my hero as well as my dad. He gave his whole life to protecting me, encouraging me, teaching me – being there for me. He is there for me still. I am still Ger Earls's lad. I thank him from the bottom of my heart for all he has given me and all that he continues to give us.

FOREWORD

by Ronan O'Gara

KEITH IS TEN YEARS YOUNGER THAN ME. IN PLAYING terms, that's a different generation. Me and my peers in the Munster squad were already a fairly battle-hardened crew when he arrived. You wouldn't be that easily impressed. Obviously he had loads of raw talent. But that's no guarantee of anything. You can't tell how any young fella is going to fare in professional rugby, no matter how good he looks.

And Keith was flashy. I mean in terms of his speed and his moves and his finishing skills. Limerick historically was famous for producing rugby forwards who would go through brick walls if they had to. It didn't often produce a player like Earlsie who was so polished and silky. But in personality he was the opposite of flashy. He was quiet, humble and hard-working. His approach to training was thorough and conscientious. So basically you had a new team mate here who wasn't your typical Munster player in one way, but was very much your typical

Munster player in terms of his attitude and character. He was just a sound, decent young fella.

Naturally enough we took to him more or less straightaway. I was mad about him, so was Paul O'Connell. We kind of minded him. He was like a baby brother to me in those years, I mean that genuinely. But sometimes I think the likes of me was maybe too influential on somebody like Keith. We were old-school. He was more like your prototype modern player that you see today. For example, he was technically very proper in how he did things. Power-lifting in the gym, he had the correct technique, very methodical, way better than many of us.

Whatever knowledge I had, I tried to pass it on to Keith and others. And he was very open to listening and learning. He wanted to improve as a player every day. But that means I also passed on a lot of the fear and self-doubt that was part of the Munster culture back then. We had an unbelievable work ethic but our psychology was wrong. We thought you had to go through mental and emotional turmoil to perform to your best. So I guess we passed that on to Earlsie too. It never occurred to us that you were actually allowed to enjoy the game! And because we were so intense about it all, I suppose Earlsie thought he had to follow suit too. None of us knew any better. We know a lot better now.

In the early years you could see him developing his speed and power nearly week by week. His acceleration was something else. That was his big point of difference. He could leave you for dead with one swerve. Within a year or two of him breaking into the first fifteen, if we were struggling in a match I'd be saying to myself, get the bloody ball out to Earlsie, he'll make something happen.

As he became more comfortable in the environment, another side of him came out. People might be surprised to hear that he has a wicked sense of humour. I mean wicked. He'd cut you in two with a dry remark. He used to love the old slagging matches. It's always the quiet ones you have to watch out for!

From time to time he would have confided in me that he was in a dark place. Earlsie has carried his burdens. I'm so pleased to hear that he is in a much happier place these times. I think he has found a peace within himself in the last two or three years – and it is showing on the pitch too. He understands that you can be relaxed and at ease with yourself going into games, rather than climbing the walls the way we used to back in the day. He has lasted long enough in the game to enjoy that more enlightened approach.

His longevity may have surprised some people but I personally always felt he could go deep into his thirties if he wanted to. That's because he was such a serious professional from day one. He didn't mess around with his fitness and athleticism, he didn't take it for granted. The fact that he was so technically accomplished, it has helped prolong his career too I feel.

I hope Earlsie realises how popular and respected he is among rugby fans. He probably doesn't. But you could see it in the reaction after he scored that brilliant try against England in the 2021 Six Nations. There might have been a few question marks over him going into that match but once again he did his talking on the field. People were genuinely delighted for him, the fact that he was still showing his bottle and class after more than ten years at the top. People had huge goodwill for him.

It couldn't happen to a better man. The fella has a heart of gold. He has stayed true to himself. He has stayed true to Munster.

FOREWORD

He has been the heartbeat of that team through an incredibly difficult last ten years. He will go down as an all-time great whenever he does hang up the boots. But that is for another day. In the meantime, I hope he keeps on dancing down that wing. I hope he keeps on keeping on.

Ronan O'Gara, September 2021

INTRODUCTION

I'M NOT SURE HOW I'VE ENDED UP DOING MY autobiography. It's not me at all to be doing anything remotely like this. I don't like talking about myself, I don't like bringing attention to myself. I try to do my job to the best of my ability without making a fuss about it. I haven't done much media stuff over the years. I've stayed away from the cameras and the microphones. They used to intimidate me. I don't mind doing interviews now but I still keep a low profile.

And in school I definitely wasn't the academic type. I wasn't the sort of student who'd be devouring books. In fact I barely opened a book after my Junior Cert. I was never great at the reading and writing. I'm still not, though I'm getting better at it. So all in all, doing a book is way out of my comfort zone.

And I guess that's one reason why I am doing it. We're supposed to get out of our comfort zone. I've learned enough along the way to know that much. It's where your progress and growth happens. Rugby has dragged me out of my comfort zone since the day I turned professional. Sometimes it has had to drag me kicking and screaming away from where I wanted to be. I hated it at times. But I'm glad now I went where it wanted to take me. Very glad. It has given me a life and a lifestyle I could only have dreamed about growing up. I actually did

dream about it growing up. Playing the game has changed my life in so many ways.

But there's a price to be paid for that too. The game has brought me to some very dark places. It has affected my mental health, at times badly. I brought some of those problems with me into pro rugby but they were made worse by the constant stress I used to feel about preparation and performance. Thankfully most of that stress is gone now. But I lived with it for the best part of 15 years and to some extent I'm still dealing with it. I've played nearly my whole career struggling with the stuff going on in my head.

That's another reason why I'm doing the book. I hope that telling my story will help me get rid of the secrecy and even shame I used to feel about it. The stigma of carrying around this private struggle all the time. I want to get it off my chest. I hope there'll be freedom in doing it, a release from the secrecy. If it helps other people too, especially young men, to open up about their mental health issues, then I'll be delighted. It will make the book worthwhile for that reason alone.

There's one other reason, maybe the biggest motivation of all. Not many people who come from the places in Ireland like I come from get the chance to tell their story to the public. I'm from "the wrong side of the tracks". To me it was and always will be the right side of the tracks but I know for society in general it is the wrong side. So, I feel I have a responsibility almost to explain how being branded like that can affect you. How it can affect your confidence, your wellbeing, your self-esteem, your whole future actually.

I had a teacher in school who told me when I was thirteen that I'd never amount to anything. This book is for all the kids who were told that, either directly or in the million other ways that you're told it, growing up in one of these forgotten places. There's an incredible amount of talent and intelligence and ability that gets wasted because they don't get the chance or because they don't feel they are worthy of getting the chance. I've been lucky enough to travel the world and meet people from all walks of life, brilliant people who've become good friends. And after all that, I can honestly say I still haven't met better than the people from my own community, in terms of their values and decency and integrity. I'm not saying this through rose-tinted glasses, it just happens to be true.

At the same time, my community was also blighted by a tiny number of people who chose to live a different kind of life. There's no point in glossing over that either. Our neighbourhood suffered far too much fear and trauma and heartache. And sadly it meant we were all painted with the one brush, we were all stigmatised for stuff that had nothing whatsoever to do with us.

I can put my hand on my heart and say I had a wonderful childhood. I was totally loved and supported by my parents. You walked out your front door and you were surrounded by loads of friends and neighbours who looked out for you. They say it takes a village to raise a child. In our village we were brought up together and you got a great sense of security from that feeling.

I want to tell that side of the story in this book. I would like to say to all the girls and boys from communities like mine that you can be who you want to be, you can go further than maybe you think, you have far more potential than maybe you realise. And that there's a lot of good people out there who will help you along the way. I got an awful lot of help along the way. I didn't do it on my own. There were times when I wanted to turn back.

INTRODUCTION

I had to learn how to be resilient. How to hang tough and stick with it until you turned the next corner.

I have learned an incredible amount along the way, about myself, about people, about how society works and about trying to find your place in it. I hope if I can share some of my life experiences here, it might inspire others, especially the boys who like me weren't mad about reading but who might be tempted to pick up this particular book and give it a go. I would love if that were to happen.

1

ON THE BRINK

THAT TRY AGAINST ENGLAND IN THE 2021 SIX Nations. It wasn't as good as I thought it was in real time. The build-up was slick alright but looking back at the finish on video, I could've stepped Jonny May a bit sharper. It was sharp enough to get the job done but it was more a shuffle than a step. I took my time about cutting inside him! Thrilled to score it, delighted to get it, a career highlight. But the cameras don't lie and when I reviewed it later that evening, I'd have liked the step to be a bit more lethal than it was. I know I should enjoy these moments more because they don't come along very often. But I'm in the habit of being self-critical. Any sportsperson serious about their trade will be self-critical because that's the road to self-improvement.

At the same time you can be too hard on yourself. I'm trying to get the balance right but it's still a work in progress. I'm definitely not as hard on myself as I used to be. I've spent most of my career punishing myself for not being better. And if I wasn't beating myself up in my mind, I'd be beating myself up in my body. In fact the physical toll got so bad in the previous three years that if I had my way, I wouldn't have scored that try against England because I wouldn't have been on the field. I'd have been retired.

Six months earlier I'd told Johann van Graan I was retiring with immediate effect. It was a Monday morning in September 2020. Leinster had beaten us in the Pro14 semi-final a few days earlier. That result hadn't improved my mood either but it ended Munster's season and I was sure it was the end of my career too. Myself and my wife, Edel, had discussed it over and over in the previous months. We'd both agreed it was time to pull the plug. Edel will tell you the previous three years were hell. I was at the end of my tether and I think she was at the end of her tether dealing with me. Something had to give and it was going to be my career.

The truth is that from about 2017 to the end of 2020 my lung capacity was only functioning at about 50 per cent. Maybe it was more than that but it felt about half of it had been cut off. Like, I couldn't fill my lungs with air. I couldn't take the deep gulps of oxygen you need to take when you're running round a field for eighty minutes. It felt like there was a small soccer ball sitting in my chest and it wouldn't let my lungs expand. It felt like a bear was hugging me. I just couldn't get my ribcage to expand. So I was constantly gasping for breath. One piece of action and I'd be panting hard. One carry and I'd be praying the ball wouldn't come near me for another couple of minutes.

I was covering it up, I was hiding the problem and getting through game after game on pure desperation and stubbornness and match experience. The irony is that I was playing some of the best rugby of my life in that period. I started every game in the 2018 Grand Slam campaign. I received the Players' Player of the Year Award for that season, which was a huge personal honour.

But to give you an idea, the following summer, in a pre-season camp before the 2019 World Cup, we were doing a sort of grappling session one day in training on the grounds of Carton House. The idea was that you'd have the ball and your man would have thirty seconds to try and rip it away from you. My partner this day was Johnny Sexton. Johnny started wrestling with me and after about ten or fifteen seconds I had to give up. It was the first time in my life I gave up on anything on a rugby field. But I wasn't able to keep going. I couldn't get the air into my lungs. I couldn't hold onto the ball. I was just too weak and fatigued. I had to go down on my hands and knees to get my breath back. Then we had to do a run after the wrestling session but I wasn't able to. I stayed down on my hands and knees. One of the physios came over to me and I was close to tears.

I was living with this situation every day for maybe four years in all. It was an absolute torment. I was getting huge amounts of physio but all it was doing was patching me up to survive the next game.

I had all sorts of scans and x-rays and medical opinions but nobody could get to the bottom of it. The best they could come up with was that it was related to my back. I'd always struggled with back issues anyway, probably because I'd damaged it doing weights too young. My father Ger was playing with Young Munsters in the All-Ireland League and he had a makeshift gym in our back yard. I used to sneak in when he was away at work and be lifting various weights. I had kyphosis as well, a slight curvature on my upper back.

By the time the problem became a crisis I was regularly getting back spasms. I couldn't even pick up the kids for fear of causing a spasm. If they wanted to go rollerblading or on the trampoline, Daddy couldn't join in cos he was minding his back. I couldn't even walk the dog. On top of that I was dealing with an undiagnosed hiatal hernia that was churning up acid reflux in my stomach. The food I was eating was driving it mad. I'd be belching and burping all the time, the sick would be coming back up in my mouth. A few months ago they put a scope down my throat and found that my oesophagus was burnt from the acid, it was red raw.

Physically I was a mess which meant that mentally I was a mess too. It was a complete mind bender. But because the medical people couldn't get to the bottom of the problem, a few of them started dropping hints that it could all be in my head. This pissed me off even more. I was unbelievably frustrated about that. I've learned enough about my mental condition to know my brain and to know when I'm in a bad place emotionally and psychologically. This time there was something definitely wrong with me physically.

One of the running repairs was acupuncture, putting needles in my chest and my abs to try and get a bit of relief from the spasms. At half-time in games I'd be getting needled to loosen up the back spasms I'd picked up in the first half. Sometimes it worked, sometimes it didn't. There were days I went out and felt okay and thought I'd maybe put it behind me only for it to flare up again the next day.

A couple of x-rays showed I had degenerative discs in my

spine so they guessed that this might be the root of the problem. Arthritis or something like it. So I was sent to a rheumatologist and he prescribed Enbrel, a medication for arthritis. I was injecting it into my thigh for a year. Nothing improved. Coming up to the 2019 World Cup I was on the physio bed first thing in the morning, after training in the afternoon, and evenings too. I was taking two or three hot baths a day. In Japan I was soaking myself in their Onsens, their mineral baths, all just trying to survive from day to day.

For years I had physios working on me who went beyond the call of duty trying to fix me. Ray McGinley in particular stuck with me through thick and thin. If I was earning soccer player wages I'd put Ray on my payroll and keep him for myself, he's been that important to me. A lot of the time their treatment would work for a short while too and afterwards I'd feel great, but once I went training again the next day, I'd be knackered all over again. It was all maintenance work but it was very high maintenance and ultimately unsustainable.

Every day going into training, I was dreading it. Would I be able to get through the session? I wanted to do every session. I didn't want to be hanging around just doing a few laps and a few warm-ups. I didn't want to be treated as a special case. But a lot of the time I had to ease off and not share the same workload as everyone else.

Lots of days I did no training at all. I ended up feeling guilty and paranoid about that. Was I losing the respect of my team mates? I was still getting picked at the weekends but I wasn't doing the same amount of daily graft that they were doing. It didn't seem fair to me and that troubled me. I'd usually manage to hang in in games and get through them but there were games when I wasn't even able to do that. I remember when Munster played Saracens at the Aviva in the European Cup semi-final in 2017, they were on the attack early doors. I blasted into a ruck trying to disturb their ball. The effort lasted about ten seconds and I was gasping for air after it. I just felt my chest cavity closing in on me like there was this big pressure sitting on my chest. And I remember thinking, 'Oh my God, there's another seventy minutes of this to go'. I was taken off after an hour or so.

In hindsight it was stupid of me trying to keep going, especially in the big games. I think I should have just bailed out and told everyone I wasn't able anymore. But in Limerick and Munster rugby the golden rule growing up was that you didn't give up. You never gave up. You played through the pain barrier, no excuses. I was old-school like that too so I just bulled along and said nothing. But at home I'd unload it all on Edel. Many a night in bed I'd be telling her I can't do this anymore and every morning I'd get up and do it again.

But by September 2020 I'd run out of road. The 2019/20 season had been suspended in March because of the pandemic and I'd plenty of time to mull it over during that spring and summer. When it resumed in August I was still battling with the same problems. There was still no sign of a solution and I was just sick of the whole damn situation.

And that's what brought me to Van Graan's door a few days after the 2020 season ended. It was in one of the Munster rugby offices at our high performance centre in UL. I told him the whole story, I told him I was quitting. I told him I was drained mentally and physically. Johann sat and listened. He was very understanding. I think he was a bit shocked as well. He asked if I could give him thirty-six hours to think about it. He came back to me a few days later and laid out his reasons why I should reconsider.

He was rebuilding the Munster squad, there were exciting times ahead, a lot of young talent was coming through and he'd love to have me onboard as one of the experienced voices in the squad. That was definitely something that was giving me a quandary alright, the prospect of playing with the new generation. Johann also said that they'd review my whole medical experience with this condition and try to get to the bottom of it once and for all. They would do a sort of full NCT on me. In the meantime the physios would work on my right ankle and knee and hips because they'd been giving me a lot of gyp too.

Then Stephen Larkham called to my house and we had a great chat. I have massive respect for Stephen as a coach and for his achievements as a player with Australia. He'd been through the mill as well with injuries and we talked a lot about the psychological darkness that comes along with them. He advised me to have a rethink. He said I'd be retired long enough. But the main thing for me was that he showed he cared and that he understood what I was going through.

I made no decision at the time, either to stay or go. I just continued with the rehab, undecided about whether to pull the plug or not.

A few weeks later Andy Farrell rang me. The 2020 Six Nations was resuming in October, would I be available for training camp? We had two games left, against Italy and France. I appreciated the call but I turned him down. I didn't tell him what I'd told Johann but I told him I wasn't fit, I was as well to continue with my rehab in Limerick. Andy was sound about it.

But then Jordan Larmour got injured playing for Leinster after the Ireland squad was announced so myself and Andy had another conversation and I said I would go in. I'd been having second thoughts anyway. Who was I to be turning down my country? When the Ireland head coach comes calling you say yes every time.

My head wasn't in the right place when I said no the first time but I was clear about it this time. I said to him, yeah, I've got through this the last few years so I might as well do it one last time. He said there'd be no pressure to play in the Italy game, just come in and do the rehab with us. Then Garry Ringrose got injured playing against Italy and Andy asked me could I make myself available for the France game. I just told him straight out that I wasn't right in myself and I'd be a liability to the team. Even to say that was a big deal for me.

It had taken me ten years to win something with Ireland and now there was a chance of us winning another championship, depending on the results on the day. Normally I'd have been desperate to play in a game of that magnitude but it was a sign of how bad I was feeling.

I rejoined the lads in Carton House. As it turned out, France beat us in Paris and England took the title. Two weeks later we had Wales in Dublin in the Autumn Nations Cup. I was put on the bench for that one. I was sent out to warm up behind the goals with about fifteen minutes left to play. And I remember cursing and swearing with vexation. One of the lads asked me what was wrong and I was like, for fuck's sake, this fuckn thing is back again. I couldn't even manage the warm-up without seizing up inside. They sent me on for the last nine minutes and it was plenty, I was just about able to survive.

We were playing England in Twickenham eight days later. It turned out to be a very lucky break. Phil Glasgow, head of physiotherapy and rehabilitation with the IRFU, was looking after me at Carton House. Phil has huge experience in his field, he was chief physiotherapist for Team GB at the Rio Olympics in 2016. I had discussed my whole medical history with him. Phil would go through our routine and loosen me out and do all the soft tissue work. He'd have his fingers buried in my diaphragm trying to stretch it all out.

And because we were going to London he decided to contact the breathing specialists he knew there and set up an appointment for me. I'd be travelling over with the Ireland squad so we'd be exempt from the Covid-19 quarantine.

We flew over on the Thursday. I got straight into a taxi from the airport with Stephen Mutch who'd just started as lead physio with the national team. At this stage the team for England had been announced and I was selected. So my anxiety levels were starting to escalate again.

We arrived at the Institute of Sport, Exercise and Health on the Tottenham Court Road. I got all the MRIs done and various ultrasounds as well. The consultant we were meeting had all my reports and scans from Ireland too. Another doctor spotted something in a scan that she wanted to have a closer look at. The two of them conferred and came to a conclusion. It was my liver that was possibly at the root of the whole problem. The consultant said he'd seen the same symptoms in a cyclist and a rower he'd worked with. They figured that the ligaments holding it in place had been loosened over the years, probably from getting banged up playing rugby. As a result the liver was sort of floating a bit, it was sliding up into my chest and pushing up against my diaphragm and that's what was affecting my back and breathing. It was a breathing dysfunction caused by the liver not being held in place. It seemed to make sense. I was just relieved they didn't find some sort of terminal disease because that was a thought that had crossed my mind more than once over the previous three years.

But I had a game against England forty-eight hours later. What was I supposed to do about that? They said the only thing I could do was strap it up. Strap up the ribcage as tight as possible and hope it would keep the liver tied down. It wasn't a very high-tech solution but it was the best they could come up with.

Stephen Mutch taped me up about an hour before the game. He used this really strong medical strapping. It felt like a straitjacket and there were times in the previous few years when I was close enough to being put in one.

I jogged out for the warm-up and a miracle happened. I was breathing free. I was filling my lungs. I was taking in huge gulps of oxygen right down to my guts. It was hitting the sweet spot. I could feel the satisfaction of filling my lungs.

The strapping was doing its job. It was holding everything in place. I could feel the tension of it against my ribs every time I breathed in and breathed out. Christ, I was buzzing. I was suddenly feeling ten foot tall. I was like, here we go, this is class. Bar the few minutes against Wales, I hadn't played a game in ten weeks but I didn't care. I could run, I could tackle, I could hit rucks and I could do it over and over without feeling I was asphyxiating.

We lost to England but I was just delighted to be back on a field feeling normal again. I lasted the full eighty minutes. That was the game where I left this long black tunnel behind me and came back into the light of day. It felt life-changing.

It was definitely career-changing. All of a sudden I was mad for road again. The retirement chat with Johann van Graan was a fading memory. Instead of quitting I was back starting in the 2021 Six Nations and capping it all off with the try against England – and a win against the old enemy too.

By then the IRFU had offered me a new central contract for another year. My current one was due to expire in the summer of 2021 and for the previous twelve months I was sure it would be the last. I signed in March for a deal that will take me up to the summer of 2022.

I got great satisfaction out of signing this one, having come through the three years of darkness. The fact that it was a central contract made it all the more fulfilling when you consider the amount of brilliant back-three players who have come through the system. There are loads of them snapping at my heels, I know that, and the day is fast approaching when I won't be able to keep them at bay.

I'm not one for talking myself up but I think the fact they offered me a new deal was reward for being a conscientious professional. For looking after myself and doing all the extras day in day out for ten years and more. Deep down, and this was very personal to me, I felt like it was just reward for persevering through the nightmare. Nobody knew how bad it was, except probably for Edel. To survive all that and come out the other side and get a new contract was one of the most satisfying moments of my career.

I suppose it's the old cliché come to life. The darkest hour is before the dawn. It was fairly bleak the day I walked into

Johann's office to tell him I was finished. A few months later I was raring to go like a young fella. It wasn't the end of the story, it was the turning of a new page and the start of another chapter just when I thought the book was about to be closed for good.

2

MOYROSS AND ME

I FIRST MET EDEL M^CGEE WHEN WE WERE IN OUR early teens. She was the first girl I met who wasn't from Moyross. I clapped eyes on her one day in Fitzgerald Park, home ground of Thomond RFC, after an Under 13s cup final. I knew pretty much straightaway that she was the one. Luckily enough she thought I was the one too. We started hanging round with her friends and my friends. We started going out. We've been together ever since. We have three daughters together. She has been my rock, my friend, the person I rely on for just about everything outside of rugby. I'm trying not to sound too corny so I'll just say she is a wonderful mother and a very good person.

We went to the same secondary school, St Nessan's Community College, but she was from Woodview, a housing estate on the other side of St Nessan's. The school and the big gates and walls separated us so I had to do a lot of climbing and jumping over all sorts of security fences and sneaking over people's back walls to see her. Obviously I wasn't going to let any barriers come between us!

We started dating when we were about thirteen. I'd be climbing over the wall most evenings to hang out with Edel and our friends. I had to cross the school's big open field to get to the wall. The field had a stone path through it. My route would bring me through different parts of Moyross. One night when I was sixteen I hopped the wall as per usual on my way home. I was close to my house when I heard footsteps behind me. I could feel footsteps behind me. I took a quick glance over my shoulder and saw two fellas wearing hoodies and baseball caps. I was wearing a hoodie and baseball cap too. They were following me and getting closer. It was pitch dark, I couldn't make out who they were. I started walking faster. A narrow black stony pathway would bring me through the houses and round to my home place in Dalgaish Park. I didn't fancy getting caught on that walkway. It was a scary enough place at night anyway. After a dozen metres of walking fast I just panicked and burst into a sprint. They started running after me. The bit of pace I had came in handy. I tore down the path but I knew I wouldn't be able to get the key out of my pocket and open the front door before they caught up with me. So I started shouting for my father at the top of my voice. "Dad! Dad! Dad!". I hurdled the garden wall and turned round to them as they were closing in and whipped off my cap to show who I was. I said, "What the fuck?" And they looked at me and realised I wasn't who they thought I was. And they just said, "Uh, we thought you were someone else", and turned around and walked away. My heart was pounding out through my chest. It frightened the daylights out of me.

I thought about it for months afterwards. What would they have done if they got me? Maybe they were planning to get me in the dark area and go to work on me there. I was thinking how different it could've been if they decided to attack first and ask questions later. I reckon they thought I'd been in a certain house, that they were waiting for a target to come out of it and when I appeared they figured I was him. They got their wires crossed. It's the closest I've ever come to being personally threatened during the gang feud that lasted in Limerick for a decade.

Truth be told, most of the time you'd forget it was happening, even though you knew it was simmering away in the background. Then it would erupt again in various parts of the city and it would be all over the TV news and the newspapers for a few days. And after that, everyone would get back to their daily lives until the next episode happened. Moyross wasn't the worst affected area, not by a long distance, but there were shootings and stabbings and killings there too. The place already had a bad reputation and this only made it worse. But actually for most of the time it was just normal living. Me and my mates never really worried about it. We'd be there kicking a ball on the green from morning till night and we were happy out. We were too young and naïve to know any better, I suppose.

But the thing is, what we didn't appreciate was that our parents were doing all the worrying for us. They had to be constantly on the look-out for where we were, who we were with, where we were going. In hindsight I think the feuding and the constant barrage of media coverage took away their peace of mind. They couldn't rest easy.

I could never understand why my father hated me wearing

hoodies and baseball caps. That's what every young lad wore on the estate so why should I be any different? But that was the reason why. Mistaken identity. You could be mistaken for one of the gang members. It's what happened to me that night. Or you could just be in the wrong place at the wrong time. Dad was always on to me about the hoodies and baseball caps. He wouldn't let me out in them. He'd make me change into a shirt and jacket, no cap. Of course I'd smuggle them out of the house anyway. A few times I was hanging out with my mates somewhere on the estate and he'd drive around in the car with a change of clothes for me. He literally drove up, got out of the car and made me change my clothes.

Dad was totally paranoid about protecting me and I think I ended up inheriting a shade of that paranoia too. That's one of the lesser-known effects of growing up in an atmosphere of fear. It heightens everyone's anxiety. It puts everyone on edge. Your peace of mind gets eroded. Every parent becomes anxious when their child isn't at home. There's just this anxiety hovering around in the background while people are getting on with their daily lives. At the time I didn't think any of it was bothering me at all. I was too busy running around playing sport and hanging out with my mates. Moyross was just one big playground to me and my friends. We were having a great time. But in hindsight I realise now that some of that anxiety was seeping into me too. Like every child I was picking up the signals from the grown-ups and absorbing them into me without knowing. Edel tells me I'm awful paranoid about things and she's probably right. I'm slow to trust people I suppose, I'm always on guard in one way or another. I'm sure some of my team mates have found me a bit of an oddball in ways.

But I suppose most people haven't seen a fella in a balaclava firing bullets outside their front door. It was a beautiful summer's day and I was out playing pool with my cousin in our back garden. We had this little pool table at home and the day was so good we decided to bring it out to the garden and play a few frames out there. Next thing we heard a load of shots. Really loud bangs. So I dropped the pool cue and ran through my house and out to the front porch. And there was this fella wearing a balaclava and he's holding a handgun out and firing shots at a bunch of lads who are running down the road. As soon as we saw it we dashed back inside terrified. Dad came out and slammed the front door shut and told us to stay inside. Next thing there was nothing but silence. We waited ages for something else to happen but all was quiet. The next morning Dad went out to work. He had started his own business as a floor fitter for schools and hospitals and commercial premises. He had bought a new van, it was parked outside in the driveway, but when he turned the key in the ignition it wouldn't start. So he lifted the bonnet and suddenly there was a shaft of sunlight coming through it. The bonnet was hit and the engine had a bullet plugged in it. The gunman maybe was trying to scare off these fellas with a volley of shots, I don't know. But it wasn't a great start to my father's working day, I'd have to say.

I should emphasise that this only happened to us once. It was not a regular occurrence, it never happened before or after. I don't think our family ever felt targeted or in immediate danger. I think it was more the fear that on a random day you could just be in the wrong place at the wrong time. But otherwise we were fine. There was a lot of respect for Dad in the community because of his reputation as a leading rugby player in Limerick at the time and because he was a hardworking family man. And he was involved a lot in organising football games on the green for all the local boys and girls. He'd be down after work of an evening getting a kickaround going and generally trying to be a good person in the community. Ninety per cent of the people in Moyross were great neighbours. They had a heart of gold. They'd do anything for you. It's just there was always this small anti-social element who'd cause trouble way out of proportion to their numbers. Joyriding was a regular source of entertainment for them. A bunch of young fellas robbing cars and driving them at top speeds around the estate. I would often wake up to the sound of a robbed car flying up and down the road outside and the engine revving and handbrake turns being pulled. I think the joyriders chose our road because if the guards came they'd be able to jump out of the car and escape through the alleyway. No cars could get through there.

I remember one night being in bed asleep and waking up with a shock because there was this awful bang outside. It was like someone had crashed through our front door. I ran to the bedroom window and down below was a car that had just ploughed through the pillar on our driveway and into the neighbour's garden where it came to a halt after knocking over their front wall as well. The driver got out and scarpered, leaving this crumpled up car behind him with smoke rising out of it.

The problems in our area were mainly to do with anti-social behaviour like this until the drugs started up in a big way. With that came the crime wave, the feuding gangs, the shootings and assaults and intimidation. I always had my sports and my family to keep me on the straight and narrow. But a lot of the lads I would've grown up with began experimenting with drugs and a few of them went down the wrong route. It was easy money, it was during the Celtic Tiger years and a lot of respectable people with plenty of cash were indulging themselves too. The supply had to come from somewhere. There was unbelievable amounts of money to be made. Again, Moyross was not the main hub of this business but enough people got involved to bring the crime war to our doorsteps from time to time. Our area was never going to escape unscathed.

You were fairly used to seeing Garda patrol cars coming in and out of the estate, questioning lads and searching them and sometimes making arrests. Then as things heated up you were starting to see armed detectives arriving in unmarked cars and jeeps and eventually police helicopters flying overhead too. I remember walking to school one morning and there was a big white tent on the path we would usually take, there was people in white overalls, forensics people examining someone who had been murdered during the night. You wouldn't be paying too much attention to the teacher on days like that.

Nobody really talked much about these incidents, or at least not to us children anyway. I'm sure the adults talked about it behind closed doors. Nowadays I suppose children will get counselling if there's been an act of violence in the community. There wasn't any counselling or talking about it back then. Like, you'd be told, you'd be warned, what roads to stay away from, what people to stay away from, and that was about it. But it was kind of in one ear and out the other.

I remember another time seeing a fella being stabbed. I was upstairs in our house and I heard a load of shouting coming up from the street below so I went into my parents' bedroom for a look out the window. There were three or four fellas in the corner across the road, late teens I suppose. They had surrounded another lad, he was the centre of attention, they were pinning him in, and one of the other blokes was jabbing away at him with a knife of some sort. I must've been around ten or eleven at the time. Suddenly they all split, running away. And the fella, the victim, he staggered away holding his stomach.

A cousin of mine was killed in a car accident when I was twelve. Thomas Boyce was nineteen, my father's nephew, they were very close, always knocking around together. I was coming out of the national school one day, Corpus Christi, and my aunt's husband was waiting for me at the gate. He told me to get in the car, he was bringing me to their house. I remember thinking this was a bit strange. It was down in the house then they told me about Thomas and the car accident. He was in the army, he'd just come back from a tour of duty in the Lebanon. He was driving through Tipperary and collided with a lorry.

A few weeks later I was home one afternoon, I was still in my primary school uniform, Mam and Dad were out working. I was sitting down on the couch and thinking about Thomas and it just hit me that I'd never see him again. It just hit me that that was what death meant. You'd never see the person again. It just freaked me out then, the realisation that when your father and mother died you'd never see them again. Next thing I broke out into the shivers. I was trembling. I was starting to sweat like mad and my breathing was really fast and shallow. The first time it happened I thought I was going to die myself, it was so strong. I was vibrating from head to toe and trying to catch my breath. I didn't know what to call it at the time but it was a full-on panic attack. I was proper scared. Eventually I calmed down. I never told anyone. I never told anyone about the panic attacks I had right throughout my teens. We went to a lot of funerals in those years, suicides, cancer, drownings, violence.

For a finish you ended up getting a bit numbed by it all. I was always fearing the worst. I wasn't religious but I was superstitious. I wouldn't go anywhere without my rosary beads. I'd be blessing myself because I thought something bad would happen if I didn't. I'd have a different set of rosary beads for each person who died in my family and I'd have a mortuary card and I'd have to kiss each one three times in bed at night to make sure they'd be okay in heaven or wherever they were. I'd say a prayer three times for every person who was dear to me. I had no interest in Mass or religion but I went through these rituals every night for a few years. It's no wonder Edel says I was "very deep" for a young fella. She says I was "very quiet" and "a bit odd". I must have been a great catch altogether! Honestly I don't know how she put up with me at times but Jesus I'm glad she did.

Overall it's fair to say I didn't come from what you'd call a typical rugby background. My home place was a bit rough around the edges alright. I wouldn't want my children to witness what I saw. They are growing up in what you'd call a nice part of town. It's lovely and peaceful. But I miss the old community spirit we had in Moyross. I miss the way everybody knew everybody, the warmth and openness and the feeling that we were all in it together. I grew up with the best of people. I miss that fantastic sense of community we had and I miss it a little bit for my kids too.

3

ROOKIE IN RED

MY FIRST MORNING AS A PROFESSIONAL RUGBY player, I did my weights and speed work. Then a gang of us had breakfast in the sports bar in UL and started playing darts for a few hours. It was a Monday morning. The Friday before was my last day working construction. Up at the crack, out to a building site on the South Circular Road in the cold and dark, chasing wires up walls and into attics and through the joists of roofs and all that. Sockets, smoke alarms, second fixings – there was loads to learn. I was registered with FÁS as well. You'd be going out to a classroom in Shannon to study the manuals and learn a bit about electrical circuits and the technical side of things. I took to the job pretty well.

During the early months I came home one day and fixed a loose socket that was hanging off the wall in my father's shed. It had loose wires, he got a shock off them once or twice when he was plugging something into it. So I tidied it up and put a proper socket box on it and I was delighted with myself. I actually got a few bangs myself from live electrics. I remember being on a new house-build one day and one of the other tradesmen had broken a socket so I had to go and fix it. But with my inexperience I forgot to turn off the fuse at the fuse board and I touched the live wire and gave myself a right old whack. The odd time in a newspaper article you'd see someone mentioning your "electric pace". I was fairly electric that day alright.

I did six or seven months of my apprenticeship. I'd like to have kept it on but it just wouldn't have been possible time-wise. But I'm glad I had a bit of work experience in the real world before becoming a pampered rugby professional. I'd worked summers with my father when he was a self-employed floor fitter. That was hard graft and long days. I delivered bread with my uncle when he was driving for Irish Pride. You'd be up at four or five in the morning heading with a full van for places like Croom, Kilmallock, Bruff and back into the city. I worked part-time in a bar and did a day selling Wexford strawberries on the side of the road. One day was plenty, flogging punnets of strawberries for a fiver to the odd passing motorist who'd pull up to make a purchase. I think I got forty quid for standing all day on the side of the road. I didn't see a career in it.

In January 2007 I graduated to a development contract after eighteen months in the academy. Declan Kidney was head coach and he'd been monitoring my progress. I think he reckoned it was time to wrap me up in cotton wool a bit. He'd see me coming into training in the evenings in my building site gear so I was basically trying to be a serious athlete while doing a full day's work as well. Deccie thought I should be given the chance to go fulltime at the rugby. My father and him had a preliminary discussion about it and then the Munster CEO, the late Garrett Fitzgerald, got involved. He recommended that I get myself an agent to look after my career. John Baker represented Paul O'Connell so we got John on board too. We met in the Clarion Hotel – it's now the Clayton – on the Dock Road, myself and Dad and John and Garrett and I signed on the dotted line. The money was fairly modest but I didn't care about that. It was my first pro contract, I was on the first rung of the professional ladder.

The lads throwing darts with me that day would go on to become team mates and friends, Ian Dowling, Barry Murphy, Ciaran O'Boyle, Mossy Lawler, Jerry Flannery. Unfortunately it wasn't going to be all fun and games – Declan Kidney had warned me to stay away from the PlayStation. He warned me he'd rip up the contract if he heard I was going home every day and spending hours on the PlayStation. But sure what else was a lad of nineteen with time on his hands going to do?! It was better than spending my afternoons in the pub and bookies anyway. And Deccie was hardly going to follow me out to the house in Moyross to keep tabs on me.

I settled into the daily routine surrounded by all these legends of Munster rugby and more or less kept my mouth shut and my ears open for the next couple of years. The senior game was a whole new ball game compared to the underage scene and these fellas had incredible knowledge and experience to pass on to rookies like me.

My electrical apprenticeship was over; my rugby apprenticeship had begun. I would learn loads too in the rough and tumble world of club rugby. I did a season with Thomond RFC in the AIL Division 2 and then transferred to Garryowen for 2007/08. It was an unwritten rule with Munster that I'd register with an AIL Division 1 club, which ruled out Thomond and Young Munster. At Garryowen we made it to the AIL final against Cork Con in May 2008. Our semi-final was a local derby with Shannon at Coonagh. That's a game you'll always want to win and on that occasion we were dominant. Garryowen had pipped Con by a point in the final the year before and this time round Con had their revenge, winning by ten points in Musgrave Park. That was the end of my club career.

I made my Munster senior debut on April 7 2007 against the Ospreys at Liberty Stadium in a Magners League match. I came off the bench after sixty-five minutes to replace Anthony Horgan. A week earlier Munster had surrendered their Heineken Cup crown in the quarter-final against Llanelli at Stradey Park. So they were fielding a lot of squad players for Ospreys and they decided to give me a taste of the action too. I was a bag of nerves on the bench waiting for my chance. I was still coming to terms with my new station in life. I was playing with lads that were still heroes to me rather than team mates. They were European champions the previous season so it was all a bit surreal for me to actually be playing with them now. And on the opposing team that day was another legend, Shane Williams, the Welsh try scoring machine.

All I remember is that someone played a ball through to Williams and I went to tackle him and caught him high and gave away a penalty. Ospreys won that day but still, my family were delighted. They got to see me make my debut on television. My grandfather Billy Earls was proud as punch. The next day Thomond U20s had a second division final against Clonakilty in Musgrave Park. The winner would be promoted to the first

division. Dad was coaching the team at the time along with
Aidan O'Halloran. Deccie gave me the green light to play. I
ended up busting my AC joint and that was the end of my
season.

I made the bench for the Heineken Cup final a year later. It
was the first time I'd ever been involved in a European game. I
was getting minutes here and there during the Magners League
that season. It was a toss-up between Kieran Lewis and myself
for the last jersey on the big day. I didn't find out until the
Thursday that it was going to be me and then we flew out to
Cardiff on the Friday. I had to brush up on our playbook fairly
lively.

Again, it was all a bit surreal to me. I had been following
Munster's famous European odyssey as a fan like everyone else
for the previous decade. And Jesus here I was now on the team
bus on our way to the Millennium Stadium and the streets of
Cardiff an absolute sea of red. I had watched those scenes on
the TV for years. And now I was on the bus looking out at
the supporters cheering and holding up their pint glasses and
waving to us and banging on the sides of it. I welled up a bit. I
got emotional. This was really living the dream.

I had an outside chance of getting on the field. At one stage
Rua Tipoki got split open and I had to warm up but they
patched him up and he carried on. Dougie Howlett had a late
try chalked off and I think I might've got a few minutes if it
had been allowed because that would have made the game safe.
Obviously the dressing room was a very happy place afterwards.
It was all sweetness and light. Which made a change from the
usual effing and blinding and being ratty and pissed off with
each other. There was always someone cranky about something!

I'd be keeping the head down listening to them scotching and swearing at each other. They were like brothers arguing with each other all the time. That was how they showed their love for each other I suppose!

I received a medal that day but I don't consider myself a Heineken Cup winner. I wasn't part of it, I had nothing to do with it, I didn't contribute. There were fellas there who'd given their lives to it; I'd just rocked up that season. In fairness, the lads made me feel very much part of it. They were giving me the cup to hold up and when we did the open top bus tour of Limerick they were handing it to me as well to give it a boost but I was a bit sheepish about it. I found it a bit embarrassing although I knew the Limerick people were proud of me and happy for me.

I seldom went pubbing and clubbing and when I did, it was usually non-alcoholic drinks. Being disciplined, sticking to the straight and narrow was always in my head. But Christ I made an exception for it the night we arrived back into Limerick with the cup. Eventually the squad got back to the Clarion Hotel in the early hours of Sunday morning and sure there was no point in going to bed at that stage. All the wives and partners were there too. I ended up greeting the dawn with I think Paul Warwick and Dougie and Tomás O'Leary and a few other diehards.

I was a useless drinker until I got going and usually I wouldn't get going because I'd bail out along with John Hayes. He wasn't a party man either, the two of us would smoke bomb when everyone else was on the lash. Some of the lads had hollow legs, they could pour it down the gullet for days if they wanted to. This was one of the few days and nights I went the distance. We did the bus tour of the city on the Sunday, ended up in the Sin Bin nightclub and then back to the Clarion to greet the dawn again! Back at it again then Monday afternoon with Mossy Lawler in the Corner Flag on Henry Street with a few of the other lads joining us throughout the day. The Corner Flag is closed now sadly, it was a great Young Munsters house. I had my eighteenth birthday party there, it was run at the time by Paco Fitzgerald and his brother Eddie. We had many a brilliant night there.

Two years earlier I'd also done a bit of celebrating, albeit in very different circumstances. The Munster team had brought home the Heineken Cup for the first time in May 2006. I wasn't at that final, Edel's brother got married the same day. The whole town went crazy that time. On the Monday I was supposed to be studying for my Leaving Cert but my father rang me to say he was in Rashers O'Briens on Gerald Griffin Street with the cup. Axel and a few of the other players were there so I high-tailed it over there for a few photos. A load of the lads were in there with the cup. I can remember Axel slagging me, asking me why wasn't I at home studying for the Leaving Cert. Two years later it was roles reversed, I was signing autographs and standing in for photos with the cup with a stream of Munster fans.

In the summer of 2008 we were kings of European rugby and it never dawned on anyone that the good days would come to an end. It didn't dawn on me anyway. I was twenty and naïve. I didn't know then about the life cycles of a team, how every champion side has its prime years before the slide begins and other teams take over and have their cycle too. I understand it a lot better now.

The following season I started to motor. I made my full debut in September '08, against Edinburgh in Murrayfield in the Magners League, and had a try on the board four minutes later. The following weekend against Newport Gwent Dragons in Musgrave Park I picked up a hat-trick playing from full back. I could feel the power and speed coming through me now after a solid eighteen months of fulltime weights and athletics. And I was getting an unbelievable buzz from playing with brilliant players. Dougie was a superstar, Rog was world class and Lifeimi Mafi is up there with the best I ever played alongside. I'd rate him that high. Mafs was incredibly fit, tough and skilful. Cool as a breeze off the field, a dream to play alongside. He gave me the ball for the try I flicked up to myself against Dragons. I kind of dummy-switched with Dowls, nudged the ball through with my foot and chipped it up to myself on the run. I'll admit it, I loved that score. Would I do it now? Probably not. You get more conservative with age, more aware of your responsibilities, more conscious of not taking risks. I'd probably consider it self-indulgent if I did it now. But I wouldn't discourage a young lad from trying it. You're supposed to enjoy yourself when you're younger and play with a bit of freedom. I'd probably go down on the ball now and try and scoop it up on the run. Back then I was more or less operating on pure instinct. You'd do things and you wouldn't know how you did them or why you did them.

A fortnight later it was my first full derby game against Leinster at the RDS. The nerves were at me, Quinny was telling me in the dressing room just before we went out to back myself, that I was as good as any of the Leinster lads. It was all new to me, I was floating on adrenaline and excitement from week to week. We beat Leinster 18-0 and for someone as immature as I was at that level, this was the natural order of things. Of course we beat Leinster.

The new Thomond Park was launched the following weekend with a win over Glasgow. I wanted to be the first player to score a try at the new stadium but that honour fell to Peter Stringer instead. They gave me the man-of-the-match award that night, which happened to be two days after my twenty-first birthday. A week later it was my European debut, against Montauban in Thomond, followed by Sale in Edgeley Park. I remember looking at their team sheet that week and being half daunted and half thrilled to be facing international stars of the game like the All Black Luke McAlister, Sebastien Chabal, Mark Cueto, Dwayne Peel and the Argentinian Juan Martin Fernandez Lobbe. Mafs absolutely smashed Chabal and that set the tone, an unbelievable tackle on a fella who was probably three stone heavier than him.

Off then on the rollercoaster to the Stade Marcel Michelin in December where Clermont Auvergne beat us in front of a home crowd that you could nearly feel breathing down on you, they were that close. Our support returned the compliment a week later at Thomond Park and we turned them over on the field. That was the day Marcus Horan scored a crucial try and Tomás O'Leary made an outrageous tackle on Benoit Baby to save a certain try. It was a brilliant night, one of my first big European nights under lights at Thomond Park and the adrenaline rush was pure magic. You could feel the electricity running through the stadium. The later the kick-off, the better. You'd have a packed house and a fair few of them would have a couple of pints in them and the passion and emotion would make your spine tingle.

Of course you're never far from a crash landing in this line of work and in our very next game, away to Connacht after Christmas, we got turned over at the Sportsground. At one stage I tried a drop goal – my confidence was obviously sky high to be trying that – and I nearly hit the corner flag. So Quinny comes over to me and he's cranky and moaning and he says to me something like, come on, you can't do it all on your own. Then I tell him to fuck off with himself. Then we have a few more words. And it's funny cos I'm still only getting to grips with all this and Quinny was someone I'd looked up to for years. He'd actually played against my father in his early years with Shannon. At this stage he's a legend and a veteran, he's known me since I was a kid, and now we're sharing the same field and I'm telling him where to go. It's a good sign I suppose, it means you're becoming friends with someone when you start arguing with each other.

We started April with another win over Leinster. I was delighted to score an individual try from a good way out in front of another full house in Thomond. Cian Healy came to tackle me and I got the hand-off in and tore up the touchline and got it down in the corner. A week later we demolished a stacked Ospreys side in the Heineken Cup quarter-final. So, we went into the semi-final against Leinster three weeks later absolutely flying and hot favourites. I'd scored two more tries against Ospreys so in theory I should have been feeling invincible coming into the big showdown. One of them I'd caught off a kick-off and sprinted the length of the field with Mike Phillips chasing me all the way to the corner and actually lifting me over the side line but I was able to get it down with my hand. That one is special to me and the icing on the cake was that it was at the Ballynanty end, near to the wall I used to jump over as a young fella to get into Thomond Park. I think it was that match against Ospreys that got me on the Lions tour to South Africa that summer. The squad was announced nine days later. The Lions selectors had apparently been keeping a close eye on me that season and the two tries that night put me on the plane. I ended up rooming with Mike Phillips in South Africa.

That was all to come. In the meantime I should have been bullet-proof coming into the Leinster game. Internally though I was on edge all that week. The hype was overwhelming. Croke Park was going to be a sellout – 82,000 people – and this was going to be my first game in the famous stadium. This was on a different level. It was going to be the biggest game of my life by far.

Everywhere you went that week, there was no escaping it. It infiltrated my mind. It started weighing down on me. I had serious anxiety in the days leading up. On top of that, I was going to be starting outside centre and starting outside centre for them was the man himself, Brian O'Driscoll. That was weighing big-time on my mind too. It was Drico and Gordon D'Arcy against Mafs and me. And actually we did well enough early doors.

Mafs managed an incredible offload that sent me away and I took off down the middle of the field. I thought I was all set to go under the sticks when Isa Nacewa jumped on top of me and pulled me down. But we got the ball back and it went left to Dowls and he was tackled by Rocky Elsom who was blatantly offside. That was a big moment.

The match swung their way with Darce's try. I'd made a wrong read in midfield, Drico was on the ball and he popped it short to Nacewa, I was caught in no man's land and Isa was through the gap. He threw it left to Darce, I got back to tap tackle him but he was able to slide over.

I think my anxiety about Drico got to me there, it was in my head and I just didn't make the right decision. In fact I had serious anxiety actually during the game. I seized up with cramps at one stage, I think the whole occasion overcame me and I made a few mistakes.

Collectively we were off that day. Leinster were a team hurting. They had a huge point to prove and we didn't. You can't manufacture an edge like that. You can't give yourself a cause like that. They had a cause that day and maybe that was the difference, I don't know. Maybe Nacewa's tackle on me was the difference, I don't know that either.

I have never watched that match back on video. I was absolutely sickened after it. I remember coming home on the train that evening and it was the first time in my life I wanted to drink so I could forget about a game. I had a load of cans on the train and then a load more drinks in the Curragower on Clancy Strand that night. Didn't want to talk about it, didn't want anyone coming near me.

Our last game of the season was against Ospreys again, in Thomond Park in May. We'd already won the Magners League title by then. We lifted the cup afterwards and it meant a lot to me because it was my first time on a winning podium with Munster. Other fellas were used to it but I wasn't. We were all presented with our medals. Mick O'Driscoll somehow ended up losing his medal walking around the field after. A young lad from Moyross who'd come onto the pitch with all the other fans found it. A few days later he contacted me and told me he had the medal and I got it back to Micko.

Once the game was safe against Ospreys, Tony McGahan started whipping off the players who were due to meet up with the Lions in England the following week. I joined Paul O'Connell on the bench with a few minutes to play and the first thing Paulie said to me was, we're on the plane now, we got through that. You tried not to think about it but you couldn't help it crossing your mind, picking up an injury in an end-of-season game that would ruin your Lions tour before it had even started.

We watched the Heineken Cup final in a pub in London the following weekend and I had one hundred per cent respect for Leinster's achievement in winning it. The campaign they'd had, they totally earned the trophy. Of course, we weren't to know then that that semi-final in Croke Park was the day the tide turned. Munster's relationship with Leinster would never be the same again. We would be playing second fiddle to them for the rest of my career almost.

You can control a lot of things in a sporting career but you can't control everything. You can't control injuries and you can't control the timing of it. Your date of birth dictates that. But that was all in the future. The 2008/09 season was my breakthrough campaign. I'd broken into the Munster first team and stayed there. I'd broken into the national squad and I was picked for the British & Irish Lions. It was a magic carpet ride. It cemented my future in professional rugby for the next few seasons at least.

By the end of that season I knew enough to know it wasn't going to be all fun and games. I wouldn't be throwing darts with the lads after training every day. And instead of getting a slap off a live wire on a building site, I'd be getting a few slaps every weekend from fellas hitting you like they were lorries. I was more than happy to take them.

4

GER AND SANDRA

MY FATHER TELLS THIS STORY. WELL HE TELLS A LOT of stories but this is one that sticks out for me. He was togging out one day in the dressing room in Thomond Park for a Munster Under 20s trial match. You had the cream of the underage crop there from Cork and Limerick, mostly fellas who came through the schools system and were now in college or just starting in college. A few of them in the dressing room were talking about the courses they were doing in Uni, I suppose law and business and medicine and accounting and so on. My father was there with his great friend and Young Munster team mate Aidan O'Halloran. And next thing Aidan pipes up and says, "Well Earls, what weight was the baby last night?!" The baby was me. My mother Sandra had given birth to me the night before in the maternity hospital in Limerick and my father had been up all night with her in the labour ward. He had just turned twenty the day before, Mam was eighteen.

My father was a builder's labourer, Mam was a machinist and seamstress and clothes maker. His Munster team mates in the dressing room that day were talking about college and careers and stuff, Ger had quit school young and was now a father. The other lads were gobsmacked when Aidan broke the news. They were looking at Dad like he had two heads on him!

My parents have been together thirty-seven years now at time of writing. They only got married in March of this year, 2021. They took their time about it, you could say. But I think they operated on the basis that if it ain't broke don't fix it. In Kileely where they grew up there wasn't a big deal made about being married or not married when you had children. Couples got together young and had their babies and went to work to provide for them. Everyone mucked in, the extended families and all, and you just got on with it. A lot of my parents' friends were in the same boat, they had their children and never married.

I was born on October 2 1987. Kileely was an old working class area on the northern edge of the city. Moyross was a new housing estate only a short distance away that had been built in the early 1970s.

My first six months were spent in my mother's family's home while she and Dad waited on the housing list to get their own place. Then they moved into their first home, a bungalow in Moyross. They hadn't a stick of furniture but there was a woman leaving to go to England and she was selling all her furniture, beds and tables and chairs and all. She was looking for £300. There was a block-layer building a boundary wall around the old Thomond Park at the time. This fella was a subbie, he wasn't a nine-to-five man, he wanted to get the job done as quick as possible. So Dad went labouring with him seven days a week for a couple of weeks and put together the £300 to buy the furniture from the woman leaving for England.

Both my parents were early school-leavers. There was a youth centre down in Thomondgate for young men to learn one of the trades. Girls could learn to be machinists for sewing and making clothes. It was run by a nun, Sister Mary Carmel, and it was a great facility for young people in the area. That's where my folks did their training. They were both out earning from their mid-teens on. They'd grown up in that culture of going out to earn as soon as you were able. Dad's father, Billy Earls, was a docker. Billy and Mary had nine children. Their house was a two up two down, one bedroom for the four girls, one bedroom for the five boys. Billy and Mary's bedroom was the parlour downstairs. There was a scullery out the back. No central heating but they had piles of coats hanging up on the walls and in the winter Billy would take them all down and throw them on the beds for extra heat. He was a big strong man.

Every morning he'd set off for the docks down by the Shannon on his black high nelly bike. He had big shoulders, big hands, big arms from the work. He could be shovelling a load of coal off a ship into bags all day, or taking off bales of timber or those wooden electricity poles covered in creosote or a mountain of salt that needed to be shovelled too. The system was casual labour but Billy always got work because of his strength and his attitude. He had a good reputation.

Dad remembers him coming home of an evening and all the brothers and sisters out on the street waiting for him to appear on his bicycle. He'd be black from the coal and his back would be all marked and reddened from hauling the bags. If they were lugging salt it'd get into the cuts on his hands. In winter he'd be soaking wet after a day of it in the rain. He'd come home and wash at the sink before his dinner. Dad remembers his mother putting cream on Billy's back and neck for all the welts and scratches and sores.

Mam was one of nine too. There was always food on the table in both houses, it might be bread and tea for supper, or a bowl of porridge. They always had decent clothes even if they were hand-me-downs a lot of the time. It's only looking back that they wonder how their parents reared these big families in such small homes and with so little money but they did it and they're very proud of the upbringing they had. Mam and Dad have fond memories of their growing up in Kileely.

Dad started out playing Gaelic football for Treaty Sarsfields but he got roped into the rugby fairly young too. He hung around with a few friends who were playing underage with Thomond RFC. The club had a stalwart volunteer, Johnny Bromell, who would go round Kileely and Moyross and Thomondgate on his bike, rounding up the young lads for training.

The lads were knocking about in Shelbourne Park one day when John came along to let them know when the next training session was. Then he asked my father did he play? No. Well come up with the lads tomorrow or whenever. So he did. And that's what set Ger Earls on the road to becoming a bit of a legend of Limerick rugby. He got the bug for rugby and never lost it. He loved the tearing into it that you could do, mowing fellas down in the tackle and not minding too badly if you got mowed down yourself. You could meet fire with fire. It suited him down to the ground. His brothers played soccer but it never really appealed to him. Moyross and Kileely and Ballynanty would have been soccer strongholds but in Limerick you could cross the class divide from soccer to rugby because there were rugby clubs in working class areas. Thomond RFC is actually in Moyross. The council demolished a load of houses as part of the regeneration project in recent years so it's not nearly as built up or as populated as it used to be. But back in its heyday it was a fairly intimidating venue for visiting teams, especially from Dublin and Cork.

I remember years ago one Dublin player joking with me that it was like the movie *Fort Apache The Bronx*! I suppose for fellas used to playing their sport in nice leafy suburbs, this was like wandering into an urban wasteland. You'd have horses grazing on the green patches and dogs barking and hundreds of kids roaming around. Some of them wouldn't be beyond throwing a few stones at the opposition team bus on its way into Fitzgerald Park. There was a lot of steel fencing and gates and iron bars on the windows and stuff like that.

Rugby and soccer in Moyross were a bit like boxing in other marginalised communities. They kept fellas on the straight and narrow, or a lot of them anyway. Dad says that when they reached their mid-teens some of his mates started doing a bit of ducking and diving. Only for coaches at Thomond RFC like Seán McInerney, a good few more lads could've ended up in prison. Seán was a taskmaster but if a young lad was prepared to put in the time on the pitch, he'd give you all his time back. Dad remembers him checking their breath regularly for alcohol and smoking. He'd want their boots polished and their togs cleaned. He demanded discipline and some fellas thrived because of it. In return he'd look out for them, he knew fellas in business and in the building trade and he'd line up jobs for the lads if he could.

In places like Moyross it was very easy for lads to go one way or the other. I mean good lads, fellas with loads of intelligence and ability who could have done well for themselves in life but didn't have the direction and the minding they needed. There wouldn't be a scandal about a fella ending up in court and in prison the way there would be in a middle class area. It was common enough. So the temptation was always there to slip off the tightrope the wrong way.

So what the coaches in the local sports club were doing really was social work. They were giving young fellas their time and showing that they cared about them. That was important, just showing that you cared. They were teaching them discipline too and helping them find jobs. There was also the camaraderie and friendships that came with your team, the satisfaction of playing in competitive games and coming away with a win. I had all that growing up and my father had it in his time.

My folks say the parenting end of things was really important as well. Dad says his father was strict about him coming home at the time he was told to come home and when the kids got into their teens he'd be checking for signs of drinking and all that. Billy Earls would be up and out every morning for work on the docks too and that rubbed off on Dad and his siblings as well. The work ethic and the earning your own way in life.

So when I got into my teens, Mam and Dad in turn kept a close eye on me. I don't think I gave them much trouble, I was generally cautious enough in my behaviour, but there was always the worry that I'd be led astray by outside influences. My father will say he went over the top at times, in terms of keeping tabs on me. It was because of the gang feud that was making so many headlines at the time. That's why we had the rows over the baseball caps and the hoodies. A lot of the fellas who got attacked in the feud or did the attacking would have worn the baseball caps and the hoodies and the trainers. Dad was petrified that I'd end up an innocent victim cos of the gear I was wearing. I had a baby blue Nike hoodie at one time and a white baseball cap with a big peak on it and he hated the sight of that rig-out!

It was routine for him to get into his car and drive around Moyross if I was out and about, just checking to see where I was. He'd do it without me knowing. Like, as he says himself, "there was serious shit happening at the time." If I was staying in a friend's house overnight he'd be warning me about hanging around on the streets after dark. Sometimes we'd tent out in the garden of one of my friends' houses, which meant I wouldn't be under my parents' supervision for the night. I remember him warning me that he'd be coming round in his van later that night and if he saw me out on the streets, I'd be in serious trouble. But sure the whole purpose of the tent was to be out and about roaming the streets. The lads would be going down to the petrol station and the shop trying to buy drink and fags or whatever. But I'd stay in the tent. I was afraid of being caught. My father had a white van at the time and I'd hear a van driving round and I'd think it was him. Maybe it was, maybe it wasn't, but I wasn't taking the chance. In fairness, they always cut me a bit of slack, they'd let me off with my mates and all that, but they kept me on a short leash at the same time. Some fellas weren't given any rope at all and they went nuts, some fellas were given too much rope and they went nuts too. Some of them ended up on heroin and homeless and in prison.

One of our childhood friends, he'd actually set me and Edel

up for our first date, tragically ended up on the wrong side of life. He was a good character and great craic. He experimented with heroin a couple of times and next thing he was hooked. He was hooked for years and years to come. One night many years after he'd first introduced us, Edel and myself were coming out of a restaurant in town. We had Ella May with us, she was about one and a half. And there was a chap sitting on the pavement with his cup for a few coins. It was our old buddy. He was embarrassed when he saw us. We stopped and had a chat. He told us his story. We gave him a few quid and wished him well and went on our way.

Dad and Mam knew that as long as I was out playing ball with my friends that I'd be happy and they'd be happy. They really supported us when it came to playing sport. They knew the goodness of it. My father gave an awful lot of his spare time helping us out. He'd come home from a hard day's work on the buildings and spend a few hours out kicking around with us. In fact he used to make us our own goals and all.

I remember him coming home in the van with steel bars from the construction job and fabricating a proper set of goals with them. We even had nets. He brought home the green protective mesh that they use on building sites and hung it off the crossbar and that was the nets. We'd have to carry the goals home again in case they got nicked or vandalised or because people would be giving out about us playing football on the public green. The next day then he'd come home and we'd carry the goals back down again and play away for ages. Dad would play in goals. I'd be there with a few friends, then a few more lads would arrive and you'd have a game for a couple of hours. There was a field with a steep enough slope on it where we'd play. I think that's where I built up a lot of stamina and athleticism without me even knowing.

Thomond were a junior rugby club and a good one. My father had played for the Munster Under 18s and had broken into the Thomond first team at a young age. The club were proud as punch when himself and Aidan O'Halloran made the provincial Under 18s side. The two lads would be going away for a weekend with the Under 18s so Thomond RFC actually organised a fundraiser in the club one night so they'd have a bit of spending money that weekend.

Thomond won three Munster Junior Cups in a row in '89, '90 and '91. Dad was twenty-one when Young Munster invited him to come training with them. Tony Grant was the coach, Paco Fitzgerald was playing for Ireland at the time, and the pair of them and Johnny Murphy turned up one day at the front door of his bungalow in Moyross. It was a big deal to have an Irish international on your doorstep asking you to join his team. Ger Copley, Dad's mate in the Thomond back row, was asked as well. That made it easier, the fact that two of them were going. So they turned up at training the next night at Greenfields and a few days later were picked to play against Shannon in the Munster senior league. That was a big deal too because Shannon were a powerful outfit at the time. But he must've done alright because at the end of that season he transferred from Thomond and spent the next ten years with the Cookies. It wasn't an easy decision at the time but you couldn't turn down the opportunity of playing senior rugby. And Munsters made him feel at home because it was a working man's club too. The lads would be coming in with cement and muck on their clothes.

Dad was lightly built for an openside flanker but he had

serious pace and he was afraid of nothing. He was a big fan of Fergus Slattery, and Michael Jones of New Zealand. They won the Munster Senior Cup in 1990 which was a major feather in their cap. They got promoted from Division 2 of the AIL in '91 and in February 1993 they brought home the bacon, the big one, the AIL title. It's one of the most famous achievements ever I think in the history of domestic rugby in Ireland. The Cookies beating St Mary's, who were also going for the title, in the last game of the season at Lansdowne Road. My father is remembered for his intercept try in the second half that day, going all the way from sixty yards or so. But it was Aidan O'Halloran who landed the winning penalty from about forty yards with four minutes to go. Aidan was a class flyhalf, he was only in his first season in senior rugby I think, he scored two penalties and two drop goals on the day. Dad will always say it was an incredible team effort by every single player on the day. By the whole club and supporters really. The players were a band of brothers. They were underdogs in more ways than one.

Four of them had played on the Munster team that beat Australia in Musgrave Park the previous October, Peter Clohessy, Ger Clohessy, Derek Tobin and my father. Australia were world champions at the time. They were a massive scalp to claim. So Dad was very much on the radar for provincial honours and went on to play eight or nine times for Munster but he says he was never comfortable in that environment. He found it all a bit daunting, just being among a whole new set of people he didn't know very well. You'd have people involved from rival clubs in Limerick and Cork and he reckons Young Munster were kind of "the black sheep" of rugby at the time. There was an element of the old class distinction thing going on, a bit of looking down their noses at you. The fact he hadn't been picked for the Munster Under 20s squad a year or two earlier soured him on it too. He'd played for the Under 18s and was making a name for himself with Thomond and someone else got picked out of favouritism more than merit. It made him a bit wary of the set-up. So he'd be getting letters from the Munster branch to turn up for training with the provincial squad in Mallow and sometimes he would and sometimes he wouldn't. I think his last game for them was a friendly against Transvaal in Musgrave Park in December 1995.

The one question that keeps coming up is why he never got capped for Ireland. He's fed up being asked about it at this stage because it comes across like he's always cribbing about it. He doesn't want to be seen like that. He's too humble really to be making a big deal about it. So I suppose I can say it for him instead. He should have got capped. In fairness, there was plenty of fellas not as talented or as brave who got capped. Again, there was an element to it of his face not fitting. Dad didn't look like your typical Irish rugby player. He had tattoos. He didn't have an office job. He worked with his hands. He just didn't fit the bill.

The tattoos were gas. They weren't done in your normal tattoo parlour. They were done when he had a few pints on him one night when he was about sixteen, by a fella who had one eye, under a flashlight in a handball alley. He had the letters SANDRA done across the knuckles of his hand. Eventually he got them removed because they were a gammy job. Nowadays tattoos are very trendy with rugby players but they weren't back then. Nice boys didn't have tattoos! So, there was the class divide thing going on there. Certainly, various alickadoos in the

IRFU would've taken one look at Ger Earls and shaken their heads. No, he's not one of us. But Dad would have absolutely loved to have played for Ireland. He's a patriot to his heart. He'd have loved to wear the green jersey. Even if you get one cap, you can always say you represented your country. That's the thing about it, it does follow you around for the rest of your life because once you're capped, nobody can take it away from you. It's kind of like you've been capped for life, not just a game. So the opposite thing is true too. If you never got capped when so many rugby people think you should have, that follows you around for life too. It's why it keeps coming up. In fairness, I don't think they can all be wrong.

The closest he came was in March '92. Ireland were going badly, they'd been beaten by Wales, England and Scotland in the Five Nations. There was a long break until the France game. To shake things up, the coach Ciaran Fitzgerald and the selectors organised a sort of trial game for one of the free weekends. There would be an Ireland A selection against an Ireland B selection on the main pitch at Lansdowne Road. Sort of probables versus possibles. Dad scored a try for Ireland B in the first half. They switched him at half-time to Ireland A and he scored a try for them second half. The team would be named the next day. Afterwards Paco Fitzgerald and a few of the other players were telling him it was looking good. He'd played well. Ireland had a lot of backrow options missing through injury too. They didn't have a specialist openside. His hopes were sky high. He says he felt so close to it he could taste it. The next day all the players re-assembled for the squad announcement and there was no mention of Ger Earls at all. Not even on the bench. He was devastated really.

Ireland got a pretty bad beating in Paris. Less than a week later the selectors announced a thirty-man squad for the tour of New Zealand that summer. There was a lot of first-choice players who were going to be missing through injury or whatever so they were having to dig fairly deep into the playing reserves to fill out the squad. But he wasn't named in that either. Out in New Zealand they had more injuries, fellas were dropping like flies. So they called out a player for backrow cover who'd been injured most of the season and who'd played one junior game for his club before getting the call.

So, when I look at it, it doesn't stack up. But my father doesn't want to say he was hard done by, he'd hate it if he was seen coming across that way. It's more me looking at the whole thing and coming to my own conclusions. And he'll be the first to admit that he didn't help himself at times with his attitude and discipline. The Cookies always had a bit of a reputation for that! They've often been accused of playing with a chip on their shoulder. Maybe it's true, maybe Dad had a bit of that too. But it's just not as easy to go round nice and relaxed in yourself when you think people are looking down on you or discriminating against you because of where you come from.

I was only a child at the time so I don't remember any drama about being picked or not picked for Ireland. But he was taking me to club games in Fitzgerald Park (Thomond) and Tom Clifford Park (Munsters) from as soon as I could walk. As I got a bit older I became steeped in the whole scene, I'd be on the bus and in the dressing room and on the sideline. I'd be bringing out the kicking tee for the kickers. I'd be at every game he was playing, a lot of the training sessions too. I was eating it and sleeping it. I was there the day he got knocked out and swallowed his tongue. I had my Munsters jersey on with the No.7 ironed onto the back of it. I must only have been about six or seven. He got a knee straight to the head and he was knocked out cold. All the players gathered round him and club officers and the referee and the doctor. It wasn't a great sight to see for a kid. The doctor got his hand into his mouth and pulled the tongue up from his throat and he started breathing again. The ambulance came and took him away.

He was always going hell for leather in games, there'd be punch-ups and melees on a regular basis. He was in his fair share of dust-ups. He never shied away from it. He'd prefer to wade in and get knocked out rather than not go in at all. I knew him as my father, a nice caring man who was always looking after me. Then I'd see him boxing the head off some fella! Himself and Trevor Brennan had some ferocious scraps. They were like Mike Tyson and Evander Holyfield going at each other. One time in Greenfields they were going at it hammer and tongs and a few of my aunts had a few words for Trevor in the clubhouse after! He's a great fella is Trevor, Dad and him are good friends, he's gone on rugby tours organised by Trevor's travel company.

Another time, Buccaneers came down to Greenfields and it was more like a wrestling match than a rugby match. The game was delayed because the teams had similar colours and Buccaneers hadn't brought an away set of jerseys. So someone had to go into town and buy a set of white togs for Munsters to be able to tell the difference. Tom Clifford Park was packed that day. I was on the sideline.

The match started and it wasn't long until the fighting started too. There was boots and fists flying. There was fellas spitting out blood with their saliva. Dad of course was in the middle of it. At one stage I had to run on with the kicking tee after another fracas was sorted and he just winked and smiled at me like it was all great craic.

Then I go into our dressing room afterwards and our lads launch into a few verses of their club song *Beautiful Munsters*. That's what gets the party started. A load of Buccaneers players arrive in and they're laughing and joking with the Cookies players. Naturally enough, the beer is flowing too. There's fellas with big swollen lumps under their eyes and busted lips and red welts on their faces and they're drinking away with the fellas who inflicted the damage like they're the best of friends!

Mam, meanwhile, was working part-time then in a small factory unit in Kileely making school uniforms and stuff like that. She made a lot of my clothes in her spare time. School uniforms and trousers and tracksuits and so on. I had all the gear I wanted from the shops. My jerseys and togs were always spotless too. She'd wash and iron them, bleach the togs so they'd be sparkling white, my boots would be shining. When Munchin's were playing in the Munster schools senior cup in 2006, we didn't like the jerseys because they were too big for us. They didn't look right. So I brought them all home to Mam and she re-stitched every single one of them so they'd fit properly and we'd look the part on the day. When I started playing for Ireland you'd get two pairs of shorts per game. I was fussy about the way they fitted me. If they weren't right I'd bring them home to Mam and she'd drop the waistband if it was too high or take them in if they were a bit too big.

I remember before a Six Nations game at the Aviva in 2010. My father and mother were there of course, beaming with pride. I'd handed over the spare pair of shorts to Mam to get them fixed. She did the job on her sewing machine, brought them to the match and took her seat. A few minutes before it started she came down the steps to the fence and called over Dave McHugh, who was running the line that day, and gave the shorts to Dave and told him to pass them on to me. Dave was a bit taken aback I think!

My international debut was in Thomond Park. I brought my Ireland jersey home that evening and gave it to my parents. Dad tried it on for the craic. He'd have loved to have had his own but this was the next best thing I suppose. Now that I'm on over ninety caps he likes to say that I won enough for the two of us. Back in his day the jerseys were big loose rough yokes. Nowadays they're skin-tight. So it's fair to say my father struggled to get into my jersey that night. In fact it nearly choked him it was so tight. He could've done with Mam loosening the stitches on it a fair bit. That was a happy day.

5

THE LION CUB

I MADE SURE TO HEAD STRAIGHT BACK HOME AFTER training that morning. The squad for the British & Irish Lions tour of South Africa was going to be named live on Sky Sports at lunchtime.

It was April 21 2009, a Tuesday. Edel and I were living in our first house in Castletroy. She was out at work so I phoned my father to come over and be there just in case we had some good news to celebrate. In the weeks before, the newspaper speculation was that I had a chance of being "the bolter" on this Lions squad. I didn't even know what a bolter was. I found out it meant a player who might be the surprise packet, the fella who was picked late in the day or out of the blue. I don't think I was even in the conversation the previous Christmas. I was still only breaking into the Munster first team. I hadn't received one of the preliminary letters from the Lions selectors that they send out to a long list of players months before the squad is picked.

I hadn't attended one of those preparatory days that happen during the Six Nations on a download week where you get your photo taken in a Lions jersey and your measurements taken for the clothes and you fill out various forms. None of that. I was back playing with Munster anyway to get game time.

I was still only a fringe player with Ireland. I'd two international caps and played eighty-nine minutes in total. It was my form with Munster in the spring of 2009 that had got people talking. After the Ospreys game nine days before the announcement Paul O'Connell got me to fill out the forms and make sure my passport was in order and all that. Paulie was going to be the Lions captain but the composition of the squad was top secret so he didn't let anything slip. It was just in case I might get the nod. But he must've had some idea at the same time! Anyway, he wasn't telling me. I'd have to wait for the big day like everyone else and I had no idea what was in Ian McGeechan's head. He was the boss, it was up to him and his fellow selectors.

Gerald Davies, the tour manager, made the announcement live on Sky standing at a podium with a screen behind him. Each time he announced a name, a photo of the player would pop up on the screen wearing the famous red jersey. Dad and his brother, Uncle Robert, had come over to join me.

Davies read out the backs first. He came to Tommy Bowe, then Tom Shanklin, Jamie Roberts, Brian O'Driscoll and . . . "Keith Earls, Ireland". Ger and Robert went apeshit. They were roaring and cheering and laughing and beaming with pride. Dad knew the history of the Lions, it was an awesome thing to be picked, a massive honour for your family and your club and the people who had coached you since you were a boy. You were one of the best rugby union players in England, Ireland,

Scotland and Wales if you were picked. It meant the world to him.

Of course I was delighted too. And shocked. I was just sitting there thinking what in God's name had happened. It was insane. I couldn't get my head around it. I was a Lion! I had watched the *Living with Lions* documentary dozens of times, the famous film about the 1997 tour of South Africa. Three years earlier, in the St Munchin's school annual, they'd done their pen pictures of each Leaving Cert student and their ambitions for the future. They said my ambitions upon leaving school were to marry my childhood sweetheart Edel McGee and to go on the next tour with the British & Irish Lions. It was a total fantasy. I mean the second ambition not the first. Fellas from Moyross didn't get to play with the British & Irish Lions. I was living in a two-bedroom council house with my baby sister in her cot at the end of my bed because we didn't have another room. No one from Moyross had played rugby for Ireland. No one from Moyross that I knew had become famous or wealthy or successful. I had no role models to follow. No role models who could show you what was possible because they had already done it. I think it would have made a difference if there was someone who'd paved the way and could say to me, you can achieve it and you have the right to be there. So playing for Ireland felt like a massive achievement in itself. But the British & Irish Lions just seemed to be a world away from where I was coming from. They were gods, these fellas. Stuff like that didn't happen to a lad like me. I never felt entitled to something like that.

I was always a glass half-empty type of person. I'd be waiting for the bubble to burst. Even when I broke into the Munster and Ireland teams and kids started coming up to me on the street in

Moyross or when we were on holidays in Kilkee, I'd be very self-conscious about it. They'd be telling me I was their favourite player and I'd be embarrassed. I'd be trying to deflect the praise away. It's very hard for a Limerick person to take a compliment! Maybe an Irish person, I don't know. But I never found it easy and I still don't.

That's why fellas like Paulie and Rog were so influential for me. They became my teachers as well as my team mates. They were incredibly kind to me and supportive and encouraging. From the first day I joined Munster they were looking out for me. They filled me with the reassurance I needed. What Paulie had achieved coming from Limerick was a huge inspiration to me man and boy. And now here I was, about to tour South Africa on a Lions campaign with him as my captain.

I was trying to take in all these thoughts and emotions when Gerald Davies read out my name. It was only months later when the documentary came about the '09 tour, *Living with the Pride*, that I discovered McGeechan and his staff had been tracking my form that season. In one of their selection meetings that's shown in the film, they're tossing around names and Sir Ian is saying, Keith Earls is someone we have to pick, he can turn on a sixpence. But I didn't know that, the day my father and Uncle Robert went jumping round the room. I was trying to get my head around it!

And another quirky kind of thing was running through my mind as well. My photo appeared on the screen too wearing a Lions jersey but I hadn't been at that photo session. So they'd obviously used another head shot of me and photoshopped it onto the body of one of the other players who was wearing the jersey. And I was trying to figure out who that player was. In fairness, it probably wasn't one of the prop forwards anyway.

A record fourteen Irish players were named in the squad, eight from Munster. Paulie, myself, Rog, Tomás, Quinny, Jerry Fla, David Wallace and Donners O'Callaghan. The Limerick-based lads had training in UL that afternoon and the place was absolutely buzzing. My phone was pinging with text messages. All the players and staff were coming over and shaking hands with us. I can remember Quinny being as gobsmacked as myself. He hadn't been expecting a call-up at all. A few days later the official letter arrived on headed notepaper from the Lions office congratulating me and confirming I was a member of the travelling party.

Can you imagine going from the high of that to the low of what happened to Tomás O'Leary three days later? An accidental collision with one of his own players against the Scarlets in Musgrave Park and his ankle was banjaxed. His tour was over a month before it even started. I was devastated for him, we all were. Then Quinny was slapped with a twelve-week ban for the incident with Leo Cullen against Leinster in the Heineken Cup quarter-final. He appealed the decision but it was upheld so that ruled Quinny out. And a few days before we were due to fly to South Africa, Jerry Fla broke his elbow in training in England and he was gone too. You can take nothing for granted in this sport. I learned that lesson seeing my friends and team mates devastated like that. And I was learning too that you can't let yourself get too high because the lows that are coming round the corner will crush you. Staying on an even keel is vital to your mental wellbeing, if you can manage it.

At twenty-one I was the youngest player on the team plane out to SA. Luke Fitzgerald was on the tour too, I'd played against

Luke at underage level and he was a star in the making even then. Luke I think is about two weeks older than me. But I wasn't the youngest player named in the original squad. That was Leigh Halfpenny. He was twenty. But Leigh got injured and stayed at home to do rehab before joining us in early June. He played one game, then got injured again and went back to Wales a few days later. So for most of the time I was the youngest British & Irish Lion on tour. As it turned out, I was too young. I wasn't ready for a challenge on that scale. It was to be a steep learning curve and a harsh lesson.

They started me in the first game of the tour, against a selection called Royal XV in a place called Rustenburg, about an hour and a half away from Johannesburg. It was a scorcher of a day, the pitch was at high altitude. I don't think I realised how badly I was suffering from stage fright until the game started. I ended up having a complete mare.

I'd been well aware in the weeks before that various rugby people were doubting me, saying I wasn't up to this level. That had been playing on my mind. And looking back now I can see that on the day I was too wound up. I didn't relax into the game. I tried to force things because of the huge pressure I was feeling. I was trying to justify my selection, which of course was only putting myself under more pressure.

Like, if only I knew then what I know now. But I was clueless really when it came to psychological preparation back then. I was playing for the Lions but in reality I was innocent as a lamb. I just didn't know how to cope with an occasion of this magnitude. I don't mean the opponents or the crowd that day. I'd played against far better teams in front of far bigger crowds earlier that season. It was just the Lions thing, being a Lion and what all that meant. I didn't treat it as a game and that's where I got lost. I couldn't catch a ball. My arms and hands weren't working. I dropped catches and knocked on balls.

Then to cap it all, I got smashed by one of their prop forwards, he nearly broke a few of my ribs. It doesn't look much on video but it was a proper sore one. My whole chest was black and blue afterwards. The doctor described it to me as being similar to a car accident where the seatbelt does its job. In fact the Lions medical staff were contemplating sending me home, they thought it was that bad. But I was adamant I wasn't going home. I couldn't face going home after a performance like that in my very first Lions match. No way. In fairness, the physios worked really hard on me for the next week and eventually I was okay. Okay physically but far from okay mentally. I was mortified for my family back at home. They'd have been watching the match and everyone involved in Limerick rugby as well and I felt terrible for them.

The next morning back in Johannesburg, Rob Howley sat down with me for a chat. Rob was on the coaching staff, he'd been on two Lions tours himself and he knew the score. He said that unfortunately the Lions jersey can make a player feel seven foot tall or two foot tall depending on how you react to it. He did his best to reassure me.

He said I was there for a reason, they'd picked me because of my talent, I was a great player, just start relaxing and enjoying the experience. I appreciated the boost he gave me but it was really only a temporary lift.

To add to the rookie errors I made on the pitch, I made another rookie error off it. I read the press coverage of the match. Jesus, when I think about it now. As if things weren't bad enough already! It was Earls this and Earls that in every match report. That really infiltrated my psyche too. My whole sporting life up until then was one rave review after another, from I'd say the age of about ten. I had won leagues and cups in every age grade the whole way through to senior. I never once was nervous before a game. I'm not bigging myself up but I was often the best player on the field. It all came so easy to me. The '08/09 season with Munster more or less followed the same pattern. I took to it like a duck to water. And now came the bang, the crash, the first major setback of my career.

In hindsight too, the Leinster semi-final had dented my confidence as well. I just did not have the resilience to put it behind me and move on. It is hard experience that puts that resilience into you if you don't have it naturally already. And I guess because sport and rugby had come so easy to me for so long, I didn't know how to deal with major disappointments. I didn't have to know. Now it was hitting me like a steam train.

They took me out of the firing line for the next game and put me back in against the Free State Cheetahs in Bloemfontein. Myself and Luke Fitz started in the centre that day. Again I was suffering big-time with the nerves.

In the pre-match warm-up I was dropping balls and this was driving me mad. My hands were shaking, I didn't know what was going on. Then on sixteen minutes James Hook puts in a lovely chip over their defence and I run onto it in midfield, skate around two defenders and cruise home from thirty yards. Just like that. Gone from not being able to catch a ball to suddenly clicking into top gear in one flash. The mind moves in mysterious ways.

I started against Western Province in Cape Town where we

just about scraped the win. They started me full back against the Southern Kings in the Nelson Mandela Bay Stadium in Port Elizabeth. I made a good load of breaks that day and played pretty well overall.

I got one more run-out, between the first and second Test, against the Emerging Springboks back in Newlands. It was pouring rain, my father was in a pub in Cape Town a few hours before the game with a couple of friends and one of them said, "Jesus Christ I hope he's not playing full back tonight!" I was and it actually went fine. Thankfully I got a chance first half and took it, stepped between two tacklers and shot in under the posts.

And that was my lot on the tour, five games, two tries, zero Test caps. But I knew from the outset my chances were slim of making the Test team. I was delighted for John Hayes, he was called up in the middle of June to replace Euan Murray and ended up coming off the bench in the third match against South Africa to win his Lions Test tour cap. They won that match too. I have a picture at home of the two of us sitting in the dressing room afterwards enjoying a beer. I was really pleased for Paulie too that his captaincy had ended with a victory.

The second Test in Pretoria was agonising. The Springboks won it with the last kick of the game to claim the series. It was an awful downer. There could have been a big temptation to mentally switch off after the heartbreak of losing that match and knowing the series was lost too. But they didn't, they regrouped and kept it together and won convincingly in the end. O'Connell had put his heart and soul into leading that squad.

Maybe with hindsight I should be a bit easier on myself about that tour. Five games and two decent tries wasn't a bad return. But everything was coloured for me by the bad start. I was thrown in at the deep end and it was just too much for me. But I rallied okay after it. I did alright, I did my bit. It was a massive learning experience. I don't think I ever learned so much so fast about elite level rugby. In theory it should've stood me in good stead in the seasons that followed. In fact it haunted me. My confidence took an awful hammering. It took me years to get over it. I beat myself up about it. I convinced myself that I was out of my depth on the world stage. I think there was an element of imposter syndrome chipping away inside me too. Like, what was a fella from Moyross doing here on a Lions tour? I wasn't supposed to be there. I'd say that was in the mix too, in my confused head that day in Rustenburg. And even though I recovered and did okay in the other games, those thoughts were still nagging away at me. And I carried them with me for years after. I was always doubting myself. Even when I was playing well I'd be doubting myself.

There's a saying in sport that if you're good enough you're old enough. I was definitely good enough, in terms of skills and speed and all that. But emotionally, psychologically, I wasn't good enough. I was too young in that way. It's a dangerous thing to do, to put talented young sports people in at the deep end. They might be ready in terms of physical ability, they mightn't be ready in all the other ways. But I suppose selectors can't see inside your head either. Sir Ian was a gentleman. But they don't know what kind of thoughts are racing round inside your head. Sure I didn't know myself a lot of the time what I was thinking.

I carried those mental scars from South Africa around with me for the next six or seven years. Now in fairness, there was a lot of other stuff going on in my head too. But it took me a long, long time to finally put it behind me for good. I didn't enjoy my rugby during those years. My insecurities were eating away at me. It was really only when I became my own man that something clicked and I found a genuine inner core of confidence. Twelve years later I would have loved to have gone back to South Africa as part of the 2021 Lions tour. It was an itch that needed to be scratched. I would've loved to have been able to set the record straight. And when I came into form for Ireland during the Six Nations, my name was being floated again as a possible contender for the tour.

A secret part of me was hoping that I'd make it. I liked the idea of coming full circle from the twenty-one-year-old cub to the thirty-three-year-old veteran who is now a very different person to that young lad. The realistic part of me with my professional head on knew that the chances of it happening weren't great. There was a long queue of brilliant back three players from the four nations who were in contention. And I wasn't a Warren Gatland type of player either. I didn't have the height and power and weight he likes in a player. Sure enough, I didn't feature when the squad was announced in May. I doubt I figured much in his thoughts at all.

Anyway, that's how it goes. I hope as I get older I'll be able to appreciate it more, maybe give myself a pat on the back for making a Lions squad at all. It was a painful experience but I look on it now as the path that was laid out for me. If I hadn't done it then I might never have done it at all. I was injured and out of the reckoning for the 2013 tour, and overlooked for 2017. So, maybe I should be grateful for what I got. There are loads of rugby players from all four nations who had all sorts of hard-luck stories when it came to missing out on a Lions tour. I can say I did it, wore the T-shirt and all. I'm there on the roll of honour, Lion number #754.

The official letter on the headed notepaper that was sent to me in April 2009. My parents had it framed. It's hanging on the wall in their kitchen to this day.

6

HANK

I HAVE A FRIEND WHO'S BEEN HANGING AROUND with me for a good twenty years. To be honest he's a bit of a dose. He lives in my head. He's not real to anyone else but he's very real to me. I call him Hank. I took it from the film *Me, Myself & Irene* because the Jim Carrey character in it has two personalities and one of them is Hank. I could identify with it. I could be up one day and down the next. Great form or terrible form. Happy enough or don't talk to me. Don't even look at me.

The panic attacks had started when I was about twelve. Throughout my teens there was this darkness hovering around in the background. It wouldn't come to the surface every day. Months could go by and I'd be in fine form. But there was always this feeling of worry and dread deep down too. Dread that something bad was happening or was going to happen. The amount of deaths in the extended family, among my circle of friends and in the community took their toll on me. The dread kept rumbling away in the background and never really went away as I got older. I just bottled it all up inside and then it would come out in the form of Hank.

I remember well the death of Darren Sutherland because it triggered something in me. I didn't know him, I just saw him on telly after he came home from Beijing with an Olympic boxing medal in 2008. He got a hero's homecoming. In September 2009 he took his own life. I was shocked, it affected me. I was at home on my own when the news broke. It said on the news that he'd been living on his own in an apartment in London. Whatever terrible thoughts he was feeling, he must have bottled them up inside until they became unbearable. It was really the first time it opened my mind up that I needed to do something about the negative thoughts that I was dealing with. I realised where these thoughts could bring you if I didn't do something about them. I never felt suicidal thank God, it was just this empty feeling inside, like a worthless feeling. But poor Darren's death made me realise that it was just probably going to get worse and worse. I knew I should do something about it. But it's one thing knowing it and another thing doing it. I didn't know what to do or where to go. I wasn't able to verbalise it. I continued to keep it all bottled up inside for another four years. And the darkness in me just got darker.

Edel was bearing the brunt of it. It wouldn't take much to set me off. She remembers us going to Donncha O'Callaghan's wedding in Cork a few days before Christmas in 2009. She was so looking forward to it, it was going to be a winter wedding, it was snowing and all. We got stuck in traffic on the way down and we were running late. I hated traffic. It would set me off. For some reason it set me off badly this day. Edel is looking at me like I've lost it completely. There I am in my suit and dickie bow sitting in traffic and my mood goes from zero to a hundred in frustration and anger. I wanted to turn around. I didn't want people seeing me like that. I couldn't control it. I didn't understand why I was feeling like that. Eventually I calmed down, Edel talked some sense into me and we ended up having a great day.

Ella May was born with a serious medical condition on January 24 2012. My usual anxiety went into overdrive after that. It became paranoia. I thought the world was against me. I was terrified for my daughter. I never felt love like I felt when she was born. I never felt fear like it either.

It just so happened that the Ireland squad was in camp in Limerick at the time preparing for the Six Nations. We were all staying in the Strand Hotel which is just across from the maternity hospital. So I was over and back to the maternity hospital for those first days after Ella May's birth. We were playing Wales in the first game, I was being earmarked for the thirteen jersey because Brian O'Driscoll was out injured. We got to go home for the weekend after the week of training before re-assembling for the Wales game. Ella May had her usual check-up with the district nurse who calls to your house to make sure everything is going well. The nurse was worried. She said a four-day-old baby shouldn't be coughing like she was. Her breathing in her chest sounded crackly. We'd have to take her to the doctor. He was worried too. There was something not quite right with the baby's chest. We'd have to bring her to the Regional for tests. Doctors at the Regional examined her and said they'd have to take her to the Intensive Care Unit. Of course we were sick with worry all of a sudden. In the blink of an eye we went from being a happy couple to sitting in a hospital room with our baby in ICU and doctors sticking needles into her. We were in a state of shock. Then we were told she'd have to be brought to the children's hospital in Crumlin for more tests. Declan Kidney was the Ireland manager and we decided I'd give the Wales match a miss. I was in no fit state to be thinking about a game of rugby. The big question in Crumlin was Ella May's heart. Eventually the news was good, her heart was perfect. The relief was huge. Finally she was diagnosed with Primary Ciliary Dyskinesia. The PCD meant her respiratory system wasn't functioning properly. It didn't process the mucus up to her throat and nose the way it does normally. So the fluid and bacteria in the lungs that should be clearing automatically get stuck. It leads to regular respiratory infections. We were told by the doctors it was similar to Cystic Fibrosis and the treatment would be the same but not as severe.

Edel had stayed on in Crumlin while I went home. When she came home with Ella May, she found bowls of water in every room in the house. What was all this about? I was researching our daughter's medical condition online and in my addled mind I decided that the house was too dry or the temperature wasn't right. So if I put bowls of water in every room it'd make the air more moist. Basically my paranoia had taken over. I was in a constant state of fear for her.

Anyway, we settled down into our daily physio routine with Ella May. The doctors and nurses explained that she would need physio twice or three times a day every day to get the mucus up from her chest. She had a nebuliser with a saline solution for breathing through. We had a nurse and a physiotherapist coming out to us for the first few weeks showing us the proper massage technique on her chest and back, holding her upside down to let gravity do its work. We got the hang of it, Ella May got used to it, the mucus would be pouring out of her! She was absolutely fantastic through it all. Plenty of times over the years her lungs would be clogged up or her oxygen levels would be too low and she'd never complain. She could get a sudden spike in temperature and collapse. She'd be getting infections and coughs regularly. She had to take antibiotics every day. But for all that, I'd say she's only been in hospital maybe three times in nine years. Edel quit work to take care of her. Rugby was good to us that way. We could afford for Edel to stay at home rather than have to put Ella May in a crèche where there would be a greater risk of infection. Everyone is well used to the regime now. Ella May knows the symptoms and how to manage them. She has her routine now for taking care of her condition. I've done a lot of research over the years on natural remedies and Chinese medicine and the food that would be best for her, to try and limit her dependence on antibiotics. But basically she has been able to live a normal life, go to school and enjoy her childhood. We might be a bit biased, her mother and me, but we're both so proud of her. She has been an angel from the moment she was born, an absolute dote who is growing up to be a lovely person and a brilliant older sister to her two younger siblings.

Back then my downward spiral was continuing. I was being bombarded with all these negative thoughts and feelings. This fucker Hank inside me was talking all sorts of horrible stuff to me. It was polluting me inside. It even made me fall out of love with rugby. In fact I was hating it. It was making me more miserable. I didn't know how to handle defeats, I didn't know how to handle poor personal performances. I found the pressure closing in on me all the time like walls closing in on me. I went to the World Cup in New Zealand in 2011 and I hated being away from home. All the away trips in those years, all the cities I visited, all the wonderful countries, it meant nothing to me. I was just going around numb, in a daze. This used to really trouble Edel. I was living a privileged life and not appreciating it one bit. I was being given all these opportunities of seeing the world and I was just wasting them. It was all passing me by. I lost count of the number of conversations and arguments we had. I was talking more and more about giving up the game. I had it in my head that I'd just be better off being a nine to five man like every other fella. Doing my day's work and coming home in the evening to my family, instead of obsessing about the next game and the next game and the next game. I didn't want to be dealing with it anymore. I didn't want to be away from my family anymore. I wasn't getting any release during the 80 minutes of a match either. A lot of sports people will say the opposite, that they find a release from all the other stresses of life when they're on the field playing. Like it's their safe space. That wasn't my experience. I would feel the pressure before, during and after games. I didn't enjoy playing, it wasn't a safety valve for me. As soon as one game was finished you'd be worrying about the next one. It was triggering my sadness and my anger and my shit behaviour. Other times then I felt on top of the world. The complete opposite of my lowest mood. I'd be in great form for no apparent reason.

I had a bad panic attack before the Heineken Cup semi-final against Clermont Auvergne in April 2013. The match was down in Montpellier. I was rooming with Felix Jones. I was carrying a shoulder injury, my AC joint needed to be pinned. So I was

My Moyross home: This is where I'm from. This picture is taken just five metres from where my house was so that was my view from a young age. You can see Thomond Park in the background

Law man: Signing my top here is none other than Denis Law, the Manchester United legend, in the Young Munsters clubhouse

Earls treble: Three generations of Earlses with the Munster Schools Senior Cup in 2006 – my father Ger on my right, granddad Billy on my left

Cup winners: The St Munchin's team that won the 2006 Senior Cup. Our coach John Broderick is far left, Pat Cross on the right. Ger Slattery is holding the ball

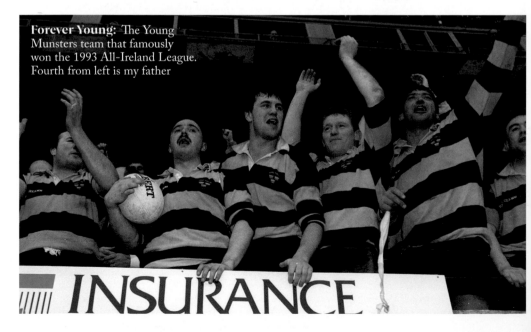

Forever Young: The Young Munsters team that famously won the 1993 All-Ireland League. Fourth from left is my father

INSURANCE

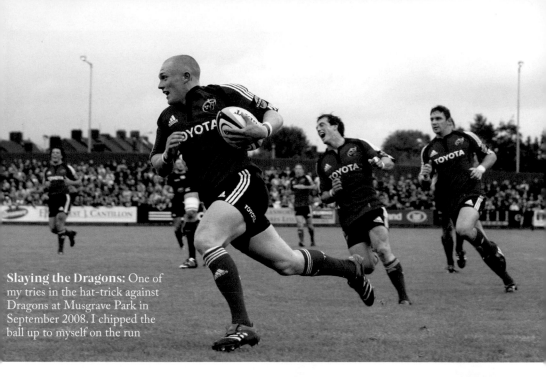

Slaying the Dragons: One of my tries in the hat-trick against Dragons at Musgrave Park in September 2008. I chipped the ball up to myself on the run

Proud parents: Myself and my parents at Templehill rugby ground in Cork in 2005. The Ireland schools side has just beaten England

Brotherly duty: A 20-year-old rugby player bottle-feeding his baby sister Jenny! They didn't teach me that at the Munster Academy

Touching down: Scoring a try for Ireland A against Scotland A at Twickenham in 2007

On the bus: Munster's Heineken Cup 2008 homecoming. I was a bit sheepish about holding up the cup

First of many: Brian O'Driscoll is first in to congratulate me after scoring a try on my senior international debut at Thomond Park. IRFU president John Lyons presented me with my first cap later on

Fractions in it: Munster vs Ospreys, April 2009, Thomond Park. Mike Phillips is desperately trying to stop me from scoring, I'm desperately trying to get the ball down. I won the battle by a hair

On the plane: Gerald Davies announcing the 2009 British & Irish Lions squad. The official letter confirming my selection is framed and hanging in my parents' home

Lions together: With my old Munster team mate John Hayes in the dressing room after the third Test

Wild and free: On safari in South Africa during the Lions tour

Quick burst: Stepping through the gap against the Emerging Springboks in Cape Town

Pumped up: The 2010 Six Nations. It's hard to contain your emotions when you've just scored a try against England at Twickenham!

Enjoying it: The Magners League final in 2011. There's a bunch of my old Thomond RFC team mates up in the stand and I'm giving them a salute with the cup

Home is where the heart is: This photo was taken by Dan Sheridan in 2010. I didn't know he'd spotted me doing graffiti in the snow. Moyross was hurting as a community and I wanted to show my solidarity. I repeated the trick with my boots a year later

An honour: Richie McCaw tackling me in 2010 at the Aviva. It was an honour to have one of the greatest players in history hanging out of me!

Tee time: Munster vs Australia in Thomond Park, in 2010. Paul Warwick landed all our points. I was happy to help him out in any way I could

Taking flight: Splashing down for a try against Italy at the 2011 World Cup. It also happened to be the day of my 24th birthday. That's my excuse anyway for the fancy finish

Having a rest: Hitching a lift on the back of a golf cart during Ireland camp at Carton House in 2013 with Tommy Bowe and Peter O'Mahony

Shoulder to shoulder: Ronan O'Gara was a brilliant mentor and friend to me during our Munster and Ireland years

Pass master: The 2015 World Cup. Ireland vs Romania at Wembley. Simon Zebo has just thrown me a fabulous pass to put me away in the corner. And not for the first or last time either

My secret: Slipping Rob Kearney to score a try against Leinster at Thomond Park in October 2013. Nobody knew it at the time but a few days earlier I'd been diagnosed with a bipolar condition

going in half-injured and they had an unbelievable team, the likes of Wesley Fofana, Sitiveni Sivivatu and Lee Byrne in the backs. I was going to be facing this monster Fijian, Napolioni Nalaga. The anxiety kept rising in me the days beforehand. In the hotel room I was trying to hypnotise myself to get the bad feeling out of me. But the anxiety kept rising in me until I was freaking out. I had a full-on panic attack. It was as bad as the one I had in Kilkee when I was seventeen. We were in a pub there, I wasn't drinking, but I got this notion into my head that someone had spiked my drink. I was convinced it was spiked and I started getting really agitated. I went outside and talked to the bouncer. I knew him, he played with Thomond, and I was insisting to him my drink had been spiked. I didn't stop until I went into a full-on panic attack of shaking and trembling and wet hands. But my drink hadn't been spiked at all. It was just my paranoia going into overdrive. Now I'm in a hotel in Montpellier before a major game and the same or similar is happening to me.

Finally it all came to a head in early October 2013. I was up at an Ireland camp in Carton House and I was sitting down on the bed in my room and just decided, I'm sick of this shit, I've had enough of it, I need to do something now, this minute. I rang the team doctor Éanna Falvey and asked him to come to my room. I told him there was something wrong with me. I blurted out what I'd been going through, or some of it anyway. Éanna heard me out. I told him about my ups and downs, my sadness and my manic happiness. Here I am sitting in Carton House living the dream, so-called, but I'm feeling so sad and vulnerable that I can't think of a worse place to be. He asked me loads of questions. He said I needed to see a psychiatrist.

He set up an appointment with an eminent practitioner. A few days later I was in this man's room telling him the long history of my condition. It was a long session. At the end of it all he said everything about my story suggested I had bipolar disorder. I was bipolar. More than likely a mild form of bipolar. It was the day before my twenty-sixth birthday.

I knew nothing about this condition. I don't think I'd even heard of it. He said it was a long recognised psychiatric condition. It was more common in people than probably I realised. And I was just another sufferer. He wanted to have more consultations with me before deciding on a course of action. But I wanted something there and then. I wanted a pill to make it better. I said I wasn't leaving the room until he gave me a prescription. I didn't want to live with the misery anymore. So reluctantly he gave me one. I was actually elated with the news. At last I finally had a diagnosis. It was real. I wasn't imagining it. It wasn't just me and my weirdness. Other people had it too. And it could be treated, I would get better. Even if it couldn't be fixed, I could get back to a good place. I left the clinic that day not frightened by the news but relieved by it. It was a massive weight off my shoulders. It felt like a huge breakthrough.

A few days later Munster were playing Leinster in Thomond Park. All of a sudden I was raring to go again. It was a RaboDirect PRO12 game. There was over 20,000 there. Five or six minutes before half-time Ian Keatley kicked a peach of a crossfield ball to me. It was nearly the width of the pitch. I was near the right touchline. It was spot on, dropping right into the bread basket but because it was travelling so far, Rob Kearney was gaining ground on me all the time. I could see Rob in my peripheral vision coming for me, lining me up. I caught it and slipped his tackle on the outside and scored. Sweet. The crowd was going delirious, cheering me all the way back down the field. And I was smiling to myself thinking, if only ye knew where I'd been four days earlier! They haven't a clue, the shit I've been dealing with for years. No one does. They think I'm living the dream. Well, I am, in that moment, but I've been living a fucking nightmare too.

That was a good night but it wasn't a happy ending to the story. My problems didn't magically disappear. I was only at the beginning of a long journey to understand what was wrong with me and how to treat it. I am still on that journey to this day. I have spent hundreds of hours online researching the science and nutrition and medication end of things. I've read loads of books. Most of all I've had to learn how to understand my own specific version of the condition. I've done a huge amount of work on myself trying to get better. It hasn't ended. It's still going on, there's regular maintenance and monitoring.

Still, that day in the psychiatrist's office was a turning point. He advised me to tell my head coaches at Munster and Ireland about the diagnosis. It was highly personal information but it was recommended to me that I tell my employers because they should be aware of it. Basically it's like telling them you have an injury, except it's a brain injury. They'd know if you have a physical injury so why shouldn't they know this too? Employers in general need to be educated about it because they have a duty of care to you, the same way they have a duty of care if an employee has a physical illness.

I was finding some real good form coming into the 2014 Six Nations. Then I did the medial ligaments in my knee against Edinburgh in the Heineken Cup in the middle of January. That was my Six Nations wiped and I was gutted. That sent me back into the gloom again, getting angry and frustrated again. And I was hating taking the tablets anyway. I felt a stigma about them, like having to admit that I wasn't well, that there was something wrong with me. Of course there was something wrong with me. But my whole self-image for years was of being a powerful invincible athlete. I decided I didn't need the tablets. I could do without them. So I stopped taking them and told no one. Fatal mistake. The old patterns of behaviour started coming back again. Manic highs and lows. Anger. Crazy behaviour. I was making life decisions I shouldn't have been making in this frame of mind. We'd be in the car stuck in traffic and I'd start going off on one again, banging on the steering wheel and shouting at the car in front of me. Edel would ask me was I on my tablets and I'd tell her I was. But I was sinking down again.

I got back from my injury in time for the Heineken Cup quarter-final against Toulouse in Thomond in April. We had a massive win, I scored a try. Toulon beat us three weeks later in the semi-final in Marseille. My anxiety was through the roof for that game. And during it too. During that game I was talking to myself but not in a good way. I was saying to myself, "You're fucking shit, you're going to drop the next ball", or "You're going to slice the next ball into touch. Wait till you see now, you'll slice it into touch." Is it any wonder I made a load of mistakes. I got pinged for a few penalties which Jonny Wilkinson converted and then I got sin-binned. There was this black tie reception afterwards in this really posh place, people going round in their gowns and tuxedos. I met Edel and my father there. I was in turmoil. I told them I was packing it in. Dad had got into a row with a Munster supporter at the game. This supporter was firing some sort of abuse at me, not knowing my father was in front of him. Edel thought it was all going to kick off.

The season limped to a finish in the middle of May and I limped out along with it. But a few weeks later Ireland would be heading on tour to Argentina and I did not want to be there. So I thought maybe I could change my attitude by giving it a jump-start. I decided I'd go on a massive bender to see if that would get me out of the rut I was in. I headed out to Killaloe and went on a long session. Even on my best days, drink and me didn't get on well. I found the hangovers really bad for my mental state. They would go on for days and really bring me down. But this was the worst I ever felt. I woke up the next day and the siege of darkness began. It was the darkest of the dark. I was never in a blacker hole. I couldn't hold back the tears. I started crying and didn't stop. Edel says she's never seen me cry like that before or since. I told her I'd secretly quit the medication months earlier. We both knew I was in no fit state to head to Argentina. I gave it a day to see could I settle down and get over it. Maybe it was just the terrible hangover. But it wasn't, I knew it wasn't, I'd been numb for a few weeks now. I rang the doctor, then I rang Joe Schmidt and told him the whole story. Joe was very understanding. He said I had to take time out and get myself right, that was all that mattered. The Ireland camp announced that I was a late withdrawal from the squad, I'd come down with a 'viral infection'. Seven years later I'm happy to talk about it. Back then it was unthinkable. There was no way I could be telling the world that I had a bipolar condition. I had told someone I trusted and their advice to me was not to open my mouth about it to anyone.

I went back on the tablets. I booked a holiday to Portugal to get out of the country straightaway. Within twenty-four hours we were in the Quinta do Lago resort. The hotel was only half-built at the time but I booked it cos I knew no one would be there who I didn't want to be around. There was just myself, Edel, Ella May and a couple of elderly people who had an apartment there as well. It was the middle of nowhere really, which suited me down to the ground. I didn't even want to go out to a restaurant for our dinner in the evenings. I wanted to order takeaways and eat them in the room. Jesus I was a right barrel of laughs. I decided to go training every day. Edel says all she can remember from that holiday is looking out of a window and seeing me running up and down a hill outside. She slags me to this day about it. Although believe it or not, I was actually in much better form because of the relief of getting away from the rugby grind.

The bottom line was that I was running away from the problem. I had got the diagnosis and as far as I was concerned that was the end of it. My condition had a name and there was medication for it. That was it, as far as I was concerned, I could turn a new page without doing any more. Edel was on to me about going to the psychiatrist for counselling and talk therapy and all that but any time I spoke to him in the following months, I told him I was feeling great. Not a bother. All good. But Edel could see the warning signs in me still. She'd try to get me to open up but I'd fob her off. She'd persist and persist until I opened up a bit and got a few worries off my chest. I'd feel the better for it but then I'd revert back to my old ways. The medication helped keep me fairly stable but really I was only kicking the can down the road.

It took me another three years to really start digging down

into it and trying to get better. I dunno, I must've been in denial
or something. I was getting by on the tablets. I was functioning
okay, some of the time anyway. But there was always a blackness
there too in my soul. And the rugby was still triggering high
levels of anxiety. Sometimes I could hide it so well on the field
that no one would notice. In fact I could hide it from myself a
lot of the time. The referee would blow his whistle and I'd be able
to switch onto the action and play away. That's how it worked
during the 2015 World Cup, for example. I was in form, I had
a good tournament overall. There was actually a bit of surprise
when Joe decided to rest myself and Iain Henderson for the
final pool game against France. Jared Payne would be starting
at thirteen. But he had a foot injury and failed a late fitness test
so I was back in the team. But that threw me because mentally I
wasn't expecting it. And I was picked at outside centre, I'd been
playing wing in previous games, and waiting for me would be
Fofana and Mathieu Bastareaud in the French midfield. It was
in the Millennium Stadium in Cardiff. Edel called round to our
hotel earlier that afternoon. As she remembers it, I was nowhere
to be seen at first. When I appeared I was white as a ghost. My
hands were wet from the sweat glands working overtime. She
says I was trembling, absolutely trembling. She went away and
she was physically sick with fear for me. I went into a toilet
cubicle before the game. I was saying to myself, what the fuck
am I doing here? Maybe I could just do a runner, out the back
door and get away from here and they'll have to put someone
else in and they'll find me later back in Limerick or somewhere.
No, don't be fucking ridiculous.

We beat France and beat them well but I hadn't much to
do with it. Right throughout the game I kept thinking I was

going to make a mistake. And sure enough, at one stage Tommy Bowe made a beautiful break, I was on his left, he gave me a lovely pass and I knocked it on. Couldn't control it. Couldn't control my anxiety. I was taken off more or less on the hour mark. The mood was brilliant in the dressing room afterwards, the boys were obviously delighted with the performance. I took myself off to the cubicle again where I cursed and cried with frustration. I was effing and blinding. I swore to myself I'd never do this shit to myself again. Then I went back out and showered and joined the lads and pretended nothing was wrong.

No matter how often I promised myself I wasn't going to put myself through it again, I did. I was trapped. Or I felt trapped. Because what was I going to do for a living if I gave up the game? I had no education and no trade. What would I do? Where would I go? I had a wife and kids. I'd have to stick with it even though I hated it. I hated it every single day.

I shared a room with Paul O'Connell during that World Cup. That's where I started listening to audio books, self-help books. I had actually started doing a bit of journaling by then. Writing down my thoughts. Paulie always had his head in a book and I was starting to do a bit of reading too about various sporting subjects and the power of positive thinking and the mental side of performance. He was great company like that. We'd be chatting about what we read. He encouraged me to keep writing down stuff.

In November 2016 I got another awful panic attack. We were playing Canada in the Aviva and two days before it in the Shelbourne Hotel I had to call the doctor to my room. Doc, we need to talk! Again. The same feelings had been creeping in for a few weeks, not wanting to be there because I was feeling so low. Then a few minutes before the game, I join the team huddle in the dressing room and I'm looking around at lads who are making their debut and they're on top of the world and I couldn't give a fuck. The huddle breaks up and I have to sneak off to a toilet cubicle to try and keep the panic at bay. It's not the usual pre-match puking that some fellas will do with nerves. Again I'm trying to hold back the tears because I don't want to be out on that field. I come out and join them for the walk out the tunnel. We're standing for the national anthems and inside I'm saying to myself, Jesus, if only people knew.

I was spending more time on my journal. I was starting to work on my positive self-talk. I was doing more and more reading and research. The more I did, the more convinced I became that I could change my brain. I would write notes to myself down on paper, little affirmations, positive things, reasons to be grateful. I started keeping a gratitude list. That became a habit, a good habit. For someone like me who was always thinking negative, it appealed to me. I was discovering the work of various specialists in this field. A lot of them had gone through tough times and they would explain how they managed to turn it around. How they changed their mindset. And one of the tools they used was journaling. Writing down your goals would help you visualise them. Writing down the good things that were already in your life. Write down that you're grateful for your health, the health of your wife and kids, your financial situation, the health of your parents and your sister, the fact that you're good at rugby. Write down that if you make mistakes on the field, you won't make them again. I was writing in my journal every night.

Rob Penney, when he was Munster coach, used to tell us from

time to time, write down your negative thoughts on a piece of paper and throw it in the fire and then they'll be gone. But I was having so many negative thoughts I'd have needed a volcano to burn them all. I wasn't ready at the time, I wasn't open to Rob's idea.

But now in 2016/17 I was open to it. I practised self-talk, getting out of bed in the morning and saying positive things. Today is going to be a good day, I'm going to do my best to make it a good day. It had clicked with me by then what the psychologists were saying, that your brain is a muscle. I have to exercise it like I exercise the other muscles in my body. It could be trained to think in a different way. It could be re-wired. I had started out as an electrician, this was a different kind of re-wiring altogether. For example, I hated flying. I had a dread of getting on airplanes. So this was one fear I decided to face. I had various audio messages on my phone and my iPad about facing your fears. Face your fears and do it anyway. I kept listening to the messages until I had myself brainwashed that I didn't fear flying anymore. It worked. I eventually got to the stage where I was actually enjoying flying. The repetition of positive messages over and over can change your thinking, I found. And in my experience it has to become a daily ritual, otherwise the negative stuff can start creeping back in on you. It's not like you've sorted the problem and we all live happily ever after. I have to keep working on my mind the way I keep working on my body.

I started getting into all sorts of books about how the mind works, about positive energy, about your consciousness and your patterns of thinking. I'd sit up every night reading this stuff that was all new to me. The more I read, the more I wanted to know. I got into the whole area of the gut-brain connection, how what's happening in your gut can affect what's happening in your brain. That led me down a whole new nutritional path. To be fair I was always prone to fads, trying this trend and that trend. But food education has made a genuine difference to me. Ray McGinley was treating me on the physio bed one day and we were talking about nutrition and he recommended this book for me, *Grain Brain* by David Perlmutter. I found it fascinating. It really opened my eyes to gluten and processed foods and how they can affect your stomach and how what happens in your stomach can affect your brain. The whole gut-brain connection. So I started cutting out carbohydrates and all the rubbish foods, pizzas, biscuits, scones, cakes, bread. It was meat and fish and chicken and vegetables and salads and probiotics and a few mineral supplements. After a few weeks I was starting to feel brilliant – mentally as well as physically. It was a revelation to me. That food could affect your mind the way it was affecting your body. It was the best I'd ever felt. I felt absolutely bullet-proof on this diet.

But then I started losing weight. At one stage I was down to 82kgs. Years earlier, when they were bulking me up, I ended up at 98kgs. But now the nutritionists were giving out to me for being too light, they said I'd burn out from the lack of food energy I needed for training. So I went back on the pasta and bread and porridge and so forth but it was gluten-free. In the Ireland training camps you had gluten-free options at meal times. I used to tell the lads it was because gluten didn't sit well in my stomach. In reality I found that cutting out gluten reduced my anxiety a lot. And my gut was feeling better too. I was eating really clean, which you should be doing as a professional anyway. The only problem was burning so many calories in training and trying to get enough of them onboard. And there was a lot of gluten-free stuff that was horrible to eat. Nowadays I've a bit more balance about it. If I've a week off and we go somewhere for a few days I'll have a nice meal with all the trimmings. I'll ask for gluten-free. If they don't have it, no bother, but you can even get gluten-free ice cream these days.

In early 2018 I started working with Keith Barry, the magician and mentalist. Joe had brought him into the Ireland camp for a talk about visualisation and I liked what he had to say. He talked about how he'd been in a bad car accident and used the power of his own mind to help him make a full recovery. A lot of what he was saying, Joe had been saying it too, there was an overlap there. I went up to him after the talk and explained a bit about my own issues. He came up to my room a few days later and an awful lot of what he had to say rang a bell with me. I was convinced he could help me.

People might laugh at this but I was open to any possibility that might make me better. For all the work I was doing on myself, I was still suffering from the pressure and anxiety of my job. I was deep into my own research on the workings of the brain and I wanted to learn more from Keith Barry. So I had a private session with him a few weeks before the start of the Six Nations campaign in 2018. I had set out my goals as they recommend in visualisation practice. My goals were to win the Grand Slam so I could walk around the pitch afterwards with my kids, the way the Munster and Ireland lads had done back in '06, '08 and '09. I'd promised my daughters for years that I'd win a cup so they could come round the field afterwards with their daddy. I also wanted to win player of the year. In my session with Keith he told me to visualise these things happening. He took me through a series of visualisation techniques. Then he went away and made up an audio recording for me, customised for my specific goals. It was thirteen minutes long. I listened to it several times the week before the first game against France. I listened to it again on my headphones on the team bus on our way to the Stade de France. The match was unbelievably tight. Teddy Thomas scored a brilliant individual try with nine minutes to go. The conversion put them a point up. With a few minutes left I failed to gather a high ball and Nigel Owens deemed it a knock-on. France had the attacking scrum and were awarded a penalty off it. The old me would've been saying, typical, that's typical now of your luck. But funny enough, we were gathered behind the posts for the penalty and I had no negative thoughts at all. We had covered that in the visualisation tape Keith had done for me. If I make mistakes I will say fuck it, nothing you can do about it, next job, move on straightaway. So, behind the posts I was thinking, we could still salvage this, I have a job to do, let's get back up the field. Then they miss the penalty, a handy-enough kick from the left of the posts for a right-footed kicker. It's a big let-off.

We go through over twenty phases after the re-start and we're struggling to get past midfield. Then Johnny Sexton dinks his crossfield ball over to me and I catch it and slip a tackle and make maybe 15 metres. Eventually Johnny lands the famous drop goal in the 83rd minute after forty-one phases that gets us the win. If I had a different mindset I could have dropped that crossfield ball. It might have freaked me out, the pressure of having to make it. Or I might have gone hiding from it. But I was in a different mindset. I was filled with positivity. I attacked that ball all-out in the air and came down with it and got us over their ten-metre line. This was during that time when my breathing was banjaxed, when I couldn't fill my lungs and I didn't know what was wrong with me. So if ever there was a case of mind over matter, it must have been this one. I had visualised us winning, I had visualised myself making important plays, and I had convinced myself that it was going to happen. And it did happen. We went on to win the Grand Slam and I got to bring Ella May and Laurie around the field at Twickenham with the trophy. It was very special. We have the photos at home, we'll always have the photos at home. I was honoured as well with the Players' Player of the Year award and the Munster Player of the Year award.

It didn't make sense given that physically I was constantly labouring to catch my breath after any bit of action and constantly worrying about not being able to catch my breath. I probably shouldn't have been there at all, when you think about it. But I was winning the battle with my mind and I was telling my mind to win the battle over my body. Instead of doing all the extras at training, I did them in my head cos I wasn't able to do them physically. I would go up to my bedroom for half an hour every day and visualise myself catching high balls, making my tackles, spinning my passes. The great American basketball coach Phil Jackson, I had read in one of his books that some of his players practised their shooting religiously after training every day but some of them practised it in their heads. They visualised themselves landing every shot.

Of course, I had heard for years the mantra about the power of positive thinking and the destructiveness of negative thinking. We all had. But just saying it to yourself doesn't help you to do one and not the other. What I was learning was that you had to work long and hard at thinking positive to make it happen. You had to give yourself the tools to do it. And visualisation was one of those tools. I had to learn how to do it and I had to practise doing it every day. But at least I knew how to practise it now. I practised it for half an hour every day during that Six Nations campaign. I still practise it. I'll start with a relaxation exercise, working from the feet up and getting my whole body relaxed. I'll be listening to a recording on my phone of Keith talking me through the process. I close my eyes and in my subconscious I visualise going downstairs into a cinema room and sitting in a comfortable seat in the dark there. And up on the screen will be images from the game I'm playing that weekend. The stadium, the tunnel, my opponents. In my mind I'm there. Then I'm making all these plays on the screen, going through moves we've rehearsed on the training ground, making line breaks, running in tries. I'll be making mistakes too but I'll get over them straightaway and make some good plays. I'll visualise myself making last-ditch try-saving tackles. I visualised it all in 2018. In the game against England a few of those 'dreams' became reality. After half-time I shot out of the line trying to intercept an Owen Farrell pass about ten metres from our line. I missed it. There was the mistake. Elliot Daly caught it but I managed to get back to him and swipe his ankle away as he was heading for the line. I had visualised executing tackles during those weeks, not on Elliot Daly but on someone.

All these changes that I was making to my life and lifestyle came together to change me for the better. I was feeling lighter in myself. I was feeling more in control of myself. I was finally getting to grips with the blackness that had been inside me since my teens. I was starting to fight back, I suppose. I was understanding that I wasn't powerless over my thoughts and feelings. I had been convinced that it was because of my own thoughts that things weren't going my way. That it was all my fault. But I understood now that I could change them. Those panic attacks were because I had no control over this constant barrage of negative thoughts. They were controlling me. The panic attacks before big games, they were like your body being hijacked by your brain. If I could control what my brain was saying to me, it wouldn't punish me as much. The visualisation ritual became the last piece in the jigsaw for controlling my fear of the sport that I'd grown up loving and had come to hate. A part of me wishes that I never had to go down into such a dark place to push myself to change and get better. But mostly I just accept it was something I had to go through. If I'm proud of anything it's that I kept turning up. The amount of times I just wanted to run away somewhere. I stuck with it.

Listen, I'm still on the medication. I hope one day sooner rather than later I'll be able to wean myself off it gradually. But while I'm still playing I will keep taking it because the game comes with such crazy highs and lows. And Hank the bastard doesn't go away that easy. But when he rears his ugly head I'm able to put him back in his box these days. I have the tools in my locker to put manners on him. Physically and mentally I'm in a good place now. But tomorrow I might not be. It's a day by day thing. I have to keep on top of it all the time.

One other huge lesson I've learned from all this. Nobody knows. Nobody knows what people are going through. Doesn't matter if you're a private citizen or a public person. Doesn't matter if you're a professional sportsman. There's a big difference between who I am as a rugby player and who I am in the rest of my life. I'm not remotely famous by global standards, thank God. But I'd prefer not to be known at all. I'd prefer to be totally anonymous when I'm out somewhere in public. I don't want 'rugby player' to be my identity. I certainly don't want it after I retire. People only know you from what you do on a rugby pitch, which means they don't really know you at all.

7

SPEED

I WAS SEVENTEEN WHEN I DISCOVERED THAT SPEED has a bit of science to it. I was naturally fast, I could run fast, it never dawned on me there could be anything more to it than that.

Then I met Tom Comyns and he got me thinking about it as well as just doing it. Tom is a lecturer in human movement science in the Department of Physical Education & Sports Science at University of Limerick. He was an international sprinter. He represented Ireland at the Olympic Games in Sydney as part of the 4 x 100m relay team. They broke the Irish record in Sydney. They still hold the record to this day.

Tom's from Dooradoyle in Limerick. When I first met him he was working on his PhD thesis. He was studying rugby players in relation to resistance exercise and plyometric exercise. This was 2005/06. I was in my first year in the Munster academy. I was still in school in Munchin's. Tom needed a few guinea pigs to do his research on and I was one of them. It had to be done before school so I'd be up at six in the morning to meet Tom over at the indoor track in UL for seven. I needed a bit of convincing to be getting out of bed at that hour to go running. I'm fast anyway so why do I need it? You either have speed or you haven't. But my ultimate goal was to play for Munster so if this was going to help, maybe I should.

Tom convinced me and I'm so glad he did. I was blessed to get that time with him. I learned the proper techniques for speed movement, for sprinting and sidestepping. I learned about 'form' – your posture, your head and torso and arms and legs. Holding your form at top speed is crucial, it will save you fractions of seconds. You see specialist sprinters, they're immaculate in their form and that's what I was learning. You're trying to push out as much power using as little energy as possible. Efficient speed. That's where your running mechanics come into it. Everything from your toes up – ankles, knees, hips, arms, shoulders, head. It should all be aligned to make you as streamlined as possible.

I learnt how to train for speed. And I learnt it young which meant I didn't have many bad habits already developed. I was a blank canvas more or less. I learnt about staying low in the initial drive and gradually becoming upright, about not becoming tense and tight, about your knee lift and leg stride. It was an important period of learning for me because if I didn't have elite speed, I wouldn't have had the career I had. One fundamental lesson I absorbed was that speed has to be trained to be maintained. You have to do your weights on your upper body and legs, and your general fitness work. The power lifting will help you become more explosive. But you have to sprint at maximum intensity at least a couple of times a week every week, sprint repetitions at full tilt. I've been doing it for sixteen years now. I can honestly say I'm as fast at thirty-four as I was at nineteen or twenty. Maybe faster. They talk about fellas "losing a yard" as they get older. I haven't lost an inch, touch wood. I know because I'm always checking my speed stats on the GPS.

At the beginning I had a good six weeks of one-on-one training with Tom. That set me up with good habits. It opened my eyes to the possibilities of getting faster and faster. The following year he joined the Munster fitness staff as a speed and movement specialist. His job was to get everyone moving faster, prop forwards included. He worked with the first team and the academy players. We'd have great sprint races with the likes of Ian Dowling, Paul Warwick, Shaun Payne, Kieran Lewis, Barry Murphy. Felix Jones when he came down from Leinster, Dougie Howlett when he came over from New Zealand. Countermovement Jumps (CMJs) were used to measure your leg power. It's basically jumping from a standing position and seeing how high you can go. Electronic gates were used for 10m and 30m sprints to time your explosiveness and raw speed. Tom has kept some of my data on file going back to those years. In 2007/08 my CMJ best was 51.5 centimetres. The next year it was 58cm and in '09/10 it was 62.8. Obviously I was improving year on year as all the training paid off.

The real craic was in the sprinting against the clock. The slagging was unbelievable. Everyone was ultra competitive about their times. My fastest 10 metres in '07/08 was 1.64 seconds. The next year it was 1.56 seconds and 1.55 the year after. So I'd gained almost a full one-tenth of a second over three seasons, which is actually a decent improvement over ten metres. Tom reckons 1.55 seconds for ten metres would be up there with specialist track sprinters. It's after ten metres that you'd start to lag behind. You'd need to be doing a different type of training that wouldn't really be relevant to rugby if you wanted to stay with them over 50, 60, 100 metres.

No one in my time at Munster has gone faster over ten metres. My best time has never been beaten. Felix came closest, he was just fractions slower. Paul Warwick was right up there too. Calvin Nash of the new generation is a flier as well. He has actually beaten me a couple of times in sprints. And that's when thoughts do creep into your head. Jesus, am I losing it a bit? But that was on the astroturf pitch and I tend to take it a bit easier on that surface. At my age you have to. That's my excuse anyway.

Nowadays they don't do those 10m tests as much but I know from my GPS numbers how I'm doing in general. If you're hitting 8.5 metres a second you're doing well. I'm usually in the 9s. I've hit over 10 a few times in games. The best I've done was 10.5. That was against Castres in the south of France in October 2017. It was like a summer's day there, nice hard ground underfoot, I was chasing back an intercept and I didn't catch him. I had a huge amount of ground to make up and this fella, Robert Ebersohn, was a sevens player with South Africa, so once he was gone he was gone. But seemingly I hit 10.5 metres per second on the chase back. I had just turned thirty. It's when you're chasing down a player that you can get into a proper foot race over a long distance. Spectators like to see it cos it's like a flat-out sprint between two opponents in the middle of a rugby match.

I had one against an Italian player in 2018. It was the last minute, we had the match wrapped up. Mattia Bellini caught an intercept about ten metres from his own line and went haring up the touchline. I was on the other side of the pitch. Anyway I hauled him in a few yards inside our twenty-two. I could feel my back and my calves cramping up on the way. I think the crowd enjoyed it as much as any of the tries we scored that day, even though it would've made no difference to the result. But it makes no difference whether it's going to make an impact on the result or not. You have to do it. Your professional pride will tell you that. You keep trying to do the right thing irrespective of the scoreboard. You have to show the supporters, the people that ultimately pay you your wages, that you care. Joe Schmidt had given us the heads-up on Bellini the week of the match, same way he'd give you the heads-up on every player you were going to be facing. He was big on reviewing individuals as well as teams. Their habits and weaknesses and strengths. I could remember him saying Bellini was a big lad with a strong fend so I was visualising all week about slapping down his fend hand if I was tackling him. I kind of half-missed the fend as it turned out but got him down anyway.

A few of the Japanese players that we met in the 2019 World Cup were fliers. Their supporters at that tournament were sensational for the noise and atmosphere they created. And they went absolutely ballistic in Shizuoka when one of their lads, Kenki Fukuoka, intercepted a pass with three minutes to go on our ten-metre line. They were leading 19-12 at that stage. Kenki was heading for under the posts when I managed to reel him in. It didn't save the game but it did keep our bonus point.

Bundee Aki made a line break for Connacht in August 2020 at the Aviva. Again we had the win wrapped up, there was just about eight minutes left. But Bundee had been wrecking our heads all day! He's brilliant to play with, he has massive energy and attitude and bottle for the fight. But when you're playing against him it can get very annoying when he's shouting and roaring and in your face. I didn't want to let him start shouting again. I got back to him just inches from the line. They scored from the recycle but at least it wasn't Bundee!

I've probably saved a fair few points over the years from chase backs, but really in my line of work you're supposed to be doing most of your business at the other end of the pitch. My first tries for Munster were a double against London Irish in a pre-season friendly at Musgrave Park in August 2008. I'd made my full debut the week before against a US Eagles selection in Connecticut. My first try in a competitive game was against Edinburgh in the Magners League a week after London Irish. A week later I had a hat-trick against the Dragons at Musgrave. I think that was the first game where 'Flight of the Earls' was used in a headline concerning my name. It's been used a fair few times since. Six tries in four games, at that rate I should have nearly 300 for Munster by now! Instead I have to settle for 59, one short of Simon Zebo's all-time record as of May 2021.

I reckoned I was all set to overtake Zeebs this season or next. Then he announces that he's coming back to Munster after three seasons at Racing 92. So the race is on again with me and Zeebs! We had ten good years together at Munster before he went to Paris so we're the best of mates and he's a brilliant character. But in sport there's this funny thing where you don't want your mates getting one up on you. The rivalry can often be at its keenest between friends. And I have to admit, it might be a bit childish of me, but I got great satisfaction out of a try I scored against Racing in November 2019. It was Zeebs's first time back in Thomond Park since he left, there was a lot of talk about it in the days beforehand. It was a Saturday night kick-off under lights and a full house was in to see it. Those are the occasions you live for.

Zeebs was playing fifteen, Donncha Ryan was back in Thomond with Racing too. Racing scored a couple of class tries in the first half hour. We were in trouble. Just before half-time our lads worked the ball left and got it out to me but I was tight to the touchline, about twenty metres from their line. Zeebs threw himself at me but I handed him off and he fell off the tackle. That got me the daylight I needed to shoot down the corridor and dive over in the corner. Jesus I enjoyed that! The crowd of course lapped it up too.

A big gang of us went out that night, Zeebs included, and I was able to give him the sort of slagging you can only give to a good mate. I'm looking forward to teaming up with him again now in 2021/22 because we always had a great understanding on the field. I scored so many tries from his passes or because of some piece of magic he pulled off in the build-up. Neither of us is getting any younger so I hope we'll be able to make the most of our time in red again. I know for sure we'll be in for some fun and games.

I knew the type of finish that was needed in that match. Sometimes you can run it in, sometimes you have to get airborne to avoid the last-ditch tackle. Sometimes you can do no more than dot it down, sometimes you can get in and get round behind the posts. Sometimes you know a straight line will win the foot race, sometimes you know the tackler will catch you so you'll need to step him. That's a question of pace judgement. Judging your pace and judging his pace and sensing which one of you is getting there faster. Then you might step him but the step might take you into more scrambling defenders. So you might have to step inside and cut back against your direction to get away from the others.

You'll be processing the scenario in your head more or less at the same time as you're doing it. It has to be simultaneous. If you take a fraction of a second to think about it you'll be swallowed up. You have to read what you need and do it at the same time.

I was fifteen or sixteen when I discovered I had a step. My father had been on to me for ages about running around fellas as opposed to just running through them! A step might save me a lot of time and trouble. I started working on my agility. A step is an essential tool in your armoury. A fella comes across to tackle you at speed and you step off your left and he's gone flying one way and you're gone flying the other. You can look very smart when you're doing it, you can look very foolish when somebody is doing it to you. There you are flying across to make a last-ditch tackle and he chops inside you and you're gone flying on your backside tackling nothing but air. It's an occupational hazard, another one. Sometimes if you know you'll need to step, you can decelerate a bit, just slow down a fraction so when you step you can drive off it and hit top gear again. You might deliberately stay in a lower gear when you know the ball is coming to you so you can put on the burners when it does come to you. It depends on the time and space you have. Everything depends on the time and space you have. The game is about time and space.

This makes it sound like I usually have it all figured out when I'm finishing a move. I don't. At my age, experience definitely does come into it. Whatever scenario you're facing, there's a fair chance you've faced it before so you will know what the situation requires. But often you're doing it on pure instinct. You actually don't know where you're going, you just know that you're going. It's often happened to me that I've scored tries and didn't know how I did it. It was only looking at the video afterwards that I could see. Sometimes it's just a blur. My eyes go blurry when the chance is there. I'm running blind.

You'll often hear commentators say that you saw a soft shoulder in the defensive line and exploited it; or that you saw a forward in front of you and knew you had the beating of him. It's often happened to me that I didn't see anything. I just got the ball and next thing I'm sliding over the line or diving over it or reaching for it or running over it. Like the one I got against the Emerging Springboks on the Lions tour in '09. We got turnover ball inside their twenty-two, I was full back, Harry Ellis threw the ball out to me, there was a line of green shirts in front of me, there wasn't really a gap. I stepped inside their scrum half and slipped the other fella's tackle and dived over just to the right of the posts. The TV commentators were giving me credit for spotting the chance, seeing the space. But the reality is I was always going to carry that ball anyway.

I didn't trust my passing at the time. If there was a brick wall in front of me I was going carrying because I wasn't comfortable enough with my passing to trust it. That's why I went for it. I didn't see that the try was on. It actually wasn't on. Now maybe their scrum half took a step or two to his right, anticipating the pass, maybe my body language sold him that idea. But it was all a blur to me. I had the ball and suddenly I was sliding over nearly under the posts.

That happened to me a lot in my early years especially. Your mind is taken out of the equation. Your body takes over and you're doing things without thinking. You're making these good plays and everything is working out for you and you genuinely don't know how you did them. One of my tries against Dragons in 2008, the ball is on the deck and I just chip it up to myself on the run. Your body is doing it, your mind is taking a back seat. They call it 'the flow state', or being 'in the zone'. I've read a few books about it lately, they say it's chemicals in your brain that trigger it, I don't know. They also say you can access the flow state any time you want. I wish you could because it's a lovely place to be. You don't feel tired, you feel you can run forever.

Between club and country I'm on ninety-three tries. I haven't been one for keeping an eye on my stats because obviously you're always moving onto the next game, the next try. But now I'm at an age where they're meaningful to me. Next season I'd like to make the ton. It would be nice to have a hundred tries in first class rugby after your name. I've forgotten a lot of them.

Only a few stand out in my memory for one reason or another. One was the Magners League final in 2011. Leinster had been crowned European champions a week earlier and were coming to Thomond to do the double. Naturally we had the hump about that. And emotionally we were in a sad place because we knew that Paul Darbyshire's time on earth left to him was short. Darbs had been with us four years as our S&C coach. We were very fond of him. He was in a wheelchair. He was dying from Motor Neurone Disease. We knew this would be his last game with us. That was the context.

Leinster were leading 9-7 with fifteen minutes to play. Rog sent over a perfect crossfield ball. Well, when I say perfect, there was a wobble on it! I slagged him about it afterwards. But it was perfect for weight and distance. Isa Nacewa was first to line me up. He was one of the toughest players I ever came up against. I caught it and danced inside Isa's tackle, which took me into Shane Horgan. Shaggy swooped on me and tried to wrap me up but I managed to roll with it and touch it down. It's up there with one of the most important tries I've ever scored. I had no right to score it when you consider the calibre of the lads who were trying to stop me. It gave me great personal satisfaction and a real good feeling cos it helped us get the win we so badly wanted.

Poor old Darbs passed away less than a month later. We felt like we honoured him the best way we could. Conor Murray was playing that day with his Justin Bieber haircut. Myself and Murr are the last of the Mohicans now, the only two players who started that game and are still on the Munster books ten years later. Quinny retired at the end of that season and Dowls was forced to quit with a hip injury. That's the last time Munster have lifted a trophy.

My second try against Ospreys in the Heineken Cup quarter-final in 2009, it was a sprint from about sixty metres. Mafs had put me in less than a minute earlier with a fabulous underarm flip pass. From the restart Dowls did great to win the aerial contest and bat it down to me just inside the five-metre line. Suddenly there was open road in front of me and I took off. Mike Phillips was over in midfield but he started to come across and eat up the ground. I figured I'd have the gas to make it home without needing to step him.

He hauled me down about five metres out and dragged my lower half over the touchline. The rest of me went sliding in face first and I planted the ball. The TMO confirmed the try was good. It was probably the one that got me on the Lions plane to South Africa.

A few weeks later Tom Comyns rang me looking for the video clip to show it in a presentation he was doing. It had more or less everything we'd practised over the previous three years in terms of the technique and mechanics of speed. He tells me he still uses it for demonstration purposes in his lectures to this day.

8

GREEN

THE MONDAY AFTER BRIAN O'DRISCOLL SCORED HIS famous hat-trick in Paris, we were doing a bit of art in school. I was twelve. I was in sixth class in Corpus Christi national school. The teacher told us we could draw a picture of whatever we liked. So I drew a picture of Drico scoring three tries with three French men crying next to him. I'm no artist but if I'd known I'd be playing alongside him one day, I'd have kept it and given it to him for the craic.

But obviously that was an impossible dream for a twelve-year-old. To be honest I still found it hard to come to terms with, the first day I shared a training ground with Drico. He was sound. It was just me who couldn't get used to it. That was in November 2008. Declan Kidney had taken over from Eddie O'Sullivan as Ireland head coach. It was only a few years earlier Deccie was warning me down in Limerick to stay away from the PlayStation. Now he was calling me into his first Ireland squad a month after my twenty-first birthday. My recent form with Munster had paved the way I suppose.

So there I was in the Killiney Castle hotel with all the household names from Irish rugby. At the press conference announcing the team I was sitting at the top table with Deccie on one side of me and Drico on the other as captain. I didn't have a lot to say for myself sitting in that chair. The cameras were clicking, I was like a rabbit caught in the headlights. It would take me years before I'd be comfortable talking to the media. My comfort zone at that time was the playing field. And if the playing field was Thomond Park, better again. As luck would have it, that was where Ireland were scheduled to play Canada in the first of the autumn internationals that year, so that was where I would make my international debut.

It couldn't have gone better. I was picked at full back. It was a shocking night weather-wise. I scored a try with my first touch of the ball in the third minute. In fairness, the crowd gave it a great old roar when I scored. I had a lot of friends and family in the ground that night.

The following weekend against the All Blacks in Croke Park, Girvan Dempsey started full back, I came off the bench with nine minutes left. It was unbelievable to me to be sharing a field with the likes of Dan Carter and Richie McCaw and Ma'a Nonu and Joe Rokocoko. Two years later we played them again at the Aviva. I saw a photo afterwards of me being tackled and I remember looking at it and shaking my head that Richie McCaw was there swinging out of me. If he'd boxed the head off me I wouldn't have minded, I'd have taken it as a compliment.

By the start of 2009 I was in the mix for a squad place for the Six Nations. We had France up first on February 7 in Croke

Park. But two weeks earlier I'd taken a knock to my knee playing for Munster against Montauban. The damage was minor but it ruled me out of consideration for France and dropped me down the pecking order. I was brought back into the extended training panel a few days later.

Beating France got an early buzz going about a possible Grand Slam. Gordon D'Arcy had returned after a long injury, him and Geordan Murphy were on the bench while Rob Kearney, Tommy Bowe, Drico, Paddy Wallace and Luke Fitz were starting in the backline. Deccie stuck with that combination for Italy and England, Darce got back in for Scotland with Paddy on the bench and stayed there for the big one against Wales on the final day of the championship. I travelled with the squad to Cardiff as the twenty-third man for cover in case of a late injury withdrawal.

I wasn't a frustrated bystander. I was happy to be going along for the ride. It was all ahead of me as far as I was concerned. I didn't expect to be breaking into the first fifteen in my first Six Nations campaign. Maybe I should have been more pushy and ambitious but I wasn't that type of fella. It wasn't in my nature. It was all new to me and I was finding the whole scene daunting enough as it was without the pressure of dealing with a Grand Slam.

It wasn't even the rugby side of things, I was doing fine between the white lines. It was more the social side of things in the Ireland camp. You were surrounded by all these stars that I had watched on TV and how was I supposed to behave around them? What's the right thing to say and the right thing to do? I didn't know what to be saying. I was always minding my Ps and Qs around them. It wasn't their fault, the lads by and large couldn't have been nicer. It was my own unease. I couldn't relax, I couldn't be myself. I thought I had to be ultra professional and act perfect all the time.

There was loose talk too that I was supposed to be the next Brian O'Driscoll. It was stupid talk, there'll never be another Drico, but I was naïve enough to let it in on me. I felt the pressure of that. I was just so bloody immature in ways. I was disciplined and mature in other ways, like staying in and minding myself when everyone else my own age was going out having the craic.

From the age of seventeen to twenty-two I didn't do the drinking and the partying, I stayed away from it all, bar a handful of times. I didn't do the big-time Charlie on it either once I started making a few quid and making a name for myself. But I was immature in not being a student of the game back then. I thought raw talent was enough. I suppose young fellas in every sport think that, the ones who walk into every underage team and win everything going. They're the fellas who often get caught out when they reach the grown-up game. They haven't really grown up themselves.

It's often the fellas who weren't juvenile stars who cope better. They've had to graft and slog their way up. They are often better students because they've had to learn more. I wasn't shy about grafting, I had a work ethic. But I was big for my age during teenage rugby and I had natural ability so I coasted through the ranks. I didn't really have to think about what I was doing. So when I reached senior rugby my mind wasn't open to all I could learn if I looked around me and took it all in. I was surrounded by players who had so much experience and knowledge. I could have learnt younger what I only learnt later through experience – often harsh experience. I had a load to learn about the defender's trade, for example. I had a load to learn about communicating with your unit. I wasn't a talker. But communication with the lads around you is crucial. Instead of learning from Drico I think I was just in awe of him.

I didn't know the name for it at the time but basically it was imposter syndrome. Deep down I was questioning did I have a right to be there training and playing with these fellas. Instead of being relaxed and taking it all in, I'd be second guessing myself, wondering if I should be doing this or doing that.

I felt I had to act in a certain way to be accepted. I have to be polite and respectful at all times. Then you'd see these lads out having a few jars and having the craic and they were as normal as the next fella. But if you're not comfortable in your own skin, it complicates things. On the pitch I'd nearly be frightened to make a decision in case it was the wrong one and it'd annoy them. In that environment I was as far away from the flow state as you could possibly be. So I wasn't in the right frame of mind to learn from these brilliant players all around me.

Drico would be giving masterclasses in defending and attacking every day on the training ground and I wasn't switched on enough to take it all in. I should've been making mental notes every day but I wasn't. I didn't take ownership of my game, I was just happy to do what the coaches were telling me to do. You look at the young fellas coming into the squad now, the next generation, and they're nearly as mature at their age as I am now. They're already aware of what they need to be doing in terms of application and studying on the job. I know it's pointless but I do look back and wish I had backed myself more when I was younger, my training could have been better, my learning could have been better. But I suppose part of being young is being foolish and immature. You can't beat yourself up for being young! And it wasn't like I lost the run of myself or anything. I did everything I was asked to do. I kept my head down and my nose clean and listened to what I was being told.

Anyway, no more than Munster winning Europe in '08, I felt no ownership of Ireland's Grand Slam achievement in '09. I was on the inside but really I was an outsider. I've got the medal and all but I don't consider it an achievement. The lads who'd spent years and years building up to that triumph, it was their day of days. I hadn't put in all those hard yards. It was their team not mine.

When we got back to Dublin Airport the next day, myself and John Hayes split from the rest of the camp. They were heading into a big reception outside the Mansion House. Thousands of people would be turning up. But I didn't want to be hanging round a party that I hadn't helped to make happen. Hayes wasn't mad about that scene either, he liked to get home to his farm in Limerick, and I wanted to get back home too. So I got a lift with him and was back in time to watch it all on the six o'clock news.

I made my Six Nations debut the following year, against Italy in Croke Park, taking over from Andrew Trimble after he got injured in the second half. I started against France a week later in Paris. They gave us a good beating and that was our reign over as Grand Slam champions. We still had the Triple Crown to aim for and just because we'd won the Slam a year earlier, didn't make it any less attractive in my mind. I'd grown up hearing about Triple Crowns and I wanted one for myself.

We turned over England in Twickenham with a double from Tommy Bowe and one for myself. Johnny Sexton put me away in the corner. It was a massive moment for me, scoring a try at

Twickenham. Tommy doesn't often get mentioned as a speed merchant but he could really fly when he hit top gear.

We had Wales in Croke Park next. I started on the wing but was shunted into the centre after Darce went off injured early in the second quarter. A couple of minutes later Drico was releasing me with a pass through a gap and I was scoring at the Hill 16 end of the ground. That wasn't lost on me. I knew a bit of GAA history. I'd watched the All-Ireland finals in hurling and football. Any time a player scored a goal in front of the Hill crowd it always seemed special. It was a thrill for me to score in front of the fans on that famous terrace.

On the hour I had my second try after brilliant work by Tomás O'Leary. It was a strike move off a lineout that actually went wrong at first. Tomás's first pass hit the deck but Brian was onto it in a flash and popped it back up to Tomás who threw a dummy, then hit me with a lovely ball and I scored in the corner. That try probably sealed the deal. It was a classic example of Drico making things happen out of shit situations. He had unbelievable smarts and balls.

Now for Scotland. It was all set up for us. It would be our last game in Croke Park before we moved back to the new Lansdowne Road. We were supposed to go out on a high. We'd put the cherry on top with the Triple Crown. Maybe all the expectation distracted us. Maybe our minds weren't fully on the job. I don't know what it was but we played putrid and Scotland did a number on us. Jesus that was a sickener. I was desperate for a bit of silverware to call my own.

I was carrying a groin by then and it wasn't getting any better. By the time we played Leinster in the Magners League semi-final in the middle of May, it was hanging off me. I barely got through the game. And Deccie was announcing his squad two days later for a summer tour of New Zealand and Australia. I was named in it but had to withdraw a week or so later. I could barely run without getting a shooting pain in my groin and lower abs. It got so bad I was literally rolling out of bed in the mornings and falling onto the floor so I could get onto my knees first before trying to stand. I was diagnosed with osteitis pubis. I'd need several months of rest and rehab.

I was back in the squad for the 2010 autumn internationals in November. I came off the bench against South Africa, New Zealand and Argentina. When you're only getting minutes here and there you're hungry. You don't want to be forgotten about. You want to be in the frame for a starting spot. So, every little bit helps. In fairness, not too many people got upset when I had a try disallowed against Argentina. But I did. I was only on the field ten minutes. Rog chipped the ball ahead and myself and their winger had a dash to get to the touchdown. I got my hand to it first. I know I did. You always know in these situations whether you did or not. Anyway they kicked it up to the TMO for a look and he decided the Argentina lad got to it first. He didn't. I was pissed off. It was the eightieth minute, we were 22-9 up, and Darce scored another try in injury time anyway so no one was too bothered about my sob story! But the thing is, every try you score at that level is precious. You don't get the chance to score too many of them in the international arena. They're hard enough to score without them being chalked off when they're perfectly legit.

I started and finished all five of the 2011 Six Nations and drew a blank. The first four I was on the left wing, the last one, against England in Dublin, I was at full back. That was a really good team performance. England were in town to win the Grand Slam. But we had our own priorities, we needed to finish the tournament on a high after a very mixed campaign. Everything clicked with us on the day.

I really enjoyed playing fifteen. At that stage I was seen as a utility back – full back, centre, wing, wherever I was needed to fill a gap. I've been pretty much a specialist winger for the last seven seasons but I've played outside centre for Ireland fourteen or fifteen times, either starting or being moved in when someone's gone off injured. I've played twelve as well. Myself and Drico used to chop and change when we were the centre partnership and I reckon I could slot in there easily enough now too. I've enough experience to do the job. The last five or six seasons I've defined myself as a winger who can play thirteen or fifteen and actually for the 2021 Six Nations I was covering thirteen as well. If Robbie Henshaw went off injured, Jordan Larmour would come to the wing and I'd move inside.

Our first game of that 2011 championship was against Italy away, the one where we just survived by the skin of our teeth thanks to Rog's late drop goal. This was the time of the gang wars in Limerick. Bad headlines about it were being splattered all over the newspapers. It was hurtful for Limerick people to be seeing this all the time. Then Moyross was coming in for an awful lot of negative publicity too and that was really hurtful because we were only a small community doing our best and we felt powerless. It was bothering me.

So the year before, we were training on the back pitch of the Aviva Stadium. It had been snowing heavily and I got this brainwave that I'd carve out the word MOYROSS in the snow! A photographer got a snap of it. It went down well back in my home place so in 2011 I decided I'd make another little gesture of support. Adidas were my boot sponsors at the time. Adidas and me parted company just before the 2019 World Cup. They never told me why. It was just business I suppose. In professional sport you'll get dropped like a hot potato when you're deemed no longer useful. Roy Keane said we're all just pieces of meat in pro sport. I know what he means. Nearly every fella who's ever been in a pro set-up in any sport will know what he means. I have seen the revolving door spinning. Munster is a great family club, a community club, but it's a business there too. It has to be I suppose. But I've seen fellas who won European Cups and they get to a certain age and they're told there's nothing there for them anymore. There isn't another contract. That's how it works. I know the chop is coming for me too, unless I get to walk away on my own terms. I would like to be in control of that decision when the time comes, but you never know.

Anyway, I've been wearing Nike gear the last few years. But back in 2011 I got onto my Adidas contact and asked him if he could rustle me up a special pair of boots with 'Moyross' printed on the side of them. And he came up with a lovely pair of lime green jobs with the name stencilled on in black near the heel. I wore them for the captain's run in the Stadio Flaminio the day before the Italy game. The photographers zeroed in on the word and I was plastered all over the papers the next day with the boots. They were delighted back in Moyross. My father and mother got loads of lovely messages from friends and neighbours and passed them on to me. When Munster won the Magners League final four months later, I brought the whole squad into Kinsella's in Thomondgate, the local bar that me and my father used to drink in at the time. We had many a great night in Kinsella's over the years, knocking back a few and playing darts and pool and rings. But the place was nearly a shrine to me at the time, I got a fair old slagging from the lads once they copped all the photos and newspaper cuttings on the walls.

The summer and autumn of 2011 were all about the World Cup in New Zealand. We didn't fly out on a high note. England gave us a beating at the Aviva in our last pre-tournament friendly at the end of August. I was playing thirteen. Manu Tuilagi tore us apart that day and I was supposed to be marking him. That was the first time I came across Manu. I think it was the first time I ever came across a back of his size and power. He was fucking enormous. And he was solid muscle. He swatted me out of the way for their first try after four minutes. Normally you'd go low in the tackle on a big man but this fella's legs were so big and powerful there wasn't much point doing that either. You come across plenty of big men in this job but you don't come across many like Tuilagi when he's on the rampage. Thank God.

We played USA in the first game of the World Cup in the Taranaki Stadium, New Plymouth. It was a filthy day with wind and rain. The worst conditions I've ever played in and that's saying something. I was back on the wing. We didn't play well but sometimes it's no harm to have an off day the week before you've a massive match. We've often done it at Munster, consciously or unconsciously. Just muddle your way through one game and save a bit in the tank if you're throwing the kitchen sink at the next one. It can lull opponents into a false sense of security too. They have to carry the favourites' tag, you're coming in under the radar.

We had Australia next. I don't know if a bit of it seeped into their squad but the Aussie media and public were expecting their lads to put us away without too much trouble. Behind closed doors though, we were building up to a major performance and we delivered it. The Aussies were shellshocked afterwards. I was a bit shook myself before a ball had even been kicked. I was going through one of my periods where I was trying every fad that was going. Caffeine gum was trendy at the time so I took two of them before the game and next thing I was getting a dose of the jitters. I love my coffee now but I wasn't a big coffee drinker at the time so my body wasn't prepared for the caffeine hit at all. This felt like I'd just drunk ten espressos! Oh my God I was shaking all over. James O'Connor was taking their kicks that day. I was standing behind the goals for one of them thinking if this ball comes near me I'm not going to be able to catch it. Sure enough it landed in on me, bounced off my chest and I had to make a double-grab to hold onto it. That was the end of the caffeine gum for me.

Otherwise it was a fantastic night in Auckland. I'd say the Irish fans who were in Eden Park that night will never forget it. There were thousands of them there. They did us proud. It was near enough a complete team performance but Cian Healy stands out in my memory. He was awesome that night. I'd gotten to know Cian from the schoolboys scene years earlier. I first came across Cian at Clongowes Wood when we were teenagers. The provincial schoolboys teams would all come together in Clongowes where we'd train together and then play against each other. I never saw a young fella so big and powerful in all my life. He was doing back flips off the chairs and landing on his feet. And then he had speed on top of that. Tuilagi was like him, only bigger and faster. We got on great, we played on an Ireland schoolboys team together, then the Under 19s, Under 20s and Ireland As. We had a camp one weekend down in Limerick and I had Cian back in the house, he was playing darts with my father up in the attic.

I was back in the centre for the Russia game in Rotorua and picked up two tries. A week later I got another double against Italy on the day of my 24th birthday. A few family friends were in the crowd with placards wishing me happy birthday. That was in Dunedin. The stadium is fully covered so the atmosphere generated by the Irish support was absolutely electric. I couldn't help myself when Andrew Trimble put me away in the eightieth minute. The match was in the bag, it was a great break by Trimby, the Irish crowd was celebrating so I decided to join in with a big splashdown over the line. Dad was giving out to me about it – make sure you get the bloody ball down first! Edel was back at home pregnant with Ella May and sending me photos of her bump. It was grand for me, it was tough on her being on her own back in Limerick. The wives and partners of rugby players have to spend a lot of time at home while we're away in training camps and travelling the world. I sometimes think that they think we're on a permanent holiday camp. In fairness, we are usually treated like royalty on tour. We got some time off in New Zealand and had a few great days out, albeit I wasn't drinking. We were down in Queenstown for the first week, it's a resort town on Lake Wakatipu with all sorts of adventure sports and surrounded by mountains. It's an incredible place. It was like being in a winter movie with all the snow and beautiful scenery. We went out to a restaurant one night, the whole squad, and someone decided it'd be a good idea to play credit card roulette. So we all threw our credit cards into a bowl on the table. The last one out would be left holding the short straw. And would you believe it, I drew the fecking short straw! Conor Murray and me were the last two names in the bowl. Conor was panicking because he was on academy money at the time and I was saying to myself, Jesus I've a baby on the way! My memory is that the bill came to something like 1800 New Zealand dollars. I had to face the music, or so I thought. I went up to the counter to take care of it but unbeknown to me the lads had a quick whiparound and came up to me with an envelope with about $1400. Everyone had chipped in. I still had to fork out $400 but it could've been a lot worse!

We topped the group and got Wales in the quarter-finals. This was supposed to be the handier side of the draw because we'd avoided South Africa. But Wales had us in their sights and outplayed us on the day. I made a few costly mistakes in defence. I scored a try after half-time which Rog converted to bring us level. But that was to be our last score of the game. That was the first time I ever encountered the backlash from the public. I don't mean personally, just the sense that you've let down an awful lot of people who were cheering you to the rafters only a week earlier. It's a fickle business, as everyone knows. I was unbelievably down about it that night. I wasn't even tempted to break out on a session. But a lot of the lads did, they had a head of steam to blow off after an anti-climax like that and after ten weeks of living inside the bubble. I remember shuffling around the streets of Wellington with Paulie that night, kind of being his wingman as he drowned his sorrows. The highs and the lows. They're like twins in this game, you don't have one without the other.

****

In February 2012 in Paris we're in the dressing room at the Stade de France, all psyched up and raring to go. Then someone comes in and announces that the match is off. The pitch is frozen. This is about ten minutes before we're supposed to go out on the field. The ground has no undersoil heating. The referee has done a late inspection, a very late inspection, and decided it's not safe. So there we are in the dressing room, all dressed up and nowhere to go. This is a Saturday night. Suddenly we've a free night in Paris and I'm thinking we might as well make the most of it. Ella May is eighteen days old and between all the panic and the medical emergencies after her birth, I haven't had a chance to actually celebrate the arrival of our wonderful daughter. So I say to the lads, come on, we'll wet the baby's head in Paris.

We didn't spare the horses that night. All we had to wear was our No.1 suits, our official Ireland squad suits. We ended up in a nightclub pouring down the booze. I met up with Paul Warwick at one stage. Paul was living in Paris and playing with Stade Francais. He'd left Munster in the summer of 2011 after four great seasons with us. People used to get us mixed up on the field because we both had fair hair and tight haircuts. Fellas would be complimenting me on something I'd done in Thomond Park that Paul had done, and vice versa. I end up going back to his apartment that night for a drink and he has loads of Stade Francais gear there and he's giving me stacks of it to bring back to the lads in Limerick. I get back to the team hotel where the session is still going strong. All I remember is waking up in bed the next morning with somebody spooning me and it's not Edel. It's fecking Pete O'Mahony! What the fuck is he doing here?! I give him an elbow. He's looking round him and he hasn't a clue either. We're both still drunk. And for good measure I'm togged out head to toe in Stade Francais gear over my suit.

That summer we head for New Zealand. We're back in Eden Park for the first Test of three, nine months after that night of nights against Australia. I'm partnered with Drico in the centre for the first time, me at twelve, him at thirteen. There's a lot made of the difference between the two positions but it depends on what your coach wants. Some coaches want a big twelve who'll bash it up and get you the gain line and a faster thirteen who'll get into space. Some will want two ball-players there operating as auxiliary outhalves at times. The All Blacks give us a good going over in that first Test and I tear a pec muscle. The doc rules me out for the rest of the tour but Deccie knows I have good powers of recovery, I can normally shave a few weeks off the usual rehab time for an injury.

Darce is back in the centre with Drico for the second Test, in Christchurch. The team is playing very well, they're leading 10-9 at half-time. We look like we might salvage a draw out of it until Dan Carter steps up with a last-minute drop goal. But I'm excited about the third Test cos I'm back in the team and in my innocence I reckon we've a great chance after running them so close the week before. But that only served to fire them up to a different level altogether. They got a kicking in the local press for that performance. And our lads are running on empty after a full twelve months on the road without let up. We had fired the last of our shots in that second Test. New Zealand go to town on us in Hamilton. We can't cope with their intensity and ferocity. The likes of Sam Cane, Israel Dagg and Sonny Bill Williams run riot on us. I'm back playing on the left wing. Ten minutes after half-time Hosea Gear is steaming down the opposite wing. I'm tearing across to get to him. I make up the ground. He knows I'm going to catch him. So he actually slows down and waits for me and instead of me lining him up, it's him lining me up. I try to go high on him and he smashes me in the face with his forearm and makes it over the try line with Fergus McFadden hanging out of him. I'm knocked out cold, lying on my side. In fairness to Sonny Bill, he has the decency and the presence of mind to come over and tend to me. He rolls me over onto my back to see if I've swallowed my tongue. He tries to take my gum shield out. My tongue is safe so it's okay. Trimby comes on for me but for some reason I'm put back in six minutes later, then I'm permanently removed seven or eight minutes after coming back on. The final scoreline is 60-0. I find it hard seeing it in black and white even all these years later. It is the most humiliating game I've ever been involved in. The speed and power of the All Blacks, it's an exhibition of total rugby. They're running lines, their handling and passing, it's incredibly slick and quick. The faster you try to execute the skills of the game, the bigger the chance they'll break down. They're doing it all at high speed and everything is sticking.

Mind you, losing to Italy in Rome the following March wasn't a barrel of laughs either. It was the first time Italy had ever beaten Ireland. It's the last time they've done it too. That's the kind of history you definitely don't want to be part of. That match had warning signs written all over it before a ball was kicked. Everything that could go wrong did go wrong. We were decimated with injuries beforehand and it got worse during the game. I had to come off after twenty-five minutes with a busted shoulder. Luke Marshall was gone three minutes later. And

Luke Fitzgerald, who'd replaced me, only lasted eleven minutes. Iain Henderson had to come on for Luke Fitz with O'Mahony being shifted out to the wing. Pete spent the rest of the game out there. Then Drico got sin-binned for ten minutes. All before half-time!

That was Deccie's last game in charge. The IRFU decided to replace him a few weeks later. I was sorry to see him go. He'd been very good to me, professionally and personally. He'd given me my first break by bringing me into the Munster academy. He'd given me my first senior Munster and Ireland caps. He had a great way about him. He was brilliant at reading players, I mean reading them as people. He knew when to leave you alone and say nothing. He knew when fellas needed to be pushed harder. He had a great skill in judging the mood of a squad and what to say and what not to say. He surrounded himself with good technical coaches to take care of that side of things. He managed the whole ship very well. He was a bit eccentric too, in a good way. He'd come out with a few mad lines from time to time. But he had that bit of humanity about him which made you warm to him and trust him.

That was a few days into April 2013. By the end of April we'd have a new man in charge. We would soon find out that Joe Schmidt was a horse of a different colour. It was going to be a whole new ball game altogether with Joe in charge.

9

CAREER GUIDANCE

I WAS ACTING THE MAGGOT IN CLASS ONE DAY AND the teacher told me to get out and go down to the library. This was my first year in St Munchin's, early in the new year, so January 2001. I wasn't happy there. It was no fault of the school's. I just wanted to be with my childhood friends, they were all in St Nessan's Community College in Moyross. That's where I wanted to be. But here I was on the other side of the city, in Corbally, and my behaviour was becoming disruptive cos I was just unhappy there. My parents had decided to send me to Munchin's because it was and is a great rugby nursery and because they thought I'd be safer there, away from the aggro and the tension in Moyross. They wanted to keep me out of the way of trouble but the funny thing was, I ended up in more trouble in my new school.

I'd made a few new friends in Munchin's, including Ger Slattery, a lad I only knew from playing against Richmond. Ger

Sla was big for his age too and the two of us had a few run-ins on the rugby field. We played against each other the whole way up through the underage grades. But we hit it off straightaway in Munchin's and became good buddies. He was in my class. After initially dreading the idea, I settled in well there. Then for some reason Ger and a few other lads I'd gotten to know were moved to a different class and I was left feeling isolated again. That was when I started acting up. I was being disruptive in class. Nothing serious but talking and messing – enough to be annoying the teachers. I'd already been suspended for getting my head shaved. I'd been shaving my head since I was ten. But they didn't approve of it in Munchin's, it was more a middle class sort of school, it still had boarders at the time.

Anyway, the teacher throws me out of class this day for acting the maggot. If you were thrown out of class you had to go down to the library to calm down. I'm just at the door of the library when another teacher appears, a career guidance teacher as it happens. He asks me why I'm not in class. I tell him the teacher put me out for messing. And he looks at me real nasty and says to me I'll go nowhere in life. He walks away with those words ringing in my ears. To be honest, those words have stayed with me to this day. I never forgot them. I'm only starting to understand how shattering they are for a kid to hear. "You'll go nowhere in life."

I hang around the library until the bell goes and class is over. I make my way back to the classroom. The teacher has left but all the boys are there. Then I explode. Hurling is big in Munchin's as well as rugby. Loads of lads are there with their gear and hurleys for training after school. I grab one of the hurleys and start walloping it off the desks. I go up to the blackboard and I take a few flakes at it. I bate it off the teacher's desk. A few fellas have their lunches out with fruit and all. So I start grabbing apples and oranges and flaking them off the walls. Basically I've lost the plot. I'm fucking mad with anger. I'm wrecking the place. Then the next teacher arrives in, a priest, and he sees the scene. He marches me up to the office of the school principal. The priest tells him the story and the principal says I'm immediately suspended and I'm not welcome back. He phones my mother to tell her. Your son has been expelled because of his conduct. Someone goes and gets my bag and coat from the classroom and they're handed over to me and I walk down the avenue and out the gates. I'm dreading my father coming home from work that evening. He's going to go ballistic with me. Mam has told him what happened. But I'm not able to explain to him why I erupted like that. He thinks it's because I wanted to be expelled all along. It's only a few days later that I'm able to get the words out. To tell him what the career guidance teacher said to me. Then he goes ballistic again when he hears that. He phones the school and demands a meeting with the principal. At the meeting he tells the principal the full story. Your man is taken aback. He tells my dad that I can't come back to Munchin's but they'll help get me another school. Long story short, I'm enrolled in Nessan's. I suppose you could call it a free transfer. And I'm absolutely delighted! I'm back with all my mates, I'm back with Edel too. They used to be texting me with all the news and craic that was going on in the school, I always felt like I was missing out. I had the best two and a half years of my school days in Nessan's.

I don't think my new teachers reckoned they had a star pupil on their hands. But the ones who had an interest in sport were happy enough to see me. My very first day in Nessan's coincided with a rugby game down in Cork and I was straight into the team. We were leaving at half nine that morning so I'm about half an hour in class on my first day and I'm out the door to play a match. On the second day, I go on the mitch. Two of my buddies told me it was national mitch day so they were going to skip school and I should go with them. I knew I shouldn't but I succumbed to the peer pressure and headed off down the train tracks with the lads. We were gone for the day. But the next day we were hauled into the office to explain ourselves. I had a hard time explaining to my folks why I ended up going on the mitch on my second day in a new school. Was one school not enough to be thrown out of? They let me off with a warning, another one, and I settled down fine.

But whenever there was a choice between the books and a ball game, it was no choice at all. I was gone out the door. It started in national school. I remember going to track and field meetings in Nenagh and Waterford, competing in the sprints and the javelin and whatever other event took my fancy. I played Gaelic football in Corpus Christi too and ended up on the Limerick City team that played West Limerick in the Sarsfield Cup in the Gaelic Grounds. Just running out on that famous field was a thrill for a young Limerick fella, I couldn't get over the size of it.

Pretty much every sport came easy to me. I just found it natural. Anything that involved a ball and running around, I just loved it from when I was knee high. Researching this book I came across a few paragraphs in the *Limerick Leader* from September 1995. So I'm seven going on eight. I'm playing for Northville United soccer team, later to become Moyross United. We've drawn 2-2 with Corbally United in Carew Park. By May

'97 I'm scoring two goals for Distillery, another Moyross team, against Coonagh. May '98 a hat-trick against Star Rovers. I'm playing loads of soccer through these years, it's huge in Moyross and Ballynanty, some of my uncles are really talented players. Everyone is out playing it on the streets and the housing estates. I usually played either in goals or up front, depending on the circumstances. I signed for Ballynanty Rovers when I was twelve. One of my best friends, his father was coaching there, a lot of my friends were there and they were playing in a higher level league as well. Balla were a big name in junior soccer and still are. They had their own pitch out towards Meelick, Bateman Park. I enjoyed the game but I don't think I ever took it serious enough to make it a career.

I was selected on a Limerick Under 14s squad. The Star Rovers manager was in charge of the Limerick side at the time. He saw me playing in goals for Balla a few times. One day I happened to be saving shots left, right and centre. He came over to me after and said he was bringing the U14 squad to Cork. Would I like to go? Truthfully I didn't like to go anywhere. I didn't like leaving my little bubble in Moyross. But I went down anyway. I only knew one or two lads, the rest were all from different teams, and I just felt uncomfortable so I opted out of the squad after that. I figured it wasn't for me. Even so, my name was being bandied about as a future prospect in goals. I played for the Limerick District Under 16s and was invited to an Ireland Under 16s trial in Jackman Park in Limerick. It was a big deal at the time but I didn't really appreciate that. There were lads from all over Ireland there. We were togged out in the full Irish kit and all. Afterwards the coaches told me I was very good at the basics but I was far too quiet. And it's true, I was very shy at the time. They told me I needed to be a lot more vocal as a goalkeeper. I never heard anything more from them and I wasn't too bothered one way or the other.

I was more at home in the rugby community. Tony Cronin was a great character and stalwart of Thomond RFC. He called down to our house one evening wondering would I come up and train with the Under 10s. I was eight. I went up to Fitzgerald Park the next evening and it took off from there. There was a blitz a few weeks later and I caught an intercept and went tearing off up the pitch. I had visions of doing what Dad had done against St Mary's in the AIL only a few years earlier but I was hauled down before the line and I was broken-hearted!

In 2000 we got to the final of the famous Pat Lawlor tournament. It's a massive annual tournament for Under 12 teams, they come from all over Ireland. Thomond played Ennis in the final. It went to extra time but it was still level at the end so we played on and on until eventually the organisers decided to call it a day and share the title between us. I scored a try in that match. I'm already big for my age and getting used to running over fellas rather than round them. I was a proper bosh merchant in those years.

Unfortunately I stopped growing when I was about sixteen or seventeen and ended up having to go round fellas for a living rather than through them. I'm playing out of my age grade in those years and swapping positions around. In my own age group I'm playing openside flanker because physically it suits me and because I want to be like my dad. Then I could be playing centre or outhalf for the next grade up. One year I played three finals over three consecutive nights at U14, U15 and U16. Thomond were strong underage in those years, we won league and cup medals the whole way up from U12s to U18s. I did a lot of the place-kicking back then. I had a big boot on me, not much technique but I could give the ball an almighty lash. Taking the goal kicks in soccer, I used to drive them way downfield. In rugby I was landing penalties aged fifteen from the halfway line if I got the right contact on the ball. I practised my place-kicking in Thomond Park after school and on holidays. Me and my friends had the run of the place when we were young. It was no problem getting in or out. We were playing Young Munsters in a league game one day when I was sixteen. This was in Fitzgerald Park. We got a penalty on the 10m line, close to the touchline on the right hand side. I was a right-footed kicker so the angle didn't particularly suit me either. I called for the kicking tee. A few spectators started sniggering and making smart remarks. Obviously they reckoned I was being a bit ambitious, or maybe deluded. Anyway, I put down the ball, lined up the kick and slotted it. All the way. "Who's laughing now?" I said to them as I jogged back.

It wasn't like me at all to be giving backchat in rugby games. That was the code of discipline that was drilled into you. My father used to drum it into me. Always show good manners to the match officials and your opponents. Stand up for yourself at the same time but keep your mouth shut and play the game. But in soccer the same code didn't apply. Everyone would be shouting at the referee, me included. I used to get frustrated playing outfield. You couldn't get stuck in to fellas the way you could in rugby. I got stuck in a few times and ended up getting sent off. I used to hate my father coming to my soccer games just in case the frustration got the better of me and I ended up in the referee's notebook or even worse, on the sideline. I remember one time we were playing Star Rovers in the UL Bowl. Dad was supposed to stay away but I noticed him out of the corner of my eye standing there trying to blend in with the crowd. So I went over to one of my team mate's mothers and asked her to go over and tell my father to go away! I knew he'd be so disappointed if I got into trouble with the opponents or the match officials so I didn't want him there.

Coming into my late teens I was training and playing for so many teams, something had to give. I was suffering from burnout. I was losing the spark. It was just overexposure and pure fatigue. My father was onto me about cutting down and specialising in one sport. I don't care which one you pick, he'd say, but pick one.

At this stage the rugby was starting to get serious. It was all heading in one direction I suppose. It was time to drop the soccer. I was much better at rugby anyway. It suited me more. I loved the feeling of getting the ball in your hands and taking off and running as fast as you could go. Dad knew I was cut out for it although he never forced me to choose what I played. But it must have been really disappointing for him when I left Munchin's because he knew I'd get a great rugby education there. But Nessan's had a team as well and that was good enough for me. In fact I played hurling and soccer there too. I'd play for any of their teams if it meant getting out of the classroom. I remember once playing in goals for the hurling team with a plank of wood out of the woodwork room! We were using the smaller hurleys they use for underage games but I wanted something bigger to give the ball a proper wallop so I got hold of this fairly rough length of timber for the job. Myself and Dad used to have puckarounds regularly. He always kept a few hurleys in the house. He was a big supporter of the Limerick hurling team too.

Nessan's had only the one pitch for all codes, every home game was played on that field. The classrooms were all prefabs, they'd be fairly cold and miserable in the winter. I remember the first time I was ever in Glenstal Abbey, it was like visiting another planet. We were playing them in a junior cup game, I was fourteen at the time. I didn't have a clue that such a place existed. It was beautiful, a big long driveway with trees either side, lovely old buildings and loads of manicured lawns and playing fields. There was a couple of monks in their gear strolling around the grounds. I just never knew there were places like this. I didn't mind, I was really enjoying Nessan's anyway. One of the reasons I wanted to go there was because they taught woodwork and metalwork. Munchin's was too academic for me, I wanted to get my hands on stuff and make things. I loved the metalwork and woodwork. They were the only two classes where I really applied myself. I got high grades in both in the Junior Cert. I learnt how to make coffee tables, chairs, tools, even a helicopter. It was real proper work and I was good with my hands.

Even though it wouldn't have been known as a rugby school, we actually had a few decent teams at Nessan's in those years because so many of us were training and playing with Thomond as well. In 2004 we had a massive win over Glenstal in the Junior Cup. That took us into the fourth round where we'd be playing Castletroy College. It was a big achievement to make it that far. The game was on our pitch, the whole school turned out for it, we had hundreds cheering us on. The coaches wanted me to play centre that day but I was playing most of my rugby in the back row and I wanted to stick to that position. My father wore seven, I wanted to wear seven too. I wasn't for budging. I was far too headstrong. It was a big mistake. I think we'd have won it if I played centre. That was the closest we got to a breakthrough in Nessan's. We were one game away from the quarter-final. Then a matter of weeks later I went to the Munster schools senior cup final in Thomond Park because Munchin's were playing in it. My mate Ger Sla was playing hooker. I was gobsmacked by the occasion. There was like 7,000 people there. The atmosphere was brilliant, there were TV cameras there and all. Munchin's beat Pres Cork and the Limerick support went nuts. I'm watching this thinking, Jeez I'd love a bit of that. That game opened my eyes. I was steeped in Limerick rugby but the whole schools senior cup thing had passed me by. I was oblivious to it. In fairness, I was oblivious to a lot of things. I didn't know what was going on around me a lot of the time. But I knew I liked what I was seeing that St Patrick's Day in Thomond Park. So I hatched a plan. I decided I'd try and get back to Munchin's, three years after they threw me out of the place. I hadn't held a grudge against the school as such. It was only one teacher who had made the bad remark to me, you couldn't blame the whole school for that. I was to blame too because of my behaviour. And the few people in authority I'd clashed with, they were no longer there. So I was prepared to go back, if they were prepared to take me back.

John Broderick was a teacher there and coach of the team that had just won only the school's fourth ever senior cup. John would have taught my father and Edel's mother in Nessan's before he moved to Munchin's. He was also affiliated to Thomond where he was coaching underage teams including his own son Eamon.

So John had known me since I was a child. He'd been good to me during my first year at Munchin's and I always felt bad over what happened because of the way he'd looked out for me at the time. Anyway, I decided to give him a call. I didn't tell my parents or anyone. I think he was surprised to hear from me. I was fairly sheepish calling him but I asked him what were the chances of me going back? I had my Junior Cert exams that summer, I could be starting the Leaving Cert cycle in Munchin's that September? Leave it with me, said John. He spoke to a few people at the school, then he rang my parents. My father got a bit of a land. He had the talk with me. Was I sure? Was there going to be any messing this time round? No, I told him, there'd be no messing, I wanted to go back to play senior cup rugby. Alright so. Munchin's agreed to take me back at the start of the next school year. Word got out in Nessan's. Our PE teacher was gutted, he was pleading with Edel to get me to change my mind. I was sad to be leaving and so was Edel but I think she figured afterwards it was for the better. She got her head down to study for the Leaving Cert. It was probably no harm that we were in different schools for those few years.

In the summer of '04 I was recruited into the new Munster rugby academy. I was part of the first batch of recruits that also included Billy Holland, Donncha Ryan, Duncan Williams and Tomás O'Leary. More and more my path was being laid out for me. I was heading in the right direction. Thankfully I never looked too far ahead of me. It was a case of keep the head down and keep going.

I thrived in the rugby culture at Munchin's. The difference this time was that I wanted to be there and I had a clear goal in mind. I wanted to win a Munster schools senior cup. Pat

Cross, a legend in Limerick rugby, coached us along with John Broderick. We had good coaches, good players and a good work ethic. Senior schools rugby was serious business and I was blessed I copped onto it before it was too late. It helped set me up physically and mentally for my transition to the pro game. It probably paved the way for me. CBC Cork beat us in the 2005 semi-final with a try in injury time, the last play of the game. We were shellshocked after it. That was the start of March. At the end of the month I was picked for the Ireland schools team to play England at Cork Con's ground in Templehill. That was a real milestone for me at the time, to get that sort of recognition at national level. Cian Healy and Luke Fitz were on that team too. Cian had a huge influence against England that day, Vasily Artemiev from Blackrock College scored two tries. A week later we had a big win over Wales in Pontypool and the following Friday we beat France in Dubarry Park with three penalties from Brian Collins, our outhalf from Castleknock College.

I didn't have time to celebrate. The same weekend I was on a flight out to South Africa. The Ireland Under 19s were at the World Cup and they needed a few reinforcements. It was all happening! It was an unbelievably fast turnaround. Four days after the France game I was sitting on the bench in Durban for the Under 19s against Japan. I came on for Rob Kearney with twelve minutes left. I stayed on the bench for our final game against Scotland.

Then it was back to Munchin's in September for the '05/06 academic year. At that age you don't have a whole pile of perspective on life. As far as I was concerned the whole world revolved around the Munster schools senior cup. Nothing else mattered. I had complete tunnel vision. I had one year left to do it. It was all or nothing. As a result I put huge pressure on myself that season, in hindsight far too much.

In December '05 I was picked on the Ireland U19 A team to play a touring Australia side in Donnybrook. I was pissed off because they hadn't picked me for the full international side. Anyway I scored a good individual try early doors, a chip and chase, which must have registered with the selectors because they brought me into the first team proper to meet the Aussies in Ravenhill four days later. Ger Sla was promoted from the A side too. That Australian team had names who'd become very famous in the following years – Quade Cooper, Kurtley Beale, David Pocock, Christian Lealiifano, Lachie Turner. I made a couple of good breaks in that game. I went into their dressing room afterwards to swap jerseys and a few of them were complimenting me on my speed – Jeez you're quick, mate! Thanks very much! David Pocock was stripped off and I could not believe the muscles on him. He's seventeen at the time and he's packed solid with muscle.

Back in Limerick it was full steam ahead now for the senior cup. We had Rockwell College in the quarter-final in Thomond Park in February. We won but I was devastated. I was sent off and a red card meant an automatic suspension. I'd miss the semi-final against Crescent College two weeks later and if we won that, possibly the final too. I'd scored a try against Rockwell and set up another; I kicked two conversions and two penalties. The semi-final was a Limerick derby, it was going to be tight, we needed all hands on deck. And it looked done and dusted that I was going to miss it. I was sent off in the sixty-first minute for getting involved in a row. Ger Sla was on the ground and two of their lads were milling into him. I saw him on the ground and these two lads standing over him and throwing digs at him. So I ran in and landed a few of my own. The ref came in to sort it out. Then the touch judge intervened. He went over to the ref and for some reason picked me out of the skirmish for special mention. He told the ref that I'd punched one of their lads when he was on the ground and defenceless. But it was Sla who was on the ground. These lads were standing. Anyway the ref took the touch judge's word and sent me off. I had a blazing argument with my father in my bedroom that night. He said I was after throwing away a Munster schools senior cup. I said I did everything he'd taught me to do. If one of your team mates is in trouble you go in and you help him and you never back away from that. He said fair enough. It was news around town at the time. It was in the *Limerick Leader* the following week, how I was going to miss the semi-final and final.

The board who governed the schools competitions was having its meeting in Thomond Park a few days later. They'd have the referee's report. That was where I'd be handed down my suspension. Rightly or wrongly, we didn't think we'd have many allies at that meeting. I turned up with John Broderick. And Jesus didn't John pull a rabbit out of the hat. He had a video recording of the game, including the incident. Liam Óg Murphy was our blindside flanker. Liam Óg's mother is American. And she had a camcorder that she brought to the game. Typical American mom, fair play to her! She'd captured the incident clear as day. It showed me fighting alright but it was a fair fight. They were standing up, I was standing up, we were throwing digs. There was no footage of me punching a defenceless fella on the ground because it didn't happen. The video was conclusive. We stated our case and the board had to accept the evidence of their own eyes. I was off the hook. I was free to play in the semi-final.

Ger Sla was from a similar background to mine, both of us working class lads playing a middle class sport. We had it in our heads that because it was me and him who were involved in that melee, that was why one of us was singled out. The fella who got blamed for being in the wrong just happened to be the fella from Moyross. We had learned to be paranoid about that kind of discrimination.

We were favourites to beat Crescent but we only got away by the skin of our teeth. Eamon Broderick and myself had a brilliant understanding at centre. I loved that partnership, we'd been playing together since we were kids. Eamon found a gap after ten minutes and put me away. I ran it in from about fifty yards. I was off my kicking game, I missed a few handy penalties. We had a couple of real close shaves and narrow escapes. The refereeing decisions went our way that day. We scraped home by a point. We were blessed. You could say the same for the final too. Pres Cork were camped on our line for ages in the second half. They had one scrum-five after another. They actually got over a few times but we held them up. Our defence was incredible. We had prepared for this kind of siege in the previous weeks. We knew it was coming and we were ready to meet it. But Christ it was close. They were picking and driving and we were getting off the line to hit everything that moved. Our back row kept putting in tackle after tackle. The tension was desperate. Edel says it's the most nerve-wracking game she was ever at in her life. I was wired for it. I remember Ger Sla in the pre-match huddle saying to me, you're not supposed to be here, they all think you're a scumbag, you've no right to be here, go out and prove them wrong. I have to say, it wasn't the most diplomatic pep talk I ever got! But I'd invested two years in this. I'd left my friends in Nessan's to get this prize. On the day I left every ounce out on the field. Nine minutes after the interval our outhalf Richie Mullane made a lovely break on our own twenty-two and slipped the ball left to Eamon. He motored through a gap and made fifty yards. I was riding shotgun. He put me away and I ran it in from outside their twenty-two. In fairness, it was a nice score. Ger Sla converted it and that was our scoring done for the day. The rest more or less was the goal line siege. We survived eleven minutes of injury time. The rest was history. To this day it is one of the sweetest memories of my whole rugby career. It was vindication for the commitment I'd made two years earlier. I scored tries in the quarter, the semi and the final. It was a massive time in my life.

The final was on St Patrick's Day as usual. It was a Friday, the same day as the Cheltenham Gold Cup, as it happened. I remember it because my father was over there. He and a few friends had booked it months earlier. He had put his money down, he couldn't back out now. So he was missing the biggest game of my career. He was looking at his phone every two minutes waiting for updates from Thomond Park. I don't know if he backed the winner in the Gold Cup. It was an Irish horse that won it and everyone was celebrating but I doubt there was a happier Irish man in Cheltenham that night.

A week later the Ireland squad for the Under 19 World Cup in Dubai was announced. I should've been thrilled at the thought of it but it was the opposite. I hated the idea of it cos I hated being away from home. It was bad enough having to spend a weekend away in Dublin or Clongowes or Belfast. But I dreaded travelling overseas. I hated being in South Africa the year before and now I was supposed to be heading off somewhere I wouldn't be able to find on a map. It wasn't that it was Dubai, it was that I'd be mixing with people I didn't know. I'd be spending weeks with them. Socially I was just totally uncomfortable being around people who were different to me. I wanted to stay in Moyross. That was my comfort zone. I was as odd as two left feet. Anything outside my comfort zone intimidated me. I always felt better when Ger Sla was with me. He was going to the same trials and camps and games that I was. I'd find it difficult if he wasn't around. A lot of it was pure shyness too. It's an awful curse in ways, being shy, I used to envy the lads who were outgoing and sociable and full of chat. Ger Sla was on the Irish squad too for Dubai so that was a big help. But still. Edel says I "sobbed and sobbed and sobbed" before that trip. She honestly thought I was going to pull out of it. Anyhow, I went.

Most of the lads on that tour were doing their Leaving Cert, in fact I think a few fellas chose not to travel to concentrate on their exams. That wasn't my worry. Charlie McAleese was head coach of that team, Killian Keane was one of his assistants, Keith Patton was team manager. They'd organised study sessions for us in the timetable, a few hours every day where we were supposed to have our heads in the books. A lot of the lads were looking to get big scores in the exams for stuff like medicine and law in college. Of course, myself and Ger Sla were on our phones and messing and arsing around. Keith Patton would come in to check that we were all studying hard. I'd say he had a fair idea that me and Sla weren't killing ourselves.

We did pretty well overall in that tournament – played five, won four and finished fifth overall in the standings. England first up was the big one. They had fellas like Danny Cipriani, Danny Care and Tom Youngs. I was in the centre along with Ian Keatley. Brian Collins kicked four penalties, I scored a late try, we pipped them by a point.

A lot of that squad progressed into the Under 20s the following season. This was a new age grade, 2007 was its first season of competition. Eric Elwood came in as head coach. He was an absolute legend of Connacht rugby. You meet plenty of legends in this sport and when you're on the way up it's a big boost if you have them mentoring you on the training ground. But at that age I think what really matters is not their reputation but how they treat you. Eric had a great career as a player but what mattered to me at that time was how nice he was to me. He took me under his wing from the first day and immediately I felt comfortable with him. He took everyone under his wing actually, he just had a lovely way about him. Some coaches don't care about you or where you come from but Eric I felt made an extra effort with me. He was one of those coaches who puts his arm round you and makes you feel better in yourself. He had that effect on the whole squad. He treated us like adults, he made sure we got plenty of training gear, we all felt we were being well looked after. As a result we came together and formed a really tight bond. It stood to us several times when the chips were down. We beat Wales by two points, France by three and were hanging on 7-6 against England until Keats slotted a brilliant penalty in injury time. We were on our way to the Grand Slam. We played some really attacking, adventurous rugby too which we all enjoyed. Eric was assistant coach to Michael Bradley in Connacht at the time. A few weeks after the Slam he rang me to see would I be interested in signing for Connacht. They were offering me a fulltime professional contract. I was still on the academy deal with Munster but I wasn't tempted to move.

That summer I was off with the Ireland A squad for the Churchill Cup in England. The morning I left Limerick to join the squad in Dublin I went down to the maternity hospital to visit my mother. She was a few hours away from giving birth to my one and only sibling. The squad landed in Bristol later that day and I got a text from my father with a photo of my newborn sister, Jenny. I didn't meet her for three weeks. Some of the lads were allowed a break from the tour to go back and do exams. I asked if I could go home to meet my new sister but they were like, no Keith, you can't! That was my first tour as a professional rugby player. John Fogarty was captain. Mike Ross, Devin Toner, Fergus McFadden and Seán Cronin were also there. Johnny Sexton too. It was the first time I ever got to play with Johnny. Fourteen years later he'd be picking me out with a peach of a crossfield kick against England at the Aviva. I was nineteen, he was twenty-one. We're the old dogs for the hard road now. Michael Bradley was our head coach at that tournament. I picked up a couple of tries along the way, including one against the New Zealand Maori which didn't amount to much because they just blew us away with their power and pace. Rua Tipoki was their captain on that tour. Within a few months I was watching him close-up in a Munster jersey and soon enough I'd be playing alongside him.

Rua was thirty-one going on thirty-two when he signed for Munster. I was starting out. But I was in the world of men now – hard men and talented players who'd made it into the pro game. My teenage years ended on my birthday in October 2007. Two years earlier all I was dreaming about was a Munster schools senior cup. Life came at me fast and furious in those couple of years. Schoolboy caps, Under 19s, South Africa, Dubai, England. An Under 20 Grand Slam and most of all, that senior cup medal. I was thirteen when I was told I would go nowhere in life. At the age of twenty I had a fair idea I was on my way to somewhere.

10

SWIMMING

WHEN JOHN BRODERICK PHONED TO TELL ME I'D had the green light to start over in Munchin's, he asked me what subjects would I be choosing for my Leaving Cert. I told him to put me down for whatever Ger Sla was doing! I wasn't too fussy. I think he knew and I knew that I wasn't going back to get the points for Trinity College. Leaving Nessan's meant giving up metalwork and woodwork, my two favourite subjects. I ended up doing biology and business instead. I wouldn't be doing transition year, I'd be going straight into fifth year. A lot of my mates in Nessan's would've been quitting school after their Junior Cert. They were heading for apprenticeships in bricklaying, electrical, carpentry, car mechanics, all the trades. Or they'd have been getting jobs and starting to earn their own money. I was looking at my two years in Munchin's as a sort of apprenticeship for professional rugby. The backup plan would be an electrical apprenticeship with Eddie Fraher. Eddie was captain of Thomond RFC at the time. He had played with my father at Young Munster. Eddie was an electrical contractor. He had a pub as well just off the top of O'Connell Street, Coopers. Later it became Eric's, it's closed now. I was doing a few hours behind the bar in Coopers at weekends and holidays. All the clubs were chasing me to sign up with them after I left school but I was always going to stay another year with Thomond. But Eddie was keeping me sweet anyway. A bit of cash from the bar work and the start in the electrical trade after I finished school. As far as the club scene goes, I'll always be one hundred per cent Thomond RFC. I'd love to have done a season with Munsters because of all the good times I spent there as a young fella but it just wasn't possible.

I didn't bother the books too badly in my last two years and they didn't bother me too badly either. Edel says I got away with murder there. I was what you'd call a part-time pupil. I didn't cause any hassle and the teachers didn't really hassle me. If we were taking turns in class to do a bit of reading out loud, the teacher would skip me. That's because I told them to skip me. I just refused point blank to read out loud because I didn't get on well with words. I would struggle to read them properly.

When we had double French I'd disappear altogether. If the teacher asked where I was going I'd say we have a big game at the weekend and I'm going out to practise my kicking. Okay so. And off I'd go. Basically it was understood by everyone that I was in school not for the education but the playing fields. In my sixth year I got insured on my mother's car, a Nissan Almera. I'd been pestering her for ages about it. I was telling her it'd save her the hassle of having to drive me across town every morning. Eventually she gave in and I drove myself to school. I didn't always arrive in school, to be honest. Not on time anyway. There's a housing estate across the road from Munchin's. Some days I'd drive in there and pull up and go back to sleep for a few hours. I'd join the lads for lunch then. I think that's what Edel means when she says I got away with murder! For the Leaving Cert I was supposed to be doing the subjects at ordinary level but when the exams came I took the foundation papers where you just had to tick a load of boxes. You didn't get any points in your Leaving for foundation level but you did get out of the exam hall fairly lively. I was gone after half an hour most days. Then for the biology exam I didn't bother showing up at all. Instead I went swimming with my old mates from Nessan's at the Ardnacrusha bridge. They didn't do biology in Nessan's for the Leaving so the lads had the day off. I was outside the exam hall about to go in when the phone rang. Sure I couldn't turn them down. It was a lovely hot day. What else would you be doing?

I wouldn't recommend that attitude now. There's a reason why people say education is important. There's a reason why teachers tell you to pay attention in class. There's a reason why your parents tell you to study more. But if you don't understand those reasons at the time, there's less chance you'll do it. And in fairness, studying is hateful to a lot of teenagers. It's unbelievably boring and annoying if you're not that way inclined. How are you supposed to do it if you don't have any aptitude for it? There were fellas in my class who had no aptitude whatsoever for sport. If they were forced to do it every day it'd be a horrible experience for them. It was a bit like that with me, except the other way round. I was okay up to my Junior Cert, I passed all the subjects as far as I can remember. But after that, I could barely bring myself to open a book. It was torture. I couldn't concentrate, I had no feeling for it and not much interest in it. I came alive in the woodwork and metalwork classes; for the other classes it was like someone would switch me off inside. But then that left me without an important life skill. I don't know how the education system can fix that. Every person leaving school should be able to read and write properly but for a lot of kids, they don't suit the system, or the system doesn't suit them, and I was in that category.

Nearly fourteen years after my Leaving Cert, at a training camp in Portugal in January 2020, Andy Farrell arranged one-on-one meetings with the members of the squad. He was new in the job as Ireland head coach and he was establishing relationships, getting to know us and us getting to know him. In my session we got round to talking about life after rugby. Did I have any plans for afterwards? I told him I didn't know what I was going to do. In passing I said that I was brutal at school, I could barely read or spell, so I wouldn't be going into some sort of white collar, professional job. I had no qualifications like that. He showed a lot of empathy, the way he replied. Faz is a working class fella too. He didn't have the silver spoon growing up either. He said he knew lots of people who struggled with their reading and writing, it was more common than you'd think. He said I should just practise it more, even when sending text messages and emails, use the predictive text, and the more you do it the better you'll get at it.

A couple of weeks later we're on a weekend camp between Six Nations games and the staff have arranged one of their evening get-togethers for a bit of craic and relaxation. We're in a conference room in the hotel and Simon Easterby has put together a spelling competition, big complicated words that the contestants have to try and get right. It's a forwards versus backs job, three forwards, three backs. And as he's picking them I'm going to myself, Jesus don't pick me, Simon, whatever the fuck you do, don't pick me. Sure enough, he picks me. You're not supposed to have a choice when there's messing like this going on. You're supposed to get up and face whatever prank is happening. But I refuse. The lads are all joking and egging me on but I say no, I'm not going up there. Thankfully Faz steps in. He's remembered our chat from a few weeks earlier. So he just declares, "Earlsy doesn't do spelling competitions", and that defuses the situation. Later Simon comes up to me privately and apologises, which is very nice of him, but there's no need because he just didn't know. Funny enough, I'm not embarrassed by the episode at the time. I don't want to stand up and make a show of myself but I'm not embarrassed either when Faz says I don't do spelling competitions. Ten years earlier I'd have been mortified. But I'm getting more confident in myself as I get older and less self-conscious.

Since my diagnosis with bipolar in 2013, I've had to do a huge amount of work on myself to try and get to a better place. Out of that work came an appetite for self-improvement in general. If anything good has come out of it, it is getting to understand that you're not stuck with something forever if you don't want to be. You can change. You're not static. You don't have to be the victim of your circumstances or your conditioning. You can take control of your destiny, at least to some degree. I'm not saying it's easy. It's hard. You have to acquire the tools, you have to apply yourself, you have to put up with frustrations and setbacks and trial and error. Maybe that's why a lot of people can't get out of the rut they're in. Because it's hard, it takes time and determination and discipline. That's where all the years of training in sport can help. It ingrains into you a discipline and a work ethic. When it came to my basic literacy skills, this was another project I had to take on. There was a path to self-improvement here too. Obviously I needed to do it for my own sake. But there was another powerful motivation appearing as well. Ella May was starting to bring some homework back from school every day. And naturally she liked having Daddy to help her with it. And Daddy to his shame wasn't always able to help her. That's not a nice feeling. During lockdown last year the kids were homeschooling and I was trying to help out but in all honesty I wasn't able to help them much. Edel did most of it with them. It got to the stage where Ella May would be asking did I ever do anything in school?! Did you learn anything at all?! Well, I learned that it's probably not a good idea to go swimming the day of your Leaving Cert biology exam. It's probably not a good idea to finish school only being half-able to read and write. Being good at sport isn't enough. At the time you think it's the perfect escape hatch out of the education system, but eventually you run into a cul-de-sac.

I remember one of the first times I signed an autograph, we were on a training camp in Cork and this fella came up to me with a jersey looking to get it signed. So I signed it 'Best Whishes Keith Earls'. Then a few weeks later I saw the word written down somewhere and the correct spelling was 'Wishes'. When I realised my mistake I felt unbelievably embarrassed and vulnerable. I could feel the cold sweat coming out of me. This problem added to my paranoia too. I had to send emails and text messages every day, the same as everybody else. But I didn't know where to put in full stops or when to start a new sentence. Something as simple as that made me really uptight for fear of making a show of myself. It's something that everyone takes for granted but that only makes it worse, if you're the fella who can't do it.

I'd always be asking Edel to check the spelling of words before I'd send a text or email. She's been my teacher here as in so many things. Even in Nessan's she'd be helping me with my homework, my maths and English in particular. Like for example I didn't know how to put the address on an envelope properly. If I was asked to sign a message for a fan and post it, the first time Edel saw me doing it I wrote the full address across the envelope in one continuous line. She was looking at me. Do you not know that you go down line by line with the address? No! That's news to me. Then I put the stamp up in the left hand corner instead of the right hand corner! Now she was looking at me like I had two heads.

To this day if I'm reading a book in bed I'll be asking her to explain the meaning of words to me. She tells me I've come on in leaps and bounds the last few years. I probably have too, in fairness, but I still struggle with how words are spelled.

I've never got tested but I've a feeling I might have a touch of dyslexia. I was supposed to get tested for it last year but then the pandemic kicked in and the appointment was called off. I'm no expert on it but from what I've learnt about it over the years, I wouldn't be surprised if I was dyslexic. I'm going to get the test for it later this year hopefully. But letters and words are definitely a problem for me.

I leave letters out of words when I'm doing an email or any kind of writing. An e or an n or an a. I have to revise what I've written and check with the dictionary. I keep a dictionary handy in my office. I'll often just open a page and put my finger on a word and learn what it means and how to spell it correctly.

During the 2021 Six Nations I was asked to partake in a promo for one of our sponsors. It was basically a bit of video banter among a few players. Andrew Trimble and Donncha O'Callaghan were the hosts, myself and Tadhg Furlong were the guests. We were in the team hotel but in separate rooms because of the social distancing. We were hooked up to the lads on Zoom calls. It was one of those skits where you're asked light-hearted questions about your team mates. Who takes the longest to get dressed, who's the best dancer, who's in charge of the music, etc. The catch for me was that you had to write your answers on a whiteboard with a marker. My answer for one of them was Shane Daly, my Munster team mate. Simple enough to spell but I left out the n in Shane. I realised my mistake and rubbed it out on the whiteboard and said his name instead. I knew how Shane is spelled and yet I still missed a letter. This happens to me regularly. It's why I think I might be dyslexic. I won't know until I get it properly tested but my life experience tells me there's something not quite right in my relationship with words on a page.

It's not holding me back as much as it used to. Of course it affected my confidence when I was younger, probably contributed to my shyness in some way. But I'm pretty good at speaking now, I can stand up in a players' meeting and say what I want to say. I can do media interviews and talk shite with the best of them. I hope readers of this book will find it pretty simple to read. That's my intention. I know there's a lot of kids who come from areas like mine who struggle at school.

I'm trying to use plain, basic English here in case a few of them might be interested in reading my story. If they leave school with literacy problems I hope they realise they can get help. I'd hope they wouldn't be too embarrassed about it to ask for help. It's a basic life skill, it's a basic human right, you could say.

I'm sure I'm not the only professional sportsman who abandoned the books too young. It happens in soccer a lot. Fellas who are singled out for big things from an early age and put all their eggs in that basket. Then if they don't make it they're kind of left stranded. The culture in pro rugby in Ireland is a bit different. Fellas are encouraged to continue with their studies or to go on various courses. It's a healthier environment because of that. In my case, that avenue wasn't really open to me – or maybe it was and I just didn't see it. Anyway, I'm making up for lost time now. I'm old in sporting terms but young in terms of the time I have ahead of me, touch wood. To answer Andy Farrell's question that day, I'm planning on going into business. As for my education, I'll keep on turning up for class every day at the university of life.

11

ANTHONY FOLEY RIP

I STOPPED WORRYING ABOUT RUGBY AFTER AXEL died. I didn't stop caring but I stopped beating myself up about it. The penny dropped with me. I was taking it far too seriously. We were all taking it far too seriously. We had lost our perspective about it. It shouldn't have taken a tragedy to teach us that rugby wasn't the be all and end all.

I saw the toll it took on Axel when he was head coach. I saw the stress he was under. I heard about the abuse he got from so-called supporters. The passion for rugby in Munster is what made us famous and successful. The downside to all that passion is you can have too much of it. It can make things toxic when results aren't going well. Axel's legendary status as a Munster player didn't seem to count for much when he was struggling. Some supporters have short memories.

I can remember him all the way back to playing for Shannon against my father and Young Munster. I can remember the first time I ever set eyes on him, he was with Olive in the old Thomond Park. I must've been nine or ten at the time. I was behind the goals looking at him, this massive fella, saying to myself, that's Anthony Foley.

Then I was introduced to him one day. This is Ger Earls's young fella. He always had a nod and a word for me after that. We didn't hang out much together when I joined Munster, purely because of the generation gap between us, but we'd have a few pints together after a match or at the Christmas party.

Axel was a brilliant tracksuit coach. On the training ground he was class. His rugby intelligence shone through. It was one of the qualities that defined him as a player and it came through on the training ground too. He understood the game at a deep level. He had incredible knowledge. Working with players, teaching them and educating them in the mechanics of the game, was where he was at his best. The wider managerial job, all the demands on his time, the media duties, the business of professional rugby, all the dealing with contracts and the player market and having to keep forty fellas happy in a squad – it was a massive learning curve. It's a huge burden of work and responsibility. I'd imagine it takes a lot of getting used to, for any new head coach.

When the club took the executive decision to bring Rassie Erasmus in as director of rugby in the summer of 2016, of course there was a lot of speculation as to how Axel would handle it. In fact he dealt with it unbelievably well. He was still head coach but he was back on the training ground, doing what he loved. Rassie lifted a lot of the other pressures off him. Over the next few months you could see him coming back to his old self. He was lighter in himself, he was starting to relax and smile again.

ANTHONY FOLEY RIP

We played Leinster at the Aviva in a Pro12 game on October 8 2016, a Saturday. I had to come off with a concussion after fifty-six minutes. On the Monday I failed my HIA test so I was ruled out for the European Champions Cup game against Racing 92 the following Sunday. I was in the gym in UL the Friday before that game. Axel was walking through the gym and we had a quick word. He said to make sure I got myself right for the game the following weekend and meanwhile they'd try and get the job done in Paris. I wished him luck and he went on his way. That was the last time we ever spoke. They flew out on the Saturday. On the Sunday Edel and I were over in her mother's house in Kilmallock. I was keeping an eye on the time, I wanted to be back home to watch the match on television. About an hour and a half before kick-off my phone rang and Conor Murray's name came up. That was unusual. You wouldn't have a player ringing you so close to a game without good reason. So I answered and Murr was like, I've something to tell you, terrible news, Axel is dead.

That is not the kind of news you can absorb the second you hear it. I couldn't process it at all. What d'you mean, what are you saying? He says Axel has been found dead in his bed in the hotel this morning. Rassie has just told us. The game has been cancelled and we're all over the place, we don't know what to do. Poor Murr sounded shellshocked. I was shellshocked. Edel says I was white as a ghost when I told her. Edel immediately thought of Olive and the boys, Tony and Dan. Olive had taken Edel under her wing when we first became part of the Munster set-up. Axel was one of the veterans who had taken me under his wing. We were stunned, devastated.

We drove home from Kilmallock, I rang a few of the younger

squad lads who weren't in Paris either and invited them round to our house. A load of them came over. None of us wanted to be on our own. We just sat around talking about Axel and having a few beers. It wasn't just us who were shocked. The world of rugby was shocked. Axel was known far and wide throughout the game. Tributes poured in from all over the world.

The next week passed in a blur. The funeral was going to be enormous and we would be playing our part. Everyone was talking about it in Limerick and beyond. Rassie and the team arrived home from France. We met up for training on the Monday and Tuesday as per normal, although obviously there was nothing normal at all about that week. Our heads were scrambled, we were upside down, we were trying and failing to process all that was happening.

There was talk that our scheduled fixture for the following Saturday, against Glasgow Warriors in Thomond Park, was going to go ahead. I thought the very idea of it was ridiculous. How were we supposed to function as a team in these circumstances? It shouldn't be played. It should be called off as a mark of respect to Anthony. But Rassie got hold of us at a team meeting and laid out the reality. Rugby doesn't stop for anyone, he said, the machine doesn't stop for anyone. The game wasn't going to be postponed. We would have to play it whether we liked it or not. That put my anxiety into overdrive. I was really worried for the younger lads in particular. This was going to be an incredibly emotional occasion. Thomond Park would be packed with Munster fans coming to pay tribute to Axel. And we would have to win it for Axel. There was no choice. It couldn't be any other way. That would bring a unique pressure down on us, the kind of scenario none of us had ever faced before. Emotionally, it could be overwhelming for the team, especially the young lads. I was worried that if they made a few costly mistakes because of the emotion, it could scar them for years to come.

It goes without saying I didn't sleep well that week. I had just turned 29, I had gotten accustomed to deaths and tragedies over the years. But this was like a flashback to when I was twelve years old and suffered my first panic attack after my cousin Thomas died. I'd never be seeing Thomas again and how could that be? Seventeen years later it was going through my mind on a loop again. How was Axel gone off the face of the earth all of a sudden? What he had given to Limerick and Munster and Ireland. He was one of the reasons that Munster had become renowned as a franchise throughout the rugby world. I'd only been talking to him in the gym a few days before. There was anger mixed with the grief too, for the way he'd been treated when he was head coach.

Rassie didn't get much sleep that week either. He really showed his mettle as a leader of people at that time. On the training ground, Felix and Jerry Fla and Jacques Nienaber kept the show on the road. On the Friday the players took it in turns to shoulder the coffin from the church in Killaloe to the graveyard. Olive's eulogy was magnificent, I don't know how she did it. After the funeral then we had to switch out of mourning mode into professional sportsman mode. We went and did our captain's run. On Saturday morning we had our meal and pre-match meeting in the Clarion Hotel and boarded the bus for Thomond Park. The crowds, the scenes on our way to the ground, were something else. You could feel the emotion coming through the windows of the bus. Same again out on the field for the warm-up. They gave us a rousing reception on our way back to the dressing room. Then the minute's silence. You could feel the intensity of the silence.

By that stage, I was waiting to be released, the whole team was waiting to be released. We were pent-up with emotion and nerves and adrenaline. We exploded into the game. Murr threw a ball to me inside three minutes, I hit a gap and popped it to Tyler Bleyendaal as I hit the deck outside the twenty-two. Tyler scythed his way up to the line from there and was horsed over it as the crowd erupted. All my anxieties disappeared after that. I knew there and then we wouldn't be beaten. There was no way we were going to lose this one.

Then seventeen minutes later I'm sent off. I've picked up their hooker Fraser Brown and I don't even know how but I've lifted his leg too high and dumped him into the turf and next thing I'm looking at a red card. I thought at the time that Brown made a bit of a meal of it. Then several of his team mates piled in and were making a big song and dance about it to the ref, calling for a red card.

Glasgow had a bit of a reputation for trying to milk situations for cards. They were definitely doing it in this situation. I could hear them. Billy Holland and Pete O'Mahony were trying to say that the fella had ducked his head, that he did that himself. I was thinking, yellow card, it's not as bad as they're making it out to be. I was fuckn disgusted when the ref showed me red. As I was walking off the pitch Stuart Hogg tried to put his hand around me but I pushed him away. I wasn't buying it. I wasn't going to give him his moment of trying to be the nice guy when his team mates were carrying on like that. Then I stupidly lashed a few water bottles out of the way on the sideline and went down to the dressing room. I was alone with my thoughts in there.

I could hear the noise from the crowd above. I was beating myself up thinking if we lose this game now, it's all my fault. Of all the games to lose, and me to be the cause of it, I'd never forgive myself. And there was a stage of the match too where it looked like they were coming back but ultimately the boys blew them out of the water. It was a hell of a performance in the circumstances.

The irony of it all wasn't lost on us. We had finally produced a performance that had Axel's vision all over it. We played the way he'd always wanted us to play. He'd wanted us to be ourselves, to express ourselves, to play with freedom and flair and intensity. Basically the Munster way, when Munster were at their best. The saddest thing was that we couldn't do it more often when he was with us.

The scenes at full-time will live long in the memory of anyone who was there. Axel's two boys joined us on the field. All the emotions that we'd been bottling up poured out of us. The lads launched into *Stand Up and Fight* and I lost the plot. I wasn't able to join in for the crying. We were happy but our hearts were broken at the same time.

When the dust settled the following week I was left facing the disciplinary process for my red card. As part of my plea for mitigation at the hearing, I contacted Fraser Brown in advance to tell him I was sorry for my actions, my emotions got the better of me, etc etc etc. The hearing was in London. I travelled over with Niall O'Donovan and our solicitor. It was a load of bullshit really. The solicitor had to bang on about what a decent fella I was and how it was completely out of character for me and how nice I was at signing autographs for kids and volunteering my time for good causes. Jesus. You'd swear I was after murdering someone. But you had to go through this whole rigmarole and I was willing to jump through whatever hoops they wanted because of a fixture in Chicago on November 5. Ireland were due to play the All Blacks that day and I badly wanted to be there. But after all our kowtowing to the EPCR they handed down a two-week suspension, just enough time to keep me out of the big one in Chicago. As it turned out, I missed the chance to be part of history. I lost out on being part of the first senior Irish men's squad to beat New Zealand. I think Anthony's spirit was present in that amazing Ireland performance too. It was an inspired idea to form the figure eight in tribute to him as they faced the haka. It was a beautiful touch. I'm sure it brought them closer together and helped them achieve that landmark victory. I would've loved to have been there on the field for all that. It went hard on me, not being there. I watched it on TV in the Clarion Hotel along with my team mate Damien Varley, torn in two with emotion.

If there was a game in my life that I didn't want to miss, it was the one in Soldier Field where the ultimate tribute to a great Irish rugby man was paid, courtesy of an Irish senior men's team beating the New Zealand All Blacks for the first time ever in our history.

12

THE WAITING GAME

IT WAS ALMOST FOURTEEN YEARS AFTER MY SENIOR debut that the best team performance of my Munster career came to pass. Well, I consider it the best that I have been part of anyway. We've had a lot of good victories along the way and maybe a few great ones, but our win over Clermont Auvergne at the Stade Marcel Michelin in December 2020 tops the lot for my money. And in fairness, I can't claim that I had a lot to do with it, I had a mixed bag of a match, but I don't think I was ever prouder walking off a pitch in the red jersey than I was that day.

Clermont destroyed us early on. They had a try on the board after twenty-six seconds. They had another after six minutes. That one was a penalty try. You'll get this scenario in France a lot, where the home team comes out like a juggernaut and treats you like roadkill. We learned a long time ago at Munster that the first twenty minutes in France is often just about damage limitation. Keep your wits about you and hang on to their coat tails if you can. Keep your discipline. Keep making tackles when they're coming at you in waves and they're trying to drown you before you've got your second wind. Because eventually it will blow over, like a storm. But Jesus, Clermont weren't just trampling over us that day, they were obliterating us. They had their third try on fifteen minutes and their bonus-point fourth wrapped up in the 23rd. They were leading 28-9.

A year or two earlier, I don't think we would have salvaged anything out of those circumstances. You're on the brink of humiliation in a situation like that. Now, it's not in the Munster culture to put up the white flag, no matter how bad things are. You don't have permission to surrender. You never have permission to do that. But there are times when the writing is on the wall and you know it. Funnily enough, this was not one of those times.

We were standing behind the goals waiting for Camille Lopez to convert their fourth try. There wasn't panic in fellas' body language or in their tone of voice. It was just about getting ready for the next task. Because even in that first twenty-five minutes we had manipulated them well in patches. We were getting around them and through them by our shape and our plays. JJ Hanrahan kicked three penalties to keep us ticking over. So we stayed calm and soon enough we stabilised the ship. They started to come off the boil too after their purple patch. Mike Haley finished off a really well-worked move five minutes after their fourth try. The third quarter we chipped away with penalties, eating bit by bit into their lead. We were calm and methodical about it. We were still six behind with ten to play. Our forwards were outstanding. They got stronger as Clermont's got weaker. They drove a maul over and JJ added a super conversion to give us the lead for the first time. They sealed the deal three minutes from time with another try from close range. We won 39-31. It was a monumental job of work. In the fifty-five minutes left after their fourth try, Clermont scored just once more, a penalty. JJ kicked nine from nine off the tee. I was delighted for him personally. I was pleased for myself too cos I'd made a few mistakes and recovered from them. I put them behind me. The younger me wasn't able to do that as much. I'd let mistakes eat away at me. This time I just ploughed on.

That match was played a week before Christmas. Between Covid and Christmas preparations and everything, it probably passed people by a little bit. The achievement went under the radar. There was no one in the stadium either so there was no atmosphere. If there'd been a full house in for it, the atmosphere would have been sensational. Clermont have fantastic support and maybe their players and coaches would argue that a home crowd would've made all the difference. I don't think so. I think we'd have sent them home quiet that day. We were fuckn brilliant, if I may say so. The dressing room was buzzing afterwards. Any player will tell you, the dressing room after you've won a big game is the place to be. You wouldn't want to be any place else in the world. Tony Mullins, our kitman, will usually come in with a few slabs of beer. That's one of my favourite parts of this whole job, sitting down and enjoying the beer and banter with the lads after a great team performance.

The nice thing about it is that we're not talking ancient history here. The best Munster performance I've ever been part of happened in December 2020, not ten or twelve years ago when we were kingpins so-called. I'm in a WhatsApp group with a lot of retired players, fellas who played in those golden years. I got loads of messages from them saying it was one of the great Munster performances. That was very satisfying to hear.

The Clermont game gave me a lot of optimism about where we were going as a squad and management. You could see the new generation coming through. When you're an ould fella in the dressing room you get a great lift from the energy and attitude that good young players bring with them. And it keeps you on your toes. It keeps you sharp. It's competition. Your whole life is about competition in professional sport. Not just the teams you're playing against but the players in your own set-up who are gunning to take your place. I don't think I'm the type of fella who'd try to keep them down in any way. I hope I'm the type of fella who encourages them and supports them. I'm willing to pass on whatever I've learnt along the way, I want to pass on whatever I know about the game. At the same time, I want to make it hard for them to take my place. The only way I can do that is by maintaining my personal standards. Not slacking off in any shape or form. Holding onto your speed, your fitness, your attitude. Learning new stuff, maybe about nutrition or psychology or a game situation. If anything, you'd be trying to raise your own standards, irrespective of your age.

But I can identify with the young lads too because I remember well what it was like when you were bursting to get through to the first team and make a name for yourself. John Kelly was one of the old soldiers who sent me a message after Clermont. John told a story years ago about me coming up to him in training one day and asking him when was he going to retire! This must've been some time in 2007 so I was nineteen and he was probably the age I am now, in his thirties. John was a highly respected veteran at the time, he'd won his Heineken Cup medal at outside centre the year before. And apparently the two of us were doing a warm-up lap at training in Dooradoyle one day and we got chatting. And then I asked him, are you retiring at the end of the season?! John burst out laughing. My tone must've been fairly obvious! It seems I wasn't implying that I'd be sad to see him go. It was more along the lines of when are you packing it in so I can take your place!

John retired in December 2007. I still don't have what he has. I'm still waiting for the European Cup medal. I never dreamt I'd be waiting this long, not when I was starting out anyway. But the seasons came and went and if anything we ended up drifting further away from the holy grail.

A fundamental problem in my opinion has been the turnover of head coaches. Declan Kidney was my first one. Deccie left in the summer of 2008 after winning our second Heineken Cup to take over the Ireland job. Tony McGahan took over from Deccie. He'd been part of the coaching staff for the previous two years. I didn't warm to him early doors because I thought he didn't warm to me. Tony was an old-school Aussie who liked to dish out the bollockings. A lot of training sessions were effing this and effing that and this shit and that shit and don't bloody well do this, bloody well do that. He was a hard taskmaster. He wouldn't be sugar-coating the message. I wasn't used to that. I was used to being told how good I was. But that was schools and the underage grades. That was the boys and this was the men. I found it hard at the start. It shook my confidence. I was convinced McGahan had a personal vendetta against me. I'd be going to Paulie or Rog saying this fella is fuckn wrecking my head here. I'd be nervous going into training. Paulie and Rog would be reassuring me, telling me he was only doing it because he rated me and he wanted to put pressure on me to perform. It turned out they were right. He put me in the team from the start and kept me there. We ended up having a great relationship on and off the field and drank a few pints together on the team nights out. When he first took over, I'd imagine Tony felt I had a big reputation but that I had an awful lot to learn about grown-up rugby and he was going to make sure I kept my feet on the ground. Obviously it's always a concern in any sport, a supposed hotshot young fella, it all comes too easy to him and he arrives into senior level with the wrong attitude.

To be fair to myself, I didn't make that mistake. For my first four or five years as a pro I kept the head down. I would let nothing distract me. I was a sponge for information. I wasn't what you'd call a mature young adult, not like the fellas coming into the professional ranks now, they are incredibly level-headed and sensible. But I was mature enough to look for advice from the older lads. I was mature enough to know I was immature, if that's not a contradiction. Paulie and Rog were my sounding boards. I was always listening to them, I'd go to them with my questions and they'd help me. Rog used to get pissed off with me that I didn't know how good I was, that I didn't have the confidence to go with my talent as he saw it.

It was really only when I got established for Munster that I gave myself a bit of slack, maybe around the age of twenty-two. I definitely went through a phase where I thought I was a great fella, with my Munster and Ireland caps. I did a bit of partying and socialising around that time but actually it was fairly tame stuff too. When I signed my first central contract with the IRFU I decided I'd treat myself to one massive present. I'd buy the car of my dreams. I'd buy a Range Rover, my favourite car ever.

So I took myself into one of the big showrooms in Limerick where they had these dream machines on parade. It was only a matter of choosing which one. The fella there told me to pick one and test-drive it for a few days and if I liked it, we'd do the deal. I drove through town in that Range Rover, delighted with myself. The first person I was going to show it to was my father. So I land round to his house and proudly show it off to him. Well, what d'you think? And he takes one long look at it. There's a long silence too. Then he takes a deep breath and he says, you know what you can do with that now? You can take it straight back to the garage, that's what you can do with it. You're only wasting your money and you're not a soccer player. Take it back and cop yourself on. Well that fairly burst my bubble! I had to go back to the dealership with my tail between my legs. I handed back the keys of the Range Rover and bought a Toyota Avensis instead. Another lesson learned.

We bought a nice house in Castletroy and after a few years we upgraded to the place we have now. It's not so much a property investment as a life investment. It's our home. It's where we are raising our family. We have a lovely lifestyle and rugby has given it to us. I feel grateful every day for that. It makes me feel good that if our children want to go to college, we'll be able to pay for their education without worrying about it. The game of rugby punishes you in so many ways but it has been good to me in this way and I will always appreciate that.

But ultimately your career isn't about the money, it's about the medals. Money doesn't last forever, medals do. In May 2010 we faced Biarritz in the Heineken Cup semi-final in the Estadio Anoeta. Already there was a widespread feeling in rugby circles that the great Munster team of '06/08 was on the slide. History tells us they were right. But of course at the time you don't want to be hearing that. We actually got the first try of that game, the only try of that game, but they ground us down and Dmitri Yachvili kicked six penalties. What stands out in my memory is the great French back row Imanol Harinordoquy wearing this massive strapping round his head and upper face to protect his broken nose. It wouldn't have looked out of place in a horror movie. And then earlier that day, one of the police outriders who were escorting our bus, crashing and coming clean off his bike on our way to the stadium in San Sebastian. Biarritz beat us 18-7 and two weeks later Leinster had our number again in the Magners League semi-final.

I spent the summer resting up my groin and was only back at training a few days that August when I did all the ligaments in my ankle. So that required a trip to see the surgeon Johnny McKenna in the sports clinic in Santry. My father drove me up in his taxi, my uncle joined us for the journey. We were approaching the Red Cow roundabout on the outskirts of Dublin when we heard a police siren behind us. There was flashing blue lights too. The cops pulled us in. I'm guessing what happened was that Limerick was flooded with law enforcement at the time because of the feuding gangs. The taxi had a Limerick reg. plate and there were three fellas inside it with shaved heads and my uncle in the passenger seat had a load of tattoos. The guards put two and two together and got five. We had to get out and take everything out of the car. Who were we, where were we from and where were we going? Eventually they let us off about our business. Johnny McKenna recommended surgery on the ankle but I decided against and rehabbed it instead.

I made my first appearance of the season against London

Irish in the Heineken Cup in October at the Madejski Stadium, where I got into a bout of fisticuffs with Delon Armitage. I don't know what Delon's fighting weight was at the time but I know that I had moved up a weight division or two. I was carrying 98kgs around that time. Fifteen stone, six pounds. That was two stone heavier than my natural walking around weight. It was ridiculous. I was fat from all the pumping iron and all the pumping food down my neck. Rugby was going through a phase at the time where there was no such thing as being too big. Just keep piling on the muscle and the weight. I was well off maximum fitness because of my injuries and on top of that I was carrying this extra body mass around with me. The match kicked off and the ball stayed in play for three or four minutes and I was burning oil already. I was actually bollixed. I was lying on the ground panting like a big old dog. And Dougie Howlett was roaring and shouting at me to get the fuck up off the ground!

I was moving a bit better a month later when we beat Australia. Weather-wise it was one of the worst nights I've ever played at Thomond Park. There was a gale blowing, it was cold and rainy and the Aussies hated it. A few of them were being treated for hypothermia after with the tinfoil blankets wrapped around them. Paul Warwick put on a kicking display. I had to hold the ball for him on the kicking tee to keep it from toppling over in the wind. The weather didn't keep the crowd away, we had over 21,000 in that night. They knew there could be a bit of history in the making. My father had played on the Munster team that famously beat Australia in '92. It meant a lot that I could repeat the trick with my team mates eighteen years later. It turned out to be the highlight of the season.

In January 2011, Toulon dumped us out of the Heineken Cup. We had qualified for the knockout stages for twelve years in a row. We lost that winning streak on our watch. Toulon beat us all ends up in the Stade Felix Mayol. The golden age was definitely over now. There was no denying it after that. The newspapers were calling it the end of an era and that's what it was. In the dressing room afterwards you could've cut the silence with a knife.

Sammy Tuitupou was chatting to someone and kind of laughed or chuckled at something that was said. It was totally innocent, it was just in the moment, but some of the other lads weren't one bit happy about it. They couldn't understand how anyone would be capable of even smiling. That's dressing rooms for you. Best places in the world, worst places in the world.

Come the end of May then and we beat Leinster in the Magners League final and the changing room is all sweetness and light again! Everyone smiling and laughing and chatting and singing in the showers. It is now over ten years since we had silverware to celebrate. Ten years and counting.

Tony McGahan stepped down at the end of the following season. The Thomond Park aura was fading away too. It was no longer the fortress of old. Ulster came down in April 2012 for the Heineken Cup quarter-final and left our home crowd stunned when they rolled us over. A month later Ospreys ransacked us in the RaboDirect Pro12 semi-final at the Liberty Stadium.

Rob Penney took over that summer. Rob was very different to Tony. He was a very chilled Kiwi. He was all about culture and community and trying to play expansive rugby. It's well-documented now that Rob wanted us playing an attacking game with forwards blending with backs as often as possible.

Back to the beginning: Fitzgerald Park, home of Thomond RFC, where I first learned the ropes. The housing estate in the background is Woodview, where Edel grew up

Ouch!: I get the wrong side of George North in 2015 and pay the price with a cavity in my face and a lift on the motorised stretcher. That's Dr Éanna Falvey looking after me, as always

High fliers: At Alton Towers with Jamie Heaslip, Tadhg Furlong, Mike Ross and Conor Murray

Suited and booted: A ceremony for the presentation of our 2015 World Cup caps

Sea of emotion: Walking out at a packed Thomond Park the day after the funeral of Anthony Foley

Mentor and friend: Axel sharing some of his knowledge with me at the Stade Velodrome before our Heineken Cup semi-final against Toulon in 2014

The gaffers: I have had some serious rugby brains teaching me over the years, from Rassie Erasmus to Simon Easterby and Andy Farrell, to Joe Schmidt, Johann van Graan and Declan Kidney

Good times: Murray and myself with the silverware after our Six Nations clean sweep in 2018. I was proud to receive the recognition of my peers at the end of that season

Airborne: Catching Johnny Sexton's crossfield kick during the famous 41 phases against France in 2018

Daddy's girls: I'd always promised Ella May and Laurie that they'd be able to join me in the celebrations on the pitch one day

Wedding belles:
We'd talked about getting married since we were teenagers, Edel and I. We finally did it in 2016 in Quilty, west Clare. A hug from my wife after beating the All Blacks in 2018

Closing the circle:
After the haka that day, and before the battle, we closed ranks. Right: A pint after the game with Pete O'Mahony

Christmas present: Finishing off an intercept try against Leinster in December 2018. That's Murr bringing up the rear

Three cheers: On my way to a first-half hat-trick against Edinburgh at Musgrave Park in November 2018

Congratulations: JJ Hanrahan and Mike Haley are pretty happy with my try against Racing 92 in November 2019. After the match I caught up with my old mate Donnacha Ryan

Hugs all round: This is one of my favourite photos. Pete O'Mahony and Conor Murray arrive for the celebrations after my second try against Scotland in the 2020 Autumn Nations Cup

Lost in thought: Standing on the training ground in UL, wondering what's wrong with me, why I can't breathe properly, and when is it ever going to end?

Last stand: Shaking hands with Ryan Baird after losing to Leinster in September 2020. With a few minutes to go, I've made up my mind. It's going to be my last game of rugby. Walking off at the Aviva, I'm convinced it's over

It's not over: Five months later I'm winning my 90th Irish cap, against France. Edel sends me this photo the morning of the match. It's better than any team talk! The girls are always there to put a smile on your face

The comeback: Our win away to Clermont Auvergne in December 2020 is probably the greatest Munster performance I've been part of

Old soldiers: We go back a long way, myself and Johnny Sexton. He is the best I have ever played with

Nice one: Sharing a moment with Jack Conan after he has set me up lovely for my try against England at the Aviva in 2021. We'd rehearsed the move repeatedly in training

We weren't really cut out for that. You could find yourself out on the wing with Paulie or Donners or one of the props for company when they just wanted to be in the engine room going at it hammer and tongs. Rob's philosophy was maybe just a bit too idealistic for us. In fairness, there were games where it clicked and we scored some fantastic tries and we blitzed teams. We produced a few massive performances in major games on his watch.

The Heineken Cup quarter-final against Harlequins at the Stoop in April 2013 comes to mind. The week before, Glasgow put 51 points on us at Scotstoun. No one gave us a prayer against Harlequins. They were champions of England at the time. Our non-performance against Glasgow, there was probably a bit of rope-a-dope involved, nearly hamming it up how bad we were and holding ourselves back for a major ambush a week later. It helped that we had Paulie back after being out injured for seven months. He produced an immense display. I missed that game because of a busted shoulder during the Six Nations. I got back onto the training ground after Harlequins only for John Ryan to run into me by accident during a non-contact drill and bust the same shoulder all over again. I got back for the semi-final against Clermont but I was carrying it. Again, the lads put in a massive battling performance, down in Montpellier, but we couldn't claw back Clermont's lead. It was a game we could have won.

I had the shoulder operated on afterwards and watched the Lions on tour in Australia from a mobile home in Kilkee with my arm in a sling. A few weeks later I was heading to Vegas with a bunch of mates and I was dreading it. I had everything paid for but I was seriously doubting would I get on the plane or not. It wasn't until one of the lads actually collected me in his car and brought me to the airport that I was resigned to going. And even then I was thinking about doing a runner. Hank the bastard was in my head day and night at the time. I couldn't think straight.

I was so drained from the nerves and worry that I ended up going to bed after a drink or two while the rest of the lads went out on the town. During the days when they'd be recovering back in the hotel, I'd be out wandering around Vegas on my own. Once again, another holiday where I was the life and soul of the party.

It was the following October that I finally got some help and got my diagnosis. Then a few days later I'm scoring against Leinster and everything looks hunky dory on the outside. I never told Rob about my condition, I just wanted to keep it business as usual with everybody. Two weeks before Christmas we had a brilliant smash-and-grab win over Perpignan down in their place. They seemed to have stolen it with a try two minutes from time, only for us to steal it back from them in stoppage time with JJ Hanrahan racing down the touchline after super play by Denis Hurley and Tommy O'Donnell to keep the ball alive.

I don't think a season goes by without Munster pulling a few huge results out of the bag and this was definitely one of those. We were a long way from home, it was an incredible effort. Lifeimi Mafi had joined Perpignan the season before. We were in our dressing room afterwards singing *Stand Up and Fight* and next thing there was Mafs in the middle of it, in his Perpignan jersey, singing along with us! I thought it was brilliant. I think Mafs's heart was still in Thomond Park.

But no matter how well you play in games like that, it always seems a bit hollow if you don't have anything to show for it at the end of the season. We demolished Toulouse in the Heineken Cup quarter-final only to come unstuck against Toulon in Marseille three weeks later. I was sin-binned early in the fourth quarter for tackling their sub David Smith without the ball. Jonny Wilkinson landed the penalty, Jonny landed nearly all their points on the day. Toulon went on to win the final. Rob Penney and Munster couldn't agree terms for a new contract so Rob moved on to a coaching role in Japan. There was no question or doubt about who his successor was going to be. Anthony Foley was the natural and number one choice.

******

It was in April 2016 that Munster announced Rassie Erasmus would be joining as director of rugby on a three-year contract while Axel would remain as head coach. In June, Ireland were touring South Africa and Rassie made contact with me and Conor Murray to meet us for a chat in a hotel in Johannesburg. He was very impressive. He already had a lot of planning done. He had his opinions on the squad we had, the areas we needed improving, the coaching team he was putting together. He would be bringing Jacques Nienaber with him, his long-time friend and defence coach.

Rassie arrived for pre-season and in his team meetings he set out his philosophy for how we'd play the game. It was going to be a lot different from Rob's. We weren't going to be playing much rugby in our own half. He didn't want us conceding turnovers or penalties in our own half. We were going to try and play a pressurised game in their half. There was a touch of the Jack Charltons about it. There would be a lot of kicking and box-kicking and playing the percentages. He wasn't what you'd call a rugby romantic.

But he was the real deal as a manager, a leader, a boss man. Cardiff Blues beat us by a point in Musgrave Park in early September. This was Rassie's chance to lay down a marker and he didn't hold back. At the team review on the Monday he wasn't happy. He put a series of numbers up on a board. Like, 35, 39, 33 etc. Right, can you tell me what these numbers mean? We hadn't a clue. So he told us they were the ages of the Cardiff pack. He said that basically we'd let a bunch of old men kick the shit out of us. A few fellas were given a pass but the rest of them would have to go to him one by one afterwards and explain to him why they'd played so badly. One of the players sniggered or smiled and Rassie lost the plot with him altogether. He told the player that he could fuck off back to his club for the next few weeks and that if any other outfit wanted to sign him, Rassie would be happy to get rid of him. We were all sitting up fairly straight in our chairs after that. There wasn't a murmur out of anyone. He put the fear of God into us that day.

He put it into us many a day after that too. In training, any fella who didn't partake would be doubted. Lads who'd be carrying knocks and niggles and were on the field but not training were called the purple squad. He wanted them to train through the pain. He was old school like that. Now, if you were genuinely injured, he was reasonable enough. But if he thought you were just minding yourself because you had a niggle of some sort, he reckoned you could be the sort of player who'd be minding yourself during games as well. There wouldn't be many but you'd always have a few who were inclined to be minding themselves. Over the years you had fellas too who'd be throwing their bodies around in training, smashing one hundred per cent into lads who were only moving at seventy per cent. These were the fellas who'd be liable then to only go seventy per cent in games when the pressure was on. Rassie was looking for weak mentalities. He wanted to weed them out. He didn't have much sympathy for you if you were in the purple squad. That's why everyone loved playing for him. He told you how it was and there was no bullshit about him.

It wasn't all stick and no carrot either. He made the set-up more family-oriented, he was mindful of including the wives and girlfriends more on the social side of things. He was involved in getting the players a corporate box in Thomond Park that could be used by our partners and children. It made it easier for them on match days. It took a lot of the stress out of it for us in terms of having to organise match tickets all the time for our families. We had barbecues and get-togethers and nights out too.

The new system and new management were only really bedding down when Axel's death turned everything on its head. I don't know whether it was that on its own that transformed us but we ended up winning twenty of our next twenty-two games. That streak included wins over Racing 92 home and away, and Leinster and Leicester Tigers. We put away Toulouse in Thomond Park in the European Champions Cup quarter-final. We were back in our first semi-final in three years. At the time a part of me was thinking, maybe this is our year. Maybe it's written in the stars. Maybe it's destiny now, after all that's happened. I'm sure I wasn't the only one in Munster thinking it. Anyway, Saracens threw a bucket of cold water over that in the semi-final at the Aviva. They were a fairly awesome outfit that time, English and European champions. They had six players named in the British & Irish Lions squad that was announced a few days earlier. We just couldn't cope with their power and physicality. On top of that, we were pretty one-dimensional in our game plan. Basically it was to kick the ball away when we got it in our half of the field. We could only play rugby in their half of the field.

At the highest level, this was a problem with Rassie's strategy. It depended a lot on winning the collisions and we didn't have the size of the biggest beasts, like Saracens or a couple of the French teams. We didn't have the sheer size that Rassie would be used to back in South Africa. Against Sarries we were running into brick walls all day.

We showed another side to our game in the Pro12 semi-final against Ospreys a month later. Zebo scored a contender for try of the season. It was just on the hour mark at Thomond Park. We were recycling the ball under their posts when they ripped it out and Justin Tipuric wellied it downfield. I sprinted back and slid onto the bouncing ball near our own twenty-two. I offloaded out of the tackle to Francis Saili. Francis jinked his way out of a few tackles and popped it to Murray who slipped it to me and suddenly I was in the clear down the left. Andrew Conway was raiding along inside me. He caught it and transferred it to Zeebs who carried it home with the crowd roaring him all the way. It was a brilliant moment.

It sent us into the final a week later full of belief that we could finish a traumatic season on a high. Again you were thinking how nice it would be to win it for Axel and his family and the whole of Munster. Surely this time the gods would smile on us and we'd finally have something to cheer about. I was never more confident going into a game in all my life. It was definitely written in the stars this time. I had visions of bringing the cup to Axel's grave and telling him we did it for him. But there was to be no Hollywood ending. Scarlets played us off the park, especially in the first half. Sport doesn't do fairytales, it does reality. I thought it was going to be handed to us. I should've known better. I was around long enough to know better. If you're not good enough you'll get what you deserve. We weren't nearly good enough at the Aviva that day.

By that stage there were rumours floating around for weeks that Rassie would be cutting short his time at Munster to go back to South Africa. But the week before the Saracens game he told the players he was staying. After the game he told the press he would be staying. But in July 2017 he announced that himself and Jacques would be leaving the following Christmas. In fact, they left in the middle of November with Johann van Graan coming in the opposite direction.

It wasn't ideal because we had made really good progress under Rassie that first season and now himself and Jacques were gone with the project not even halfway completed. As a player obviously these things are outside your control. But any time there's a change in coaching staff there's an element of starting from scratch all over again. Continuity and stability are important, in my opinion, and at least we've had that now with Johann for the last four years.

But no matter who is running the show, teams have to take responsibility for their own performances too. It can't all be on the head coach. There has to be a big element of self-management, self-motivation. The culture in Munster is generally good like that. There's always another game coming down the tracks and you have to be ready for it no matter what's going on in the background. A few weeks after Rassie left we played Edinburgh in Musgrave Park. I had three tries on the board inside eight and a half minutes. Some days, not often, everything just falls into your lap. According to the statisticians it was the fastest hat-trick by a Munster player in the professional era. It was my first hat-trick since Newport Gwent Dragons in September '08. It brought me up to fifty career tries for Munster.

I played my 150th Munster match in the Champions Cup semi-final against Racing in April 2018. I wasn't in much of a mood to mark the occasion. My knee was injured and my breathing problems were really starting to depress me. I couldn't look forward to any game, knowing what was in store. Every game was just one long struggle to get oxygen into my lungs. It was a horrible feeling and there was no end to it in sight. It was scorching hot that day in Bordeaux. I was mentally drained before a ball had even been kicked. I was standing under the posts with Pete O'Mahony during the warm-up and I remember saying to him that I genuinely didn't care if this was the last game I ever played. I was that worn out by it all. I was going to throw myself about, I was going to give it everything and if it meant doing myself serious damage, so be it. As long as we win, I don't care if it's the last game I play. If we win and we get to the final and we win the final, I'd be happy to sign off with that. I'd trade the rest of my career for one European Cup. It was desperation on my part. It was kind of negative wishful thinking.

Racing had other ideas anyway. They blew us out of the water in the first half. They had the game more or less wrapped up by half-time. Since winning in '08 we'd now played six European Cup semi-finals and lost all six. That's been the story of the last ten years. Good but not good enough. Twelve months later that stat changed to seven out of seven, beaten by Sarries in Coventry. Our last game of the 2019 season was the Pro12 semi-final against Leinster and just like twelve months earlier, they had the upper hand again.

That win in Christmas 2020 over Clermont Auvergne sends us into the new year on a high. Again there's a lot of hope around that we finally have a squad ready to seriously challenge for silverware. We have our chance to prove it in the Pro14 final at the end of March. But Leinster turn up and we don't. They outplay us and they outsmart us. I'm under the pump out on the left wing. Several times in the first half they have a two or three man overlap and I'm trying hard not to panic. It's a scary place when you've thirty metres of space to cover and they have three players queuing up to go past you. It's a minor miracle that it's only 6-6 at half-time. I don't know whether it's the occasion that's got to us or not but we are way off the pace. It is unbelievably disappointing. So, is the Clermont game a false dawn – another one? I don't think so. But the consistency isn't there.

Years earlier, a result like that would've sent me down into a black hole. But I've seen enough tragedy in real life, I know how to keep my job in perspective now. Basically it boils down to doing everything you can to be the best you can be on the field beforehand, and if it doesn't work out, you can't beat yourself up because you know your preparation was a hundred per cent. In my case, that means taking care of my mental health, taking care of my nutrition, doing all my extras on the training ground, doing my visualisation, my research on the laptop, being on top of all the plays we've planned, being one hundred per cent prepared in every way. No shortcuts. I try to tick all those boxes for every game every season. I didn't always, I wasn't aware, but in the second half of my career, that's how I've lived it. Win or lose, if I can look myself in the mirror and say I did all I could, I'm able to move on pretty quickly. I come home and the joys of my life are there waiting for me. Edel is there, the kids are there wanting to be cuddled, and there's a lot of healing in that. There's a lot of healing in the love of your family. I switch off from being a rugby player and become a husband and a father. The game doesn't keep me awake at night the way it used to.

The one-year deal I signed with the IRFU in March 2021 will expire in the summer of 2022. I will look at my options then. A lot will depend on how my body is holding up. A one-year deal was fine with me. If Munster had offered me two years I'd have only signed for one anyway. I wouldn't want to be hanging around for an extra year if I wasn't able to seriously compete for a place in the first team. I wouldn't want to be the veteran who's past it and is only there handing out advice to the young fellas. I want to be competing with the young fellas to the last day of my career. So, next year I'll decide. Maybe someone else will decide for me!

Billy Holland played his last game for Munster in June 2021. Me and him had been together every step of the way, from our academy days on – from boys to men you could say. In my opinion he'll go down as one of Munster's greatest servants. He showed incredible resilience and loyalty. He came into his own as a leader after Axel died. His workload in terms of the forwards went through the roof. He took responsibility for running the lineout and with Billy there were no shortcuts. He'd be there doing twelve-hour days on his planning and research to make sure it was running smoothly. I used to say to him, when you retire I'll retire. He was great at making logical decisions whereas I could go off on a tangent and get lost in the red mist. He'd talk me back down with his logic and his reasoning and that way he helped keep me on the straight and narrow. I will miss him around the place. It's another connection to the old Munster culture gone.

******

Playing for Munster is a unique kind of job. You get to have loads of craic at training every day with the lads, you get to play in front of thousands of people in great stadiums at the weekends. It's a fantastic job to have. But Christ it can be exhausting too. It's more than just a game. If you're walking down a street in Limerick the day after a match, you'll soon enough be reminded that it's more than just a game. I stopped going to certain pubs years ago because of it. You could be out with a few friends having a lovely time but at some stage, sure as night follows day, you'd have various randomers coming over to you telling you the team is shit or you missed this tackle or you dropped that ball. These fellas would think it's only a bit of slagging or whatever. They don't know you've heard the same shit a thousand times before. You'll bite your lip and laugh along just to humour them. Inside you're thinking, piss off and leave me alone. It got to a stage where you learned to be very careful about when you'd go out for a night, where you would go and who you would go with.

So, if you're born and reared in the Munster tradition, it will never be just a job. I've seen fellas from other places sign for us and they didn't give two shits about it. To them it was just another gig. But if you're born into it, you live it and you breathe it. And that's where it can get exhausting. Sometimes I think everybody needs to lighten up just a little bit. Lighten the load a little bit, take the pressure off. I've been a member of the senior players group the last few years. I'd be advocating to ease up on all the little rules and regulations. Occasionally you end up spending far too much time discussing trivial infringements, like a fella has forgotten to wear his regulation polo shirt or something. Big deal! Have a word if you need to but don't make a big song and dance about it. But I suppose when you're coming up short every season and you're desperate to become a winning team again, every little thing gets magnified. It's hard to get the balance right between being too uptight and being nicely relaxed.

The days of having a scatter of pints after a game are more or less gone now. You just won't be able to get away with it. Physically you'll be found out at training or you'll pick up a muscle strain or something. At the same time, fellas need to blow off steam a couple of times a year too. That's the dilemma of trying to get the balance right. The new generation of professionals nearly live like monks now. From the age of fourteen or fifteen they're aiming at a pro contract. They might have their parents pushing them in that direction too. I'd be concerned that they're not getting the chance to enjoy their teenage years. And you'd wonder does it take away their personality? Does the pressure to conform quench their individuality a little bit? Because you need to be yourself at the end of the day. It took me a long time to understand that. Your best chance of making it is by being who you are.

As I write this, I'm on my summer holidays. But I won't be letting myself go. I can't afford to, not at my age. I'll be doing some sort of maintenance, cycling and swimming and running and so on. Then it will be back to pre-season for 2021/22. I made my senior debut in April 2007. That's a long time on the treadmill. But I'm not ready to step off it just yet. Once I do, I'll never step back on it again. I will be far longer off it than on it. I have to keep going. I want to keep going. We have unfinished business at Munster.

13

ACTION AND SUFFERING

ARTHURS QUAY IS A WELL-KNOWN SHOPPING centre in Limerick city. It's there at the bottom of O'Connell Street. Myself and my buddy went into town one day to buy some clothes. There was a shop in Arthurs Quay that had the cool gear. We were fourteen or fifteen at the time. We went in the front door of the shopping centre and were sauntering down to the shop when a security guard appeared out of the blue and marched us straight out the back door. "Right lads, out!" We were like, what? "Out!" And he was pointing towards the back door and steering us in that direction. We said we're only after walking in, what the hell? But there was no conversation with this chap. He just ushered us out the back door and there we were left standing on the street outside shocked and pissed off. This fella had obviously taken one look at us and made his mind up. We were wearing tracksuits, we had the tight haircuts, and the security guard decided we were trouble.

On Friday nights, Supermac's on the Ennis Road was the place to hang out because there was a bowling alley attached to it and there were pool tables and video games too. You could have a good night's fun there with your mates. Edel had a part-time job since she was thirteen or fourteen so sometimes she'd pay for the two of us, your burger and chips and ice cream and games in the arcade next door. The problem was that sometimes me and the lads wouldn't be let in. You took a gamble going down there. One night they'd let you in, the next night they wouldn't, depending on who was on the door. Again, it was the look we had. The clothes we were wearing, our haircuts, maybe even our faces. The security guards would eye us up and down and turn us away.

It was the same thing when we got older and we'd be heading into town for the night. There were a few bars and late night venues where they let in the younger crowd. Edel and myself and a bunch of our mates would be queuing outside. The girls would get in, sometimes the boys wouldn't. It happened lots of times that Edel would be inside waiting for me to come through only to find I'd been kept outside. She'd have to come back out and plead with the bouncers. The bouncers usually would say I was too drunk to be let in. But I'd have been stone cold sober. Normally I wouldn't have been drinking.

I was so strict about my fitness and my rugby, I wouldn't have had a drop of alcohol. But that was their excuse. We'd have to try and find some place else or just go home. It was very embarrassing. It was hurtful. It would ruin a night. They were judging the book by the cover.

At that time I was big and strong for my age, I had the shaved cut, I might have a couple of scars on my head from a match.

The bouncers and security guards would take one look at me and make their mind up. This fella's a bit of a gouger, we can't let him in.

Now that I'm older I can understand how a bunch of teenage boys with their trackies and tight haircuts might come across as a bit intimidating on the street or in a shopping centre. And when I was a teenager Limerick wasn't in a good place, there was a lot of fear around, so I suppose bouncers and security guards were maybe that extra bit paranoid. But it's horrible being judged like that when you're young and you know you're a good person. When you know the difference between right and wrong. When you know you've been brought up the right way. But people have their mind made up about you without knowing one thing about you.

Later on when we were doing the Leaving, Edel says friends of hers got turned down for places at third level because they were failed at the interview stage. It wasn't that they didn't have the ability, it was to do with how they looked, how they spoke, where they were from. It happened too often to be a coincidence.

Job interviews, the same thing. If Moyross was the address on your CV, you could guarantee they'd cross you off the list without even reading your CV. Really smart, talented young people with a proper work ethic, turned down because of their accent or where they're from. Getting judged before they had a chance to prove themselves.

I remember when I got my first car, I was advised not to put down my home address because the insurance companies wouldn't insure me. That was a common one. It was well known in our area. Don't put Moyross on your address or they won't insure you. And if they do, the premium will be sky high because they know you won't be able to afford it. I was told to put my aunt's address in Meelick down on my form. I refused to do that. I put my real address down. As it happened, I did get insured.

In general when it came to official things and official people, there was always this basic lack of trust between us and them, and them and us. The city council, the government offices, the police, there was just a sort of suspicion there. Mutual suspicion maybe. The guards sometimes didn't help in that respect. I know they had an incredibly challenging job to do at the time, trying to bring law and order to parts of the city. I'd have the height of respect for the work they did. In our area there was a certain group of lads who were causing a bit of havoc alright but then we got roped into the policing as well.

Myself and my mates would be hanging around outside Edel's house and next thing the squad car would pull up. This happened a good few times. They'd get out of the car and line us up and search us head to toe. And we genuinely wouldn't be involved in any of the bad stuff that was going on. But I suppose we dressed like the fellas who were involved and that was enough for the guards. They'd order us to go home and warn us that if they saw us out on the road again we'd be thrown into the paddy wagon and taken away to the station.

It happened to me when I was on my own too. They'd get out and surround you and ask you who you were and where were you coming from and where were you going. If there'd been a spate of robbing and vandalising going on, you were liable to be stopped and searched and questioned. Sometimes it happened nearly on a daily basis.

So that didn't improve your trust in people either. Then there was the teacher in Munchin's who said I'd never get anywhere in life. And the teacher in Nessan's who said more or less the same thing.

So, looking back now, I suppose from childhood onwards you're picking up these signals all the time that you're different. You're different from normal society, so-called. It's your clothes, your accent, your haircut. It's the way people look at you or speak to you or treat you. If it happens often enough, it becomes imprinted on your mind. It becomes imprinted on your self-esteem. It takes only one act of discrimination to hurt you. It will be burned in your memory. You won't forget it. And if it happens dozens and dozens of times in all sorts of small ways, you end up with a stigma about yourself.

Then if it happens that the sport you're good at belongs to a class of people who you have nothing else in common with, you'll notice it more and more. You'll feel it more and more. If you happen to be good enough to get picked for your provincial and national teams at schoolboys, you'll find yourself mixing with virtually no one else who has a background like you have. A lot of them will be going to private schools. The rest of them will be going to good schools that send their students to college. And here's me, struggling with my reading and writing as well.

Most of the boys will be dead sound. But they'll speak differently, they'll dress differently, their parents will come across to you as posh and well-spoken. And so you can't help but feel different yourself. I'm the only one here with my kind of background. It was the same with my father. So from a young age I have a fear that history will repeat itself. That I will be discriminated against too. And I'm a shy type of person anyway. Feeling like a fish out of water only makes my confidence worse.

So I'm always on guard, I always have my defences up, I can't relax and enjoy the social side of things.

This follows me right throughout my career, from schoolboys to veteran international. On the field I'm as good as anyone, off the field I don't feel I'm as good as them. I suppose putting it bluntly, I feel inferior to them. I'm the outsider, the fella from the wrong side of the tracks. They're from the right side of the tracks. They're at ease with themselves and I'm not. They seem very secure in this social environment. I'm very insecure in it. I'm all the time trying to fit in. There's always this push and pull going on in my head. I love rugby, I love being good at it, I love that it's my career – I fucking hate that it makes me feel like a fish out of water all the time. It's nearly a case of, can't live with it, can't live without it.

But from a young age I'm well aware that it's going to be my passport to a better life. It's why I'm so determined to make it as a professional. It's why I don't drink on my nights out as a teenager, even though the bouncers accuse me of being drunk.

But there's one night when I'm eighteen when every door in every pub and club in the city is open to me, if I want it. It's in December 2005. Myself and Ger Sla have played for the Ireland U19 A side against the touring Australians in Donnybrook. After the game we're told we've been selected for the Ireland U19 first team squad that will play Australia in Ravenhill four days later. But we're allowed back home for a couple of days after the A game on the Saturday. So Ger and me head back to Limerick. It's the week before Christmas. We're wearing our formal Irish team gear – a navy blazer and cream chinos and a tie with the Ireland crest on it. We're proud as punch wearing it. We meet up with our girlfriends, Edel and Erika, and head into town for the night. There was no stopping us at any door that night. We cruised in. I've gone from being a nobody to a somebody. I'm an Ireland international, I've got the blazer and the tie to prove it. They always say about rugby that it opens doors for people because of its social networks. It opens doors for me that night, even if they're only the doors of a few pubs in Limerick.

But I'm not part of that social network. I couldn't have been born further away from it. On the Saturday night of a home international I'm in the Shelbourne Hotel with the squad, the IRFU officers, the alickadoos and the corporate guests and the society types. There's the dinner and the speeches and the small talk and the back slapping. But I don't want to be there. I want to be back in Kinsella's in Thomondgate with my friends and family. That's where I belong. I don't belong in the Shelbourne. I'm way out of my comfort zone. I can feel the snobbery and the falseness. People only want to talk to you because you're a player. They wouldn't give you the time of day otherwise. Edel has had situations where people were unbelievably condescending until they discovered she was Keith Earls's partner. Then they'd change their tune.

Don't get me wrong. Not everyone in that environment is like that. You will meet some very genuine, warm people there. But to go from Moyross to social occasions like that is a massive journey to make for me. For years I found it intimidating.

I had two huge learning curves. One was how to be an international player on the pitch, the other was how to be an international player off it. Being honest, I found the first easier than the second. I remember having to learn the whole etiquette of the dinner, the big banquet back in the big fancy hotel. The first few times the waiter put the starter in front of me, I'd start eating it before the rest of the table was served. I didn't know you should wait until everyone was served. I had to learn which glass was for the water and which one was for the wine. What were all the knives and forks for?

One night the lads were asking for horseradish to go with their beef. So the next night, I can remember I was sitting next to John Hayes, I was having the beef and I asked the waiter if he could get me some horse hummus please. Some what? Horse hummus please. Well the whole fuckn table erupted with the laughing. I got a desperate slagging. It's funny now but at the time I was mortified.

I've spent most of my career feeling like a fish out of water. Moyross was my safe space. They were my people. I found the world beyond it threatening and uncomfortable. It's a strange thing to say, I suppose, but despite the trouble and danger that was always hanging around Moyross, I found it far less threatening than a place as polite and civilised as the Shelbourne. For me it was like going from one parallel universe to another. It was purely my ability at rugby that brought me from one place to the other. That was the bridge from Dalgaish Park on the edge of Limerick city to the heart of Dublin 4 society. And I kept wanting to go back across that bridge to my home place.

Very occasionally, like when Munster won the Magners League in 2011, I would bring a bit of the rugby community to my home place instead of me always having to go in the opposite direction. A load of the players came over to Thomondgate with me on the Sunday. We ended up having a great day in Kinsella's with the cup.

In 2014 then, when Rob Penney took over, he was big into

building a culture so one of his ideas was to bring us all to Dingle for a weekend of training and bonding. But there was a challenge built into the journey. Rob divided us into groups of say six teams, five or six in each team, and each team would have to plot a different route to Dingle and we'd have to stop off in various places along the way and build up a story of our trip. We had to try and make it humorous as well so I had the bright idea of bringing my crew out to Moyross and putting the lads up on a few sulkies for the craic.

Horses were a big thing in working class communities like mine. Fellas owned horses like other people owned dogs. My uncle, Robert, he was a brilliant soccer player with Ballynanty Rovers, had a horse and sulky. I'd done a bit of bareback riding too on whatever random horse might be standing in Kelly's field. Me and my buddy did it a few times over the years, not very often because personally I wasn't into it. Anyway, Robert had his horse and sulky waiting in the field for us and I got Donncha Ryan to sit up on it and take the reins. I was filming it on my mobile phone. Donncha was chatting away to Robert when next thing the horse took off and Donncha went flying out the back of the sulky!

After we recovered from the laughing the lads took turns flying up and down the field on the sulky before we headed off on our journey to Dingle. They should have built an equestrian centre in Moyross because a lot of the lads were naturals with horses. They'd kind of inherited the interest and the knowledge. There was a lot of racing and gambling with the sulkies, it was nearly like a local industry in itself. There was buying and selling for breeding purposes too. That culture could have been turned into something useful and productive for the area, I'd have thought. Some of the Munster lads were big into their horse racing, like the official horse racing that you'd see on television. I remember trying to explain to Mick O'Driscoll one day about the sulky scene but it was a different kind of horsey set to the one Micko and the lads would have been used to. David Wallace was into his yachting. In fairness, a different kind of transport to the one around my place.

It's hard to gauge how much of my discomfort was down to being from Moyross and how much of it was down to just me. I was struggling daily with a mental health condition that wouldn't even be diagnosed until I was twenty-six. But my anxiety levels would automatically go up around people who weren't my local friends and neighbours.

The lads at Munster were my team mates and friends but even there, I found the social side of things would unnerve me. Say if a few of them were going to dinner in town for a night with their partners and me and Edel would be invited along. That's a pretty normal scenario in any walk of life. But I would find the idea of it really stressful, especially in my first few years with Munster. I'd be looking for excuses to back out of it. I'd overthink it by a mile. There was no need to think about it at all. It was just dinner with friends but I'd be working myself into a knot about it the whole day. I'd be dreading the situation where strangers would come up looking for a photo or an autograph or a chat with the lads.

They'd be recognised if we were out in a bar or restaurant and people would be coming over to chat with them and the lads would be dragged off to meet more people and I'd be left in the corner on my own – Billy No Mates. I'd find that situation embarrassing so I'd try and avoid it by not going out at all. I'm sure the lads at times thought I was an awful oddball. But I hadn't an ounce of confidence in social situations like that.

I'm better able to deal with it now but I still don't like being put up on a pedestal in any way. I hate the way rugby is blown up to be something bigger than it is. I'll sign all the autographs, I'll stand in for all the photos, no problem. But I don't see myself as anything special and I'd prefer not to be seen that way. I don't like being elevated above ordinary people. I like just being a normal everyday bloke. That's why I still enjoy going on holidays to the mobile home in Kilkee. I'd have team mates saying to me, why the fuck are you going on your holidays to a mobile home in Kilkee?! But I just like being around ordinary people like myself. I like walking around and bumping into other families on holidays and playing a bit of soccer or rugby with the kids on the beach. It reminds me of my home place and the feeling of everyone mixing in together in one big community.

Rugby was always taking me away from that world. It was always pulling me one way and I was always pulling back the other way. It's why, particularly in my young years as a pro, I was such a mess nearly everywhere except the field and the training ground. It's why I hated all the international travel, the dinners, the socialising, the meeting people. I wanted to be back in my cocoon in Limerick.

And if you're so uncomfortable in your own skin all the time, it can wear you down. You will exhaust yourself trying to fit into another skin that's not your own. I lost my identity in those years – for most of my twenties really. I was trying to be someone else. I was always looking at other lads and imitating them. So every fad that came and went in strength and conditioning, for example, I would try it. I'd be hopping from one to another. I'd be very easily rattled by something someone said. If I was eating chocolate and someone said to me, is that going to make you a better player, I'd be feeling guilty straightaway. I ended up being hyper vigilant about my nutrition. I became conscious of my body image.

I put on a pile of muscle and fat when that was the trend because that's what you were told to do. If I didn't do everything right and proper, I'd feel guilty. I can't have that slice of pizza or that piece of cake or that glass of cola because it's not helping me and it's not helping the team. I was paranoid about stepping out of line. I was trying to be perfect all the time. I was lost, really, because I was trying to be somebody else instead of being strong enough to be myself.

And if you're not yourself, then who are you? I wanted to be a rugby player but I hated being a rugby player for all those other reasons. I was a home bird who had to go away all the time. I was a full back, a centre, a winger – a jack of all trades who lacked an identity. I was 98kgs, I was 82kgs. I was a private person doing this very public job. I was a rugby international with all the prestige that goes along with it but in my heart I was this stray kid from Moyross.

For the first ten years of my life I wasn't even Keith Earls. I was christened Keith Costello, my mother's surname. If your parents weren't married you were registered under the name of your mother. That was fine, it made no difference to me. Then when I was eight or nine and starting to play soccer and rugby, I was Keith Costello but I was also "Ger Earls's lad". I was "young Costello" to some people and "young Earls" to other people. So my folks eventually decided to settle it once and for all by getting my name changed to my father's surname, the way most people are named. I was happy with that too. My dad was my hero, I wanted to be like him, I was happy to take his name. They went down to St Camillus's on the Shelbourne Road in Limerick, the place where they kept the registers of birth, and filled out the forms and I was officially re-named Keith Gerard Earls. I made my communion as a Costello but my confirmation as an Earls. When I started playing rugby seriously people would say, "He's an Earls alright!"

Then you sign your first professional contract and that's where the pull away from your roots begins.

Listen, I know I wasn't emigrating to the other side of the world. I wasn't even going to England, like the Irish soccer lads have to do. It's just that I was institutionalised in Moyross. I didn't know anything about the world beyond it. I think it's part of the problem for us. We become scared of leaving the place. We stick to the place we know and the people we know. It's like we don't belong to the rest of society. This is our society and it's all we know.

It doesn't help when you're walled in. There was this big wall around Moyross. There was more or less only one way in and one way out. It was cut off from the rest of the city almost. It was like a dead end. It's nearly like it was planned deliberately that way to keep us isolated from the rest of the city. It worked fairly well, if that was the idea.

Edel says I didn't know anywhere else existed beyond my own stomping ground. The rest of the city was alien to me, never mind the rest of the country. She says I didn't lift my head up to see what was out there, beyond my own little enclave. That's true too. It was one reason why I had such a panic attack when I was called up to the U19 squad in South Africa in 2005.

For a fella who didn't even know the South Circular Road in my own town, going to a place as far away as South Africa frightened the shite out of me. And that inner fear of travelling to new places and meeting new people never really left me. It used to bug Edel that I'd be off to all these amazing places from America to Japan to New Zealand and I'd barely even notice I was there.

The bottom line, though, is that I wanted to succeed at rugby more than I wanted to stay in my comfort zone. It was a close enough battle at times, not much more than a point in it. The desire to succeed just about edged out all the dread that was constantly sapping me. If I was going to make it for Munster and Ireland, I'd have to leave my safe space. And ultimately you couldn't bottle that decision. Sure you'd never live with yourself if you bottled a decision like that.

You couldn't walk away from the talent and the opportunities you'd been given. If you wanted to make your dream a reality you'd have to take action and there was going to be suffering. I'm a big believer in that anyway. If you want to achieve something close to your heart, you have to show action, and suffering has to happen before you get success.

Everyone's definition of success is different I suppose. Going out to your nine to five job every morning and providing for your family, I'd consider that a very admirable type of success. For me I nearly had no choice because I was given this talent for sport and I had to honour it. I had to be true to the gifts I was given.

There were many times when I felt rugby was eating me up. But I know for sure that if I'd packed it in young, that decision would have eaten me up a lot worse and for the rest of my life too. I can't imagine all the regrets I'd have now if I didn't stick with it.

At the time it always seemed like a big deal, going away with some team or other to play rugby while all my buddies were out at the weekend having the craic and hanging out together. Meanwhile, I'd be hanging out with a bunch of strangers feeling lonely and uneasy. I'd be pining to be back in Limerick. My father used to be talking me down and reassuring me. He'd say I was only going away for a few days, everyone and everything would still be here when I got back.

As the years went on, I ended up losing that connection with some of my friends, our lives just grew apart. That's one of my regrets. I didn't want that to happen but with hindsight it was unavoidable.

I was asked to do groomsman at a few weddings and had to turn them down because I couldn't guarantee I'd be there. I'm hoping that when I'm retired I'll have my life back and I'll be able to pick up the threads again with some old mates.

Edel says that for all the stresses and the downsides that went with it, rugby is the best thing that ever happened to me. It opened up worlds to me that I never knew existed. It broadened my horizons and hers.

Most of our childhood friends more or less mimicked their parents, they got married young and had their kids and lived in the same area they grew up in. We've made loads of friends from home and abroad through the game. We've travelled far and wide. We've had brilliant experiences. It taught us about life and society, stuff we'd never have discovered and people we'd never have met, if I had stayed in my comfort zone.

I still think we'd have had a nice life. We'd probably both

be working and bringing up the kids and going to a match at weekends and going to our local for a few drinks. That's a good life too, in my eyes. I was just lucky enough to be able to play in those matches instead of sitting in the stand looking at them. And because of that, I ended up living a different life.

You end up learning a lot of different life lessons too. And actually one of the things I realised after all the travelling and meeting people from all sorts of different cultures was that the people I know from Moyross and Weston and St Mary's Park and Kileely and Thomondgate are the finest people you'll meet anywhere. I mean in terms of their values and decency and goodness. Their generosity and genuineness and attitude to what's right and what's wrong. I don't think I'm being sentimental in saying that. It's just that you notice that those values aren't as common when you're dealing with the corporate end of rugby, for example. There's always more cynicism and less loyalty I suppose when money is involved. There's less sincerity and less trust.

Whereas the people I grew up with were all about community and looking out for each other. Everyone was in it together. The children were minded by everybody. Your neighbours would bring back sweets from the shop for you as well as their children. If a family was struggling financially they'd get furniture and clothes if they needed them, maybe a cooker or a fridge. There was decency and empathy like that.

Our rugby coaches and our soccer coaches looked out for us and looked after us. They taught us right from wrong too. You were out on the street from morning till night running around and the neighbours would be keeping an eye out for you, making sure everything was okay. The teachers in our national school were great to us and it wouldn't have been easy for them all the time.

So I can put my hand on my heart and say I had a great childhood. I didn't want for anything, be it food or clothes or toys or holidays. There was love at home and there was love in the community. And really at the end of the day that's what every child needs.

We'd like our own kids to experience that kind of community too but it's nearly impossible to replicate what me and Edel had in Moyross and Woodview. Basically, you were fed at home and then thrown out on the street and down the park for the rest of the day. That's not the done thing now, and we're living in a different part of the city where people live more private kind of lives. Kids go on play dates now with their friends.

We bought our first house in Castletroy when I was twenty-one. I was nineteen when my father came into my bedroom one day. I was playing my FIFA video game. I had my first ever session with Munster in Thomond Park that day. And Dad comes in and he says, "I've something to tell you." And immediately I'm worried. Okay, what is it? And he goes, "Your mother is pregnant." Oh. Right. And then he bursts out laughing. I'm twenty when my baby sister is born.

For the first year or so, Jenny sleeps in her cot at the end of my bed. It's a two-bedroom house and there's a bit of pressure on space now. My parents decide to move out to Meelick which is out in the countryside a few miles further from Moyross, inside the Clare border.

Meanwhile, I've signed a good contract with the IRFU, Edel is working too, so we decide to get our own place in town. And I suppose that's when you start building a new life that's different from the world you grew up in. The life we have now, it's what our kids know. I hope it's a lovely life for them. We're doing our best to make sure it is. I'm probably guilty of spoiling them.

But we're both determined to keep them grounded and to pass on the values we got from our parents and our community. I suppose they'll find out in their own good time that life can be tough and cruel as well as lovely and enjoyable. They'll find out about work and taxes and wins and losses.

I learned maybe too young how tough and painful it can be. You'd want to protect your children from those realities for as long as possible. But at least they know what cutlery to use when we're out for dinner somewhere. Their daddy taught them that cos he's an expert on it now. He knows which glass is for the water and which one is for the wine. He's come on in leaps and bounds like that!

I've been absolutely pampered as a rugby player, we all have. The best of food, clothes and medical treatment. The lap of luxury on tour and at training camps.

I have been put up in hotel rooms that were literally bigger than the house I grew up in. I used to get the 303 bus from Moyross into town. A few years later I'm flying business class to New Zealand being waited on hand and foot. For a fella who sometimes wasn't let into Supermac's, it's a fair old contrast. It's two worlds apart.

I haven't been back to Kinsella's in a couple of years. I suppose a lot of the old fellas who sat at the bar have probably passed away now. Their children and grandchildren are probably regulars there now. It's still a great community pub. I'd say if I walked back in there now and a few of the old familiar faces were there, the craic would start up and I'd be loving it.

The thing is, though, what I have now I wouldn't change for the world either. The people I grew up with are the people who made me. Moyross is in my heart and soul. It's in my bones. The struggle for me was trying to reconcile where I came from with where I've ended up. I don't want the two things to be incompatible. I'd like to belong to both worlds. I want to be able to walk into Kinsella's and feel right at home there still. But I want to take my family to Adare Manor for a night out too, if we feel like it.

Growing up, a thing that used to be condemned was anyone getting above their station. It was seen as a bad thing if somebody got above their station.

Funny enough, you wouldn't hear it said in rugby circles. It was taken for granted that you should aspire to be doing well in life. It was taken for granted that you'd have privileges and success and a nice lifestyle. I had to stop drinking in certain pubs in Limerick because fellas would throw it in your face that you were a big shot now. Sort of like, who do you think you are now? And I'd be like, oh fuck off, I'm just out for a pint. But there was that undercurrent of jealousy there. A bit of basic begrudgery I suppose.

I've never been the type to flash the cash or flaunt whatever bit of success I've had. My father taught me that lesson the day I landed home with the Range Rover. I live my life modest and low-key. But at the same time, why shouldn't I get above my station? Why shouldn't a person from Moyross or any other disadvantaged area have the ambition to go further in society than their parents did or their neighbours did?

Sometimes we're our own worst enemies in terms of keeping ourselves down. Personally I get great satisfaction out of taking our family on a couple of holidays a year. It makes me feel good that my children will get the best education they want, no questions asked.

I like going out with my wife to a nice restaurant and ordering a good bottle of wine. It's no big deal. It's part of who I am now and I enjoy it.

I spent my twenties not knowing who I really was, searching for an identity. In my thirties, it's been better. I'm not there yet but I'm getting there. I'm growing into my own skin. My identity is father and husband. To the outside world, in as much as anybody cares, I'm a rugby player. But I can't control that. For me the most important priority is to be a good husband and father. Having kids is the greatest thing that's happened to me. That's my identity. That's my role in life. Having that clarity brings me peace of mind.

In March 2021 construction began on a new urban carriageway from Coonagh on the Ennis Road to the Knockalisheen Road in Moyross. The project had been talked about for years. People in the area had been crying out for it for years. It will connect Moyross to the city in a way it never was before. The wall that was built around us was a symbol of how much we were cut off from the rest of the city. We became a bit walled in psychologically as well as geographically. We all became a bit institutionalised.

The hope is that the new roadway will be instrumental in developing the area socially and economically. That it will improve transport links and open up the area to residential and commercial development.

It's been described as a cornerstone of the regeneration process that has been happening for over a decade now. Moyross has already changed hugely over the last ten years and more. A lot of the original housing has been demolished. A lot of families have moved out.

The original urban planning for the place was terrible. It was more or less a case of put them on the reservation and forget about them. Local government and politicians got a bad rap for it and rightly so. People who lived there ended up feeling like second class citizens. But to be fair about it, there was a lot of effort and investment made in the following decades. They built us parks and playgrounds and a community centre and a new secondary school.

But in my opinion facilities aren't going to solve every problem. People have to take a bit of responsibility also. I think they will too, with a bit of help and mentoring and guidance. Some parents need help with parenting, otherwise it becomes a vicious circle.

Lots of people have done well but some others need mentoring about the education system for their kids, about trades and apprenticeships, about mental health and a life outside the social welfare system. About working and paying taxes and making your contribution to the wellbeing of society as a whole. There's a whole world out there that they're not aware of. I know this because I was the same. I didn't lift my head up to look around me and see what was going on beyond my little cocoon. I didn't want to venture beyond it either until I was dragged kicking and screaming away from it.

I am so glad I was. I am so glad to have had so many doors opened for me when as a young fella they were closed in my face. But wherever I travelled, no matter how far away, I always brought Moyross with me. I brought the pride of being from there and the stigma too.

Maybe they were one and the same. I think there's more hope and optimism and confidence about the place now. I hope the next generation can go where they want to go, and be who they want to be, without bringing any of the old baggage with them at all.

14

HARD LABOUR

YOU'RE NOT A PROPER RUGBY PLAYER IN MY OPINION until you have learned how to defend. I came into senior rugby not knowing how to defend. Scoring tries is fun, defending is work. It's a proper blue collar job. When you're getting paid to do your job, you have to do it all and you have to do it well. You can't just pick and choose the bits you like. Learning how to defend is basically learning how to grow up as a player. I came into senior rugby naïve and immature. It happens with a lot of people I think across all sports. Sport is play when you're a child. It's still play when you're a teenager if you're marked out as the finisher, the scorer, the glory boy. Nothing wrong with that. Someone has to do it! And who doesn't like getting a bit of the limelight when you're young and you haven't a care in the world?

You bring that innocence with you into the adult game and eventually you lose it. You have to lose it. The sooner you lose it the better. Typical of me, I had to lose it the hard way. I got exposed. I was totally green about a crucial part of the game. It wasn't for the lack of courage. I liked putting in the tackles, I didn't mind putting my body on the line. But defending is a systematic thing. It's a whole system of its own. You have to study it. You have to concentrate on it and learn a lot of lessons.

Every raw young fella gets exposed during their first few years in the senior ranks. But it's not so bad if it happens, say, at club level where not many people are there to witness your growing pains. You can make your mistakes in a fairly low-pressure environment. I made mine on just about the biggest stage possible in rugby, bar a World Cup.

It was on tour with the Lions in South Africa in '09 that I got exposed. Shaun Edwards was the defence coach on that tour. Shaun was a rugby league legend who'd come over to union and was now coaching a lot of the stuff he'd learned in league. He was a defence guru. His calling card was the blitz defence. Basically getting your players moving up fast and hard in one line across the field. It sounds simple but it takes a lot of trust and co-ordination to get it right. If one or two players aren't properly aligned and alert, it can break down. Everyone has to be operating in tandem in the moment. Naturally enough, on a Lions tour he didn't have a lot of time to get the system absolutely bedded down. It meant he had an awful lot of explaining to do on the training ground to get everyone singing from the same hymn sheet. We were going through his drills over and over. And personally, I struggled to take it in. I just didn't understand the importance of this part of the game. I was still in that phase where I thought raw talent was enough. It was a hangover from my school days. Natural talent had always got me through. So, a lot of what Edwards was coaching in South Africa was going straight over my head. Maybe it was a concentration issue too. Maybe it was a bit like switching off when it came to the books in school. I couldn't concentrate then, I couldn't concentrate now either. Was it a symptom of the bipolar thing? Maybe it was, I don't know.

It's a cliché in sport that the higher you go, the more your mistakes will be punished. But it's true. The inherent flaws in your game will be exploited. It came home to roost for me against the Emerging Springboks in Cape Town. I showed the two sides of the same coin that night. The try I scored in the first half, the one I conceded in the second half. Obviously, you don't score tries on your own and you don't concede them on your own either. There's usually a systems malfunction somewhere when you let in a try. A few links in the chain have broken down. But that night in Newlands I was the last link in the chain. And what's worse, there were only ten seconds left in the bloody match. If we'd held out we'd have won it. But the Emerging Springboks get one last chance, they throw the ball wide right, I make a misread in the line and their sub, Danwel Demas, dives over in the corner. Then Willem de Waal lands the touchline conversion to draw the match. I'm supposed to be guarding that corner. Shane Williams is inside of me.

In hindsight, it's not a huge deal, it's not a career-defining moment or anything like it. But it's annoying. It annoys me when I look at it now, knowing what I know now. I should have held my position. Basically, I should have kept my nerve. But I twitch under the pressure. I pull the trigger and shuffle over to join Williams and of course they throw a skip pass wide for Demas and he has broad daylight in front of him because I'm not there. I nearly run into Williams I'm so close to him. Basic error. Lack of knowledge, lack of experience.

Twelve years later, to give a contrast, against Leinster in the PRO14 final in March 2021, I don't twitch. We're getting overrun in the first half. Leinster are coming at us in waves. A few times I'm outnumbered three to one on my left wing. They have a choice of player to pass to for a handy run-in. The only thing I can do is hold my position and hold my nerve. Don't bite down or jump in. Let them make the decision instead of me making it for them. Sometimes it can put a bit of hesitation in the passer's mind. Should he pass now or should he delay it? If I commit to the tackle, it makes the decision easy for him. So I don't. I wait and I drift and it causes just enough doubt for them to mess it up a few times. But I'm thirty-three years old, I've a fair bit of experience under my belt by then. Aged twenty-one in South Africa, I don't know enough about this kind of situation. And I'm too shy and too lacking in confidence to put my hand up and say to Shaun Edwards that I don't understand what he's trying to teach me.

May 2011, the Magners League final against Leinster in Thomond Park. I only remember this because I caught it on TV one night in the spring of 2021. Maybe I was better off not watching it! My memories of it were very affectionate until then. Leinster didn't score a try that day so I must've been labouring under the illusion that my defence was great that day. Then I'm looking at it ten years later and the reality is very different. I couldn't get over how shocking it was. Even Edel was going, Jesus Christ, your defence! She wouldn't be into the finer points of the game but she could see that much. I was shooting out of the line and missing man and ball. I wasn't keeping my positional discipline, I was making wrong decisions and poor reads. It was brilliant scrambling and last-ditch tackling that kept Leinster out on a couple of occasions.

Four months later, the World Cup quarter-final against Wales in Wellington. Again, the two sides of the coin. Shane Williams scores after two minutes in my corner. In fairness, they're probably going to score anyway but I'm caught betwixt and between, Leigh Halfpenny on my inside, Williams on my outside. I end up tackling neither. Five minutes after half-time I've a job to do to convert a chance into a try. I slide for the corner from a long way out as Mike Phillips comes across to haul me over the touchline. I get the nod from the TMO. I've had that bit of opportunism in me from a young age. I know how to finish chances. It comes naturally enough to me. The other stuff, the grown-up stuff, I don't have the instinct for it and it takes a long time for the penny to drop.

In the sixty-fourth minute in Wellington, Jonathan Davies gets a ball down the narrow side. He's infield, he's not coming directly down my channel but we're caught a bit short on that side and I've drifted in. Cian Healy is next to me. Davies waits for the tackle but it never comes. I'm looking at him and Cian is looking at him and I'm backing off, biding my time. Davies senses the hesitation and shoots through the gap between us and suddenly he's in the clear. It's the try that wins it for Wales. It's my fault. My attempt at a tackle is woeful. You should never leave a prop forward with a one-on-one tackle. It's up to me to be decisive and hit Davies.

You're branded then. You're labelled as just a speed merchant who can finish tries but doesn't have anything else in his locker. Other teams have sussed out this weakness in your game. They make plans accordingly. You've been found out for something you didn't even know was a problem until you've been punished for it. Coming back from the 2011 World Cup, I'm facing a serious deficiency in my game. It rattles your confidence badly when a sport that has always come easy to you suddenly isn't easy at all. I have to learn a fundamental aspect of the game that I realise is basically a mystery to me. I just don't understand how a defence works and what I'm supposed to do in the defensive system. Various coaches are talking about numbering up and split defences and blitz and drift and spacing and all the rest of the jargon, and it's not really sinking in with me. And I'm playing alongside serious defenders like O'Driscoll and D'Arcy and Mafi and Howlett and Tipoki. All these fellas can play too, they can cut open defences themselves, but they've got the other side to their game as well and I don't. A bird never flew on one wing; I'm flying on one wing as a rugby player. You won't get away with that. I have to re-think my attitude to my preparation. I actually have to study the mechanics of team defending and learn it more or less from scratch.

So I do. Session by session, season by season, I concentrate on it more and more. The penny drops as to how important it is. I make incremental improvements. I become more reliable on D, less porous. And when Andy Farrell comes into the Ireland backroom as defence coach in 2016, he helps me bring it to another level. Andy said something early on that really clicked with me. He was the first coach who ever said to me that defence wasn't a black and white issue. That was a revelation to me. Because coaches I think across all sports like to simplify things for players. Rightly so, too. The simpler the message is, the easier you can absorb it. But not everything can be simplified. If something is complicated, then say it's complicated and explain why it's complicated. Players love learning new stuff. It really chimed with me when Andy said that defence wasn't black and white, because I had never found it to be a black and white thing. There was a lot of grey in it for me. And then if you're told something is simple, but your experience is that it's not simple, you kinda feel stupid for not being able to understand it. So when Andy said it wasn't simple, it was like he could understand why I didn't understand it. I found that empowering. He also said another thing early doors that I found empowering. He said there was no such thing as a stupid question. I loved hearing that. I used to be one of those players who wouldn't put his hand up at a meeting for fear of sounding a bit thick. But I got over that. I've been comfortable doing it for years now. If I don't understand, I ask them to explain. Sometimes nowadays, even if I know the answer I'll ask the question anyway because I'll sense that a few of the young lads might be too embarrassed to ask. But mostly these days there's no need to cos Faz makes everyone feel comfortable enough in that environment.

I was fascinated by the way he explained defence. He talked about seeing the picture. Then seeing smaller pictures within the bigger picture, like the speed on the ball, the depth of the player, their body language and facial expressions. He puts a lot of responsibility on the wingers to read opposition attacks and call the shots. We are like the captains of the defence, as he sees it, because we can see the full picture better than the players who are in the heat of the action. We can count the numbers and see what's outside us and what's inside us and where the key space is and who have I working with me in this moment. You've to factor in how quickly the ball is coming out of their ruck, have our lads slowed it down enough, is their ten flat to the line, what's their formation behind the ball, what's our formation. How much space have we to cover? Are we 14-1 or 13-2, are the wingers, me included, moving over and back in pendulum fashion – how are we set up in this situation? Then I call the defensive play I think we need. Stay connected, drift across, shoot up, don't shoot up.

You're trying to process all this information in an instant, like you're a computer. You'd have a pain in your neck from all the looking around you have to be doing. An extra pair of eyes somewhere above your ears would be handy, there's so much stuff going on in your peripheral vision too. Out on the wings we don't go to war the way the forwards do. It can be more a mental test than a physical test. You can feel very vulnerable out there because you are so exposed and isolated. And if you make a mistake out there, your team usually pays a big price, like a goalkeeper in soccer. So, if you don't want that to happen, your concentration has to be really intense. You can't switch on your defence when your opposite number has the ball in his hands. You have to switch it on whenever they take possession of the ball, no matter how far away from you that is.

Your radar should be scanning their nine and ten at all times. But your first priority is to follow the ball. It sounds basic enough but you'd be surprised how easy it is to get distracted by the players rather than the ball. If you lock your eyes onto the ball, there's less chance of being manipulated by the players' movement. It doesn't matter what shapes they're making if you're tracking the passage of the ball. Andy is big on that. But then you have to sort of contradict that by looking at their playmakers for clues. Steal a glance at the flyhalf's face just before he receives the ball. Obviously, he is scanning the field for his next move. Sometimes you'll see it in his eyes what he's planning. Where is he looking for his options? Is he going to kick or pass? You can pick up the tell sometimes and if you've read it right, you can cover the move before it happens. Or even better, show them the space where they think they can operate but then close the space before he has executed his move. And if he does execute it, we've already read it and covered it. It's a form of manipulation. Your movement is manipulating their decisions. If it works, you're telling them lies. You're telling them you're here so he'll think he should kick it over there – but you're already on the move over there before he's kicked it. Or certainly before the ball has arrived. Obviously, this is all happening in seconds, fractions of seconds. If your forwards are putting serious pressure on their nine and ten, then it's narrowing down his options so it's easier for us to read what option he's going to take, ideally before he has taken it. Everything is connected. What our forwards do has a knock-on effect on what we do. But the higher the level, the faster a ten or a nine will react to that pressure and come up with a counteraction to beat it. They are reading the picture in front of them too. A Johnny Sexton or an Owen Farrell only needs a split second to figure out what's in front of him and come up with a solution. Any top international scrum half or flyhalf, they're nearly looking at you looking at them. It's a game of cat-and-mouse that way. It's one reason why you'll study them on tape to look for any habits or signs or tells that give you an early warning of their intentions. They might cue up their wingers for a crossfield kick with some sort of signal, maybe an arm in the air. Or one fella might clap his hands unconsciously before he kicks the ball.

So, seeing the picture is one thing but the picture keeps changing, second by second. No sooner have you read one picture than it has changed into another picture. It's like pressing the button on a camera. Once the picture is taken another picture comes into your viewfinder and you have to process it instantly in your mind. That's where your concentration becomes so important.

You're living on your nerves a lot of the time because everything is changing all the time and at high speed. It can be very stressful trying to cover every move, every change of picture, for eighty minutes. Staying in the zone for eighty minutes is a tough thing to do. I remember Joe Schmidt asking us in one of our meetings, what's the average time a person can concentrate for? According to Joe it was something like eight seconds. Doing it for eighty minutes in the heat of a match will give you a migraine.

That's why defence is not a black and white situation. That's why it's not simple. It's fucking complicated! What's more, trends and philosophies are changing all the time too. The game keeps evolving, attacks are constantly evolving, there's different shapes, everyone is trying to manipulate everyone else. Defence is evolving too, probably not as fast as attack, but people are coming up with trick plays and ideas around positioning or tiny details that you wouldn't notice watching on TV. The evolution is happening on the hoof and you have to be super adaptable to keep pace with it. These days you could be running a hard line one week and a softer system the following week. You don't have one fixed identity. A kind of hybrid philosophy is the fashion at the moment.

And at the end of it all, no one will have any sympathy for

you if they score a try and you're deemed not to have done your job. Where was Earls when they dinked that low ball into his corner? I'll tell you where I was. Their ten was going to put it up in the air and I was moving over here to cover that. Then the picture changed because a tackler was coming to block that kick so he dinked it instead. Or he shaped to kick but then he threw it out wide at the last second. Something happened and the picture changed in a flash. They can manipulate you, just as you can manipulate them. Sometimes it's not good to tell lies. You think you've bluffed them but their flyhalf has seen your bluff and pulled out his own bluff. There's a bit of a double bluff going on.

A lot of the time you read it right and you've covered the kick, or the pass, before it's happened. So you've cancelled out the danger before there was any danger and it goes unnoticed. It won't go unnoticed in the video room, which is where it really matters. That's where you're accountable. That's where the culture in your squad matters. If everyone accepts he's accountable as an individual for his actions, then you'll get honesty and improvement.

That was how I had to face my own basic weakness as a player. Face up to it, admit I had a problem and start trying to solve it. It took a long time but I got there. Maybe it got to the stage where I was so hung up about my defence, I ended up losing some of my flair in attack. I was so conscious about becoming a solid defender, I prioritised it above the thing that came naturally to me.

The last season or so I've kind of swung back the other way a little bit and tried to remind people what I can do with ball in hand. I nearly had to remind myself first of all. I think I've got the balance more or less right now. I still get a buzz out of scoring tries. I get a lot of satisfaction out of helping to prevent them too. It can be hard labour trying to do that part of the job. But if you come off the field knowing you've stuck at it for the full eighty, you'll know you've earned an honest day's pay.

15

THE JOE SHOW

I'M NEARLY EMBARRASSED TO SAY IT BUT WHEN JOE Schmidt was in charge I was kind of the teacher's pet. In fairness, there was no danger of that ever happening to me when I was in school.

At the same time, Joe wasn't the type of coach who wanted to be pals with his players. It was the opposite. He was a very demanding taskmaster. Some people believe he ruled through fear. I wouldn't go that far. I think it's more accurate to say that he ruled through excellence. But his demand for excellence was so fierce, it came with a bit of fear attached to it too. He hated when things weren't done properly. He wanted every detail done to a T. And if you didn't do it properly, he wouldn't be long letting you know about it. That's why everyone toed the line with him. You wouldn't get away with sloppiness. He'd spot it and he'd nail you for it.

He'd forgive you if you made a mistake in the heat of battle that was a genuine mistake. But if he was coaching, say, a technical skill in training and you didn't execute it correctly because you weren't concentrating, he would take it personally. He'd be bubbling up with frustration. You had an excuse if your mistake was genuine. You had no excuse if it was because you weren't concentrating on your job. If you weren't trying hard enough. If you were talking when you should have been listening. If you were messing around when he was trying to explain something. He knew what he was talking about. And he knew that he knew what he was talking about.

A lot of his authority came from his knowledge. He had incredible knowledge about the game of rugby from its tiniest mechanics to the big-picture tactical stuff. And he was intense. He was hard on himself. He worked night and day. He was as hard on himself as he was on his players – maybe harder. He put everything he had into the Ireland job. So, you had this fella who insisted on excellence, who had the knowledge and who had the personal intensity. And that is a hell of a powerful combination in any one coach. Joe was special. Someone like him doesn't come around very often. Joe Schmidt changed Irish rugby and left a massive legacy behind him that is still benefitting the game in this country to this day.

And he changed me too. He changed the way I thought about rugby. He changed the way I prepared for it. And eventually he changed my fortunes in green after ten years of missing out on the good days. I never talked to him about it but I'd imagine the way he handled me had something to do with what I told him in the summer of 2014.

He'd taken over from Declan Kidney in autumn 2013 around the same time I was diagnosed bipolar. He made an instant impact. They started the 2014 Six Nations with big wins over Scotland and Wales. They lost to England in Twickenham, a game I watched with Edel and Ella in McGettigan's Irish bar in Dubai.

Ireland won the championship with a win in Paris on the last day. I watched it at home in Limerick, delighted for the lads but cursing the knee injury that had wiped out the whole championship for me. I was also unravelling mentally having quit the medication that the psychiatrist had put me on the previous October.

My knee recovered in time for the summer tour of Argentina but my brain didn't. I was in no fit state to go on that tour. The bender I went on in Killaloe had put the tin hat on that. It put me into meltdown. I had to ring Joe and tell him the truth of where I was at. He was very compassionate about it at the time and I'd say it coloured the way he treated me over the next five and a half years. We never talked about it during that time but I think in his own subtle way he did try to build my confidence and encourage me. I think he was careful with me, maybe aware that I might be suffering inside.

Obviously, I just wanted to be treated the same as everybody else. But, for example, he'd make a point of giving me compliments in team talks. If he was showing video clips, say of good habits, he'd sometimes show a clip of me doing something well. I'd find it embarrassing, because of my shyness, but it was coming from a good place. He was trying to show me I was valued and appreciated.

In fairness, he trusted players who trained well and in general I trained well. How you trained was extremely important to him. How you trained during the week told him a lot about how you'd play at the weekend. As players we knew that too. You wouldn't have needed Joe to tell you that. Any player who's serious about his job knows he has to be serious about his training. I took it seriously. I'd be switched on for it. I never got too much wrong in training. I didn't make many mistakes. I knew good habits were important. Joe was big into players having good habits, off the pitch as well as on it. So, even if he didn't know about the bipolar thing, I'd probably have been in his good books anyway.

And in fairness too, if I wasn't performing on the field I'd have been out on my ear fairly lively as well. I understood that. We all understood that. A lot of fellas came and went who didn't measure up to his standards. I think some fellas just couldn't cope with the pressure he put on us to be at our best all the time. He was relentless that way. You could never fully relax when you were in camp.

My anxiety was always simmering away because of the high-pressure environment he cultivated. But the payoff was in your confidence. My anxiety would be sky high during the week of a match but at the same time your confidence would be sky high going into the match because you'd know you could not have been better prepared. His preparation was world class. His attention to detail was phenomenal. The upshot was that you got fantastic confidence from it. You'd have no doubts that you were ready. Every player would be switched on. Every player would know the job he had to do. And it was amazing the amount of times he planned for something to happen, and it happened. It was nearly like he could see into the future. He could see the patterns of play that were going to happen before they happened. He'd have your opponents sussed out. You found yourself going into games feeling bulletproof. The lads from Munster and Ulster and Connacht, it didn't take us long to find out why Leinster had been streets ahead of us when Schmidt was managing them. We were seeing it up close for ourselves now.

I could have done with seeing more of it in his first eighteen months but most of the time I wasn't there. Another knee problem surfaced in the autumn of 2014, a patella tendon that kept me out for months. Ireland kept on winning, they took the big scalps of South Africa and Australia in the autumn series that year. I watched the game against the Springboks in Herbert's bar in Castleconnell.

I got back to fitness in the new year and Joe included me in his 46-man preliminary squad for the 2015 Six Nations. But I didn't make the cut. He sent me back to play with Munster. I guess he just didn't trust that my body would hold up so he decided to move on without me until I had proven my fitness was solid. So I had to sit at home and watch them win another Six Nations championship and it gutted me to be on the outside looking in again.

The day they beat England 19-9 in the Aviva, I watched it from a pub in Doonbeg in Clare. I had to get out of the house and go somewhere when I was watching Ireland matches, or the big ones anyway. I had to go somewhere else to watch them, maybe because of the emotion of not being involved or something. I was always torn between wanting them to win and being totally sickened at not being there myself.

But I can put my hand on my heart and say I never wished a bad game on any of my rivals for the green jersey. I didn't think like that. Maybe it was a touch of arrogance on my part. I always believed I'd get my place back in the team. But I do know of one

Ireland player who came out and admitted that he wanted me to have a bad game when he wasn't playing. He'd feel his place was threatened if he saw me playing well. Maybe he was just being honest.

The lads did the business against Scotland in Murrayfield on the last day of the 2015 championship and then had to hope that England would fall short of the points margin they needed against France later that evening. It was unbelievable drama and by all accounts there was a great old Irish party in Edinburgh that night. And I was back at home peeling the spuds or changing nappies or picking toys up off the floor.

I actually didn't play my first game under Schmidt until the following August, a World Cup warm-up against Wales in Cardiff. It was my first Ireland Test game since March 2013 when Italy embarrassed us in Rome. We had one casualty after another that day. I was gone after 25 minutes with a shoulder injury that kept niggling away at me in the following months until eventually I had to get an operation on it. Between the shoulder, the knees and the brain, I lost two years out of the international game. So when I finally got picked by Joe for that Wales match, it was a massive relief and a massive amount of pressure too.

It might only have been a friendly but it was crucial for me. Two years is a long, long time to be away from the international game. The show moves on without you. Out of sight is out of mind. This was going to be my 40th cap but I felt like I had to prove myself all over again. I was very nervous all that week. Joe had picked me at 13 and that was playing on my mind too. Wales had moves to manipulate the opposing centres. I felt they'd be targeting me. I drove myself demented all that week, I was walking around my bedroom visualising the plays they would use to manipulate me and trying to visualise how I would adapt to those plays when I saw them coming. So, what might have seemed a bit of a nothing match to the general rugby public was actually a big deal for me. I had to perform. I had to gain Schmidt's trust.

We had a World Cup coming down the tracks and there was no guarantee I'd even make the squad. Thankfully, I did perform. I was sharp. I made breaks. I was moving well. Then on the half-hour Andrew Trimble emptied Eli Walker with a man-and-ball hit. The ball popped up to me lovely, I hit the gas and ran it in from forty yards. The game is beautiful when it gives you moments like that. It doesn't give you many moments like that.

It was my first international try in three years, my 14th in all. They gave me the man-of-the-match award, I was on cloud nine. Afterwards I was selected for the drugs test. The roof was closed on the Millennium Stadium during the game and I was so dehydrated it took me forever to produce a urine sample. I was trying to pour water down my neck but the testers were saying I couldn't because it might dilute the sample. I must've been there for ninety minutes to two hours, with them waiting for me to piss and me only dying to get into the showers and have a good wash and get the hell out of there. In the heel of the hunt it took me so long to do it that we had to head straight for the airport without me even getting a shower to wash off the sweat and the sticky spray.

That performance brought me right back into the Ireland picture, and just in time too for the World Cup. Three weeks later I came frighteningly close to being back out of it again. I was carried off on the motorised stretcher at the Aviva. It was the return friendly with Wales.

Around the hour mark I went to tackle George North. Tackling George North is like tackling a lorry that's coming to mow you down. You need to be setting yourself for impact. You need to be doing it right. I did it wrong. I got my timing off, I got my head on the wrong side and his knee banged into my face and fractured my jaw. The game was stopped, the medics came on, then the motorised stretcher came on. They lifted me onto it, strapped me down, put my neck in a brace and carted me off.

I dunno why but there I was lying on the flat of my back and I decided to give a thumbs up to the crowd on my way off. Maybe I knew I was going to be okay. My neck was okay. They brought me to hospital for scans which showed up the fracture. There was this big dent in my face too, like I'd been hit by a flying golf ball and it sunk a hollow in the side of my face. It was awful ugly looking.

Initially the doctors were convinced that my World Cup was over. They'd have to do surgery to fix the jaw and smooth out the hole in my face, like a panel beater fixing a dent in the body of a car I suppose. The surgery would mean I'd miss at least the first two games of the World Cup, which meant it would be touch and go whether I'd be selected for the squad at all. But the fracture wasn't too bad. Given time it could mend itself. So an operation was recommended by the doctors but it wasn't strictly necessary. And I could live with the cavity in my face, even if the sight of it would frighten children. The choice was to have the surgery and miss the first two games of the World Cup or take my chances and leave the fracture heal on its own. Sure it was no choice at all. I turned down the surgery and rejoined the squad.

I sat out the final warm-up match, against England at Twickenham a week later. We had another two weeks to the first game of the tournament, against Canada in Cardiff. It was just about enough time to free me up for selection.

I made the first fifteen for Canada. Then it was Romania at Wembley. The match was nothing to write home about but it was a special occasion because of the crowd – nearly 91,000 people, a huge number of them Irish. Obviously we won at a canter, I scored two tries, Tommy Bowe got another two, Zeebs lit it up from full back. Getting to play at such a famous stadium was a thrill. It meant a lot to my dad. It was a field of dreams to him. He'd grown up watching the FA Cup finals and the big England international soccer games there. I got a text from him the morning of the match wishing me the best of luck and saying that to get from Moyross to Wembley was no small achievement. It was very cool to play there and score a couple of tries and get man-of-the-match as well.

Joe moved me from wing to outside centre for the next match, against Italy at the Olympic Stadium in London, with Robbie Henshaw inside of me. After cruising the first two games, we were well off it for this one and struggled to carve many openings in the Italian defence. Robbie after twenty minutes popped a pass to me out of the tackle virtually on their line and after a quick bobble I dotted it down. It turned out to be our only try of the game.

We squeaked past Italy and moved on to France in the Millennium a week later, the match where my anxiety kicked in big time. First I was going to be rested but an injury to Jared

Payne meant I was drafted back in late on. I'd been in great form up until then. The try against Italy was my eighth in World Cups, meaning I had overtaken Drico's record as Ireland's top try-scorer at World Cups. But apart from that, my confidence was high, I could feel the sharpness and fitness in myself. I was bang in form. Then it unravelled very quickly. Having initially thought I wasn't going to start against France and their juggernauts in the midfield, finding out I was back in unnerved me. It shouldn't have but it did. I felt my preparation had been compromised.

There was pressure on to win the group and avoid New Zealand in the quarters. I couldn't quell the anxiety. I hadn't the tools at the time to do it. All the confidence I'd had evaporated. I carried a load of nerves with me onto the field and into the game and couldn't shake them off. Joe took me off shortly after the hour mark.

We beat France, though, and topped the group and avoided the All Blacks. It would be Argentina instead. But it decimated the back bone of the team. Sexton – gone, O'Mahony – gone, O'Connell – gone. Seán O'Brien was cited afterwards and suspended. That France game brought the curtain down on Paulie's outstanding career. I was right beside him when the injury happened. It was just on half-time. He was trying to poach a ball, he got hit and I just heard this horrible roar from him. I knew straightaway he was fucked. I knew from the roar coming out of him that he was in agony. I'll never forget the noise he made.

I was rooming with him in the Celtic Manor hotel that week. They brought him to hospital and the doctors did what they could and then he rejoined us back in camp. He spent the week in bed in horrendous pain, his hamstring sheared off his bone. And to give you an idea how bad my brain was at the time, I was envying him that he didn't have to worry about the Argentina game. I was thinking, wouldn't it be great to be lying in bed too and not having to face the stress of this week. I'd nearly cracked up before the France game, and in the dressing room afterwards too, and the whole thing was frightening the daylights out of me. But of course no one knew and now I was facing into another week of fear before a World Cup quarter-final. I was hating everything to do with it. And there was poor Paulie in the bed next to me trying to cope with this horrific injury when he'd have given anything to be able to lead us out onto the field against Argentina the following Sunday. Instead, I was helping him put his socks on in the morning because he was in too much pain to do it himself.

Then of course, to put the tin hat on it, Argentina went to town on us. In fairness to them, they played brilliantly on the day. They were devastating in the first quarter. I can remember looking at the scoreboard at one stage and we're well behind and saying to myself, cop the fuck on, get stuck in here, you're an Irishman, be proud of it, give it everything because that's what Irishmen are supposed to do. I suppose I was trying to cling on to something in the wreckage. Our World Cup was over.

Five months later, in March 2016, I played my 50th game for Ireland, against Scotland in the Six Nations at the Aviva. Rory Best wanted me to lead the team out to mark the occasion. I told him I didn't want to do that because getting the win was more important to me than doing that. Obviously the team winning is always going to be more important than the likes of me getting a ceremonial honour.

In hindsight, leading out the team with the ball in my hand wasn't really going to jeopardise the team in any way. But I wouldn't hear of it at the time. I told Bestie that if he tried to persuade me I'd have an argument with him. I was saying it was all about the team, not me, but probably it had as much to do with me not wanting to bring any attention onto myself, as usual. I should have done it, just for the honour of leading out your country for a match. But I was too uptight in myself back then to be able to enjoy an honour like that. We won anyway, fairly comfortably, and I did score a try, which was a nice way to mark the occasion.

In the five years plus since then, I've picked up another 43 caps. I can say hand on heart that I've enjoyed the second half of my Ireland career a lot more than the first. Getting older has its compensations. I've enjoyed the second half more because I've been able to relax more into the job. The knowledge and experience I've accumulated has made me more comfortable. I understand the job better, I understand the game better. I know the level of preparation that's required. All that experience has made me feel more secure in myself at that level. I've been there and I've done it, over and over and over. I suppose it's like any career in that regard. The more you do it, the more comfortable you get with it. That has taken a lot of the fear away. I don't suffer as much from the imposter syndrome that used to undermine me.

That season, 2015/16, was virtually a full twelve-month job. We spent June on tour in South Africa. Ireland had never beaten the Springboks on their home soil. We did it in the first Test in Cape Town. It was lovely to be part of something historic. It was Andy Farrell's first game as the new defence coach. You'd have been tested to the limit with fifteen men on the field but when CJ was sent off we had to spend nearly a full hour working with fourteen. A lot of lads put in a serious shift that day. We were under the pump but someone somewhere always came up with the vital tackle.

Joe again decided to rest me for the next Test. It was just as well because I came down with an awful virus on the Tuesday. We'd gone out to dinner a couple of nights after the first match and later that night back in my room, I spent more time in the bathroom than in the bed. When I wasn't puking I was sitting on the pot with diarrhoea. When I wasn't doing one I was doing the other. And there were one or two moments when I was trying to do both at the same time. It wiped me out completely. I lost several pounds in a matter of days. I was down to 82kgs. I couldn't even be around the lads. I was rooming with Murr and I had to move out of the room in case I passed it on to him. I watched the match in Ellis Park from my bed, in between visits to the jacks. Leading 19-3 at half-time it looked as if the lads were on the brink of a Test series win in South Africa for the first time ever. They swamped us in the last quarter to leave it one-all going into the final match in Port Elizabeth. I finally started coming round early in the last week. I was getting all the fluids into me and the food was staying down and my energy was coming back. I got back in for the third Test. We should have won that game. We were the better team by a distance. We butchered several try chances through wrong decisions or poor execution. We had them on the rack at times and just lacked the killer instinct to finish them off. A series win in South Africa would've been a massive achievement. That was a missed opportunity.

When the next opportunity came to make history, they took it. The famous win over New Zealand in Chicago that November. Of course, I was stuck in Limerick still simmering with anger that I wasn't over there with them. The day of the match I got a few photos and messages on my phone from Zebo and Murray in Chicago. They sounded very relaxed altogether. And I was like, Jesus Christ, ye're playing the All Blacks you know. But they were very chilled about it. They were like, no, there was a feeling in the air, they had a sense that something special was about to go down. It was just a vibe, a really good vibe. And sure enough, they came up trumps.

Murray was sensational that day. If you ever want to see a player in the state of flow, look at Murr in that match. He was in the zone, the flow state. He was the best rugby player in the world that day. Rob Kearney was incredible too. Well they all were, but Rob was just outstanding. But for me, I was once again caught between being happy for the lads and gutted for myself. Absolutely gutted. The lads had made history. The scenes on the field were fantastic. They had done the figure eight salute to Axel before the game. Then they'd gone out and done him proud. I was a bit shattered by the whole emotion of it all. My mood was fairly black that night. I texted Mike Sherry saying I couldn't wait to get the fuck out of this game. It was bringing me nothing but misery. I couldn't wait until I was retired. Obviously, I was being a bit hasty! Five years later and I'm still hanging around. Mike was like, just hang in there, your day will come, you'll be part of these big days too.

Two weeks later New Zealand got their revenge in Dublin. They were highly motivated and very aggressive that day. I think there was an element of them putting us back in our place for having the cheek to beat them at all. Maybe they thought that Ireland should never beat the All Blacks ever. I wasn't selected for that game.

A week later I was back in for the final match of the autumn series, against Australia. That was a terrific match, Australia were in brilliant form, the second half see-sawed one way and the other before we took the lead again in the 65th minute. It was a really well-worked move across the line before Zeebs threw it out to me on the touchline and I dotted it down in the corner. It turned out to be the winning score. It meant Ireland had beaten South Africa, New Zealand and Australia in the one calendar year. Being involved in that one took a bit of the sour taste off missing Chicago.

It meant too that we headed for the 2017 Six Nations full of confidence and raring to go. Then Scotland turned us over in Murrayfield in the first match. That was the day the police escort took a wrong turn and our bus ended up arriving late at the stadium. Joe was going mad. Our pre-match schedule would normally be timed to the last minute. Now it was all over the shop. And to make matters worse, when we got off the bus inside the ground we had to walk behind a fella playing the bagpipes.

The dressing rooms were three or four hundred yards away and here we were traipsing after this spanner playing the bagpipes and walking at a snail's pace. Joe was going ballistic, roaring and shouting. We only had about fifteen minutes to get togged out and onto the field. It was mind games. It's happened us a few times with Munster too in Scotland, people making things awkward for you in little ways. Anyway, it was a shit start to a championship where we were being talked up as potential

Grand Slam winners. But that was the Grand Slam gone there and then.

I had a decent campaign and with the Lions tour of New Zealand coming up that summer, I was being touted in a fair few media outlets as a possible tourist. A lot of rugby pundits, former players and coaches, were giving me the nod too. I think I must've made the mistake of listening to the hype because when Warren Gatland announced his squad, I was disappointed not to be included. Not crushed or anything like that but disappointed all the same.

It worked out okay in the end. Ireland had a summer tour of America and Japan lined up. It was designed mainly for the young generation coming through, but Joe decided to bring along a few of the old hands like myself, Dev Toner and Cian Healy. It turned out to be the most enjoyable tour I ever did in my career. It had a lovely, relaxed vibe. Joe basically left the three of us veterans alone while he did his schooling on the young lads. Our week in the USA was basically a holiday.

My hotel room happened to have a fantastic view of the Empire State Building. That was the sight that greeted me every morning when I pulled back the curtains.

We played their national team on a scorching hot day in New Jersey. They weren't great to be fair, so I filled my boots. Apparently I broke a few Irish records for line breaks and metres gained in a match. The stats on the IRFU website say I carried for 218 metres. I can remember being properly in the state of flow that day.

Naturally all the young lads went out on a good session in New York that night. And me with the sensible head on me stayed in and ordered a club sandwich up to my room and watched a UFC fight on the telly with a couple of the other lads. My excuse was that I was exhausted from all the running in the heat of the day! But I was just being old and lazy.

I was rooming with one of the rookies. He was the opposite. He was mad for road. He was delighted to get his international cap that day. Wild horses wouldn't have stopped him from hitting the tiles that night. He arrived in at some godforsaken hour upside down from drink.

I was in the other bed pretending to be asleep. He managed to get the door open alright but every step after that was a bit of a challenge. I could hear him slapping off every wall before he managed to find the bed. Then he spent about a half hour trying to get his shoes off. I was cracking up with a fit of the giggles, I could barely keep in the laughing.

On to Japan then for the two Test games there. We stayed in the Conrad in Tokyo, an absolutely incredible hotel, the luxury of it was unbelievable. It was times like that when you'd think of your roots and where you'd come from. Our little house in Dalgaish Park, Moyross, where my baby sister slept in her cot at the end of my bed cos she didn't have a room of her own. From there to a hotel in New York looking out at the Empire State Building and then on to this spectacular place in the heart of one of the great cities of the world.

I took my form with me from America and racked up a load of line breaks in both Tests in Japan. So at one of our team meetings there, Joe was showing examples on video of backline moves and attacking options and whatever. Next thing he puts up a bit of a montage of my line breaks and tries and there's a caption to go with it – 'Lord Earls'. And I was like, oh shit, the slagging is going to be desperate now. I could feel my face turning red. I think Joe was enjoying my discomfort as well. He actually had a good sense of humour, when he was in the mood to show it. But he was definitely looking out for me and always trying to boost my confidence.

He was very good to me. In fact, I could do no wrong, even when I did do wrong. There was one incident in the first Test against Japan where Luke McGrath was playing scrum half and he put up a box kick and I chased it. But I misread the flight of it and the ball hit me on the back of the head and Joe afterwards blamed the kick! But actually it was a perfect box kick, I'd just made a balls of it. I was a bit embarrassed about Lukey getting the blame.

I went up to him after the meeting and told him it was a great kick and that I'd misjudged it. It was no big deal in fairness. I came home from that tour in great fettle. And even though it was more like a B tour, I think it helped to fix me in Joe's mind as a nailed-on starter when the serious stuff came round. He saw what I could do with ball in hand, he wanted someone who could break lines and finish moves.

I missed the 2017 autumn series with a torn hamstring but when the Six Nations came round in 2018, I was good to go. At least I was good to go as far as Joe and the coaches and the outside world were concerned. But I had two secrets that very few people knew about. My mental health and the breathing crisis that would bring me to the brink of retirement in 2020.

For the first one, at least I had a diagnosis and medication and a strategy for living with it. For the second, I had no diagnosis, no clue what was wrong with me. The wonder is that Joe didn't spot there was something wrong with me. Usually, Joe missed nothing. He was eagle-eyed. You couldn't scratch yourself without him noticing it. But seemingly he didn't spot it. Or maybe he did spot it and decided just to keep a watching brief on it, I don't know.

Maybe I should have taken it up with him. Maybe I should have told him the truth. In theory at any rate, you are supposed to do the right thing for the team at all times. And if you know you're carrying an injury or an ailment that will affect your performance, shouldn't you tell the coaches about it? This is where it gets complicated. In theory, yes you should, in practice you won't. You won't because no player that I know of will ever volunteer to be de-selected. In rugby anyway, maybe all professional sports, you are always fighting for your place against your rivals for the jersey. It's not just a sport, it's your livelihood, your career, your money in the bank. It's one reason why fellas play injured all the time, especially in our line of work.

Rugby players are always carrying injuries. Usually the medical staff will know about it and treat it as best they can and talk it through with the player. Is he fit for the weekend, is he not fit for the weekend? A decision will be made in consultation with the player and the coaches. But sometimes it is mind over matter too. A player with a high tolerance threshold for pain can force the matter and make himself available. Fellas will play through the pain barrier if they want to play badly enough.

My case was a little bit different in that the medical staff couldn't figure out what the hell was wrong with me. I didn't know either. All I knew was that I couldn't fuckn breathe properly. And that's a fairly significant handicap when you're playing high level rugby. I didn't know what to do about it except keep doing what I'd always done, which was turn up for training and try and get through each session as best I could. It was pure stubbornness. It was the instinct to survive I suppose. It was the fight to hold onto your place. It was a case of springing into action when the ball came your way and then hoping it wouldn't come your way again until your lungs had recovered. I learned to adapt and manage my way through training sessions and through games. I covered up the problem, I concealed it and I soldiered on. Then I'd get home and I'd wonder, how the fuck am I going to go through this again? Then I'd go into training the next day and go through it again. That's how it was until finally the doctors in London came up with the answer in November 2020.

That's how it was as we headed into the 2018 Six Nations. In a roundabout sort of way, the battles I was having with my bipolar actually helped me cope in the battles with my physical health.

I'd really started working on my mental health in 2016. I'd immersed myself in research, I was doing my journaling, my self-talk, my self-image. I was changing my patterns of thinking, my habits of self-criticism. I was changing my diet in ways that were really improving my moods. I was taking the medication. I was practising the visualisation techniques that Keith Barry had taught me. I was basically in the process of re-wiring my brain. All of it helped me cope with this crisis in my breathing. I think otherwise I'd have completely panicked and let it get on top of me. But somehow I managed to manage it. I nursed it game by game and worked my way around it. My lungs weren't working but my brain was working a lot better than it used to. I had the tools to cope with it, just about. It was literally a case of mind over matter.

So when the crunch moment arrived in injury time in Paris on February 3, and Sexton put in that crossfield kick, I was looking for it, I wanted it, I didn't give a fuck about my lungs. We all did our bit during that famous forty-one phases before Johnny landed the drop goal. I was very pleased that I'd done my bit too. Murray's pass was a peach, Johnny lined it up and pulled the trigger. I went chasing the ball in case it came back off the post but in my mind I was thinking, please go over, please go over, and then she sailed between the posts and we all went apeshit. It was one of the sweetest moments I ever enjoyed on a rugby field. And afterwards I was thinking, you know what, maybe my luck has turned. Maybe there is something in this positive thinking malarkey. Maybe you actually can make your wishes come true, if you work for them hard enough and you do everything you can to force them into reality. And part of it is imagining them into reality.

That's what positive visualisation is, I think, it's using your imagination to help turn your heart's desire into reality. I really felt Sexton's drop goal was a momentum shift for me in my career. I felt like my luck had finally turned and that I had earned the right for my luck to turn. The depression I was prone to, the black moods, sort of lifted off me. Christ I felt bulletproof that evening. The adrenaline and the optimism that was coursing through me was unreal.

Of course, all the talk afterwards with the press and the public was the Grand Slam. It's on now. Of course it was on. Once we got out of Paris with a win, it was on. We weren't talking about it within the camp but we weren't denying it either. We'd set out our goals at a training camp in Spain and we'd talked openly about winning the Grand Slam. It didn't matter that we'd have to go to Stade de France and Twickenham to do it. Now we were up and running.

On the wing opposite me, Jacob Stockdale was announcing himself to the world with a fantastic scoring streak. He bagged two more tries against Scotland in Dublin. England had to win in France later that evening to keep their championship hopes alive. We were at dinner when that match finished. France won and CJ Stander turned to me at the table and said, that's it, we're after winning the championship. Some of the lads were fairly casual about it because they'd already won titles in 2014 or 2015 but I was delighted. I'd won something in a green jersey at last. But of course everyone was switching their thoughts to Twickenham a week later.

We blew them out of the water. It was one of the great days. Edel and the girls were over for it. Funny enough, I didn't have any nerves the night before. I was in a great place. Our confidence was so high and Joe had us so well prepared, it almost felt like we were destined to win it before a ball had even been kicked. We were going to win the Grand Slam on St Patrick's Day and that's exactly what we did. We were 14-5 up just on half-time. I was standing on the touchline and the lads on the sideline were screaming at me to get the message to Murray to kick the ball out. They were happy to be going in 14-5 at the interval. We all were. Next thing Murray was popping it out of a ruck to Stockdale and Jacob was chipping it over the top and winning the race to the touchdown.

At the final whistle, I took Ella May and Laurie onto the pitch. They finally got to experience what I'd been promising them for years, walking around the field with their dad and a big shiny trophy. And I was able to fulfil my boyhood dream of doing exactly the same thing. It was magic. Except for the fact that it was bloody freezing and poor Edel and the girls were shivering. And the fact that Joe Marler had hit me at the side of a ruck with seven minutes to go and I did the MCL muscle in my knee. So I was hobbling around taking the lap of honour and the women in my life were shaking with the cold but we were loving every second of it. The photos we have from that occasion are special. My father was there too and I was so happy to see him so happy. He got to see me win a Grand Slam and lift the trophy.

Parents suffer a lot if they've got a child involved in serious sport. They suffer all your setbacks and disappointments just as much as you do. Maybe more. They live your pain and heartbreak.

My mother finds it hard to go to games, even to watch them, because of how nervous she gets. It had been a rough few years for my mam and dad, seeing me struggle with all my ups and downs, mainly downs. They wouldn't admit it but I know there were times when I was so low, they'd have been relieved to see me pack it in and retire. They saw how much I was suffering and they wanted it to end. But here at last there was joy, real joy, and vindication. For me it made that day in Twickenham all the sweeter and deeper in meaning.

Back in the hotel that night I had a couple of drinks but my knee was in a brace and I was wrecked so the four of us went up to the room and just chilled out together on the big bed. I was a contented man. I had the people who mean most to me in the world around me. We could hear the shouting and roaring coming up from the ground floor where an almighty St Patrick's Day hooley was underway. One by one we drifted off to sleep. It was one of those perfect days. Back in Dublin the next evening we had a big celebration in the Shelbourne Hotel and the next morning the family flew out to Dubai for a week's holidays.

Ireland were now on a twelve-game winning streak. It came to an end against Australia in Brisbane in the first Test of the summer tour. I was taken off after 24 minutes with a knock to the head. I actually felt fine, I wasn't concussed or even dazed, but the independent doctor examined me in the medical office down the tunnel and decided I shouldn't return. I wasn't happy about it but he didn't care whether I was or not – and he was right too.

The second Test in Melbourne we played much better and delivered a first Irish win on Australian soil since 1979. I scored a try in the 54th minute. It seemed like a crucial score at a crucial time. I had an awful grapple with Israel Folau to try and stay in touch and get the ball down. Then Bernard Foley came across and I wriggled and twisted under him and planted it at the corner flag. Christ I fought might and main to get that score. Then the TMO decided I wasn't in control of the ball when touching it down. He was wrong, I got downward pressure with my fingers, but it was chalked off and I was fuckn fuming. It didn't matter, Tadhg Furlong crashed over less than a minute later and we were on our way.

Our forwards fronted up unbelievably well on that tour. They were outstanding. We had massive Irish support for the first two matches and again for the third one in Sydney. It's a magnificent city but we saw a bit too much of it on the way to the stadium. Again, a police escort that mysteriously goes the roundabout way. Anyway, we were around long enough to be able to deal with stupid mind games like that.

But this was the middle of summer now and in reality the

squad was running on empty. The Aussies came at us hard and often in the final quarter. We kept tackling and kept surviving. A big theme for us on that tour was to back up the Grand Slam. That was the standard now and we didn't want to be reverting back to the old Irish habit of up and down. Great one day, shite the next. We wanted to prove we were a proper champion team. We believed that winning a Test series in Australia for the first time since '79 would prove our status in the international game. Winning the series was a real coup and a major statement. Kurtley Beale and David Pocock were on the pitch in Sydney that night, twelve and a half years after I'd played against them for the Ireland U19s in Ravenhill.

It was a late kick-off that night so by the time we got out in Sydney a lot of bars were shutting up shop. We knocked back a load of drinks in double quick time and headed back to the hotel.

Joe and the coaching staff were in the team room and they were enjoying a few jars too. The mood was fairly merry. Next thing the craic started. We found a few rugby balls and started doing a bit of a piss-take of Joe's coaching sessions. Like, tackle situations and hitting rucks and presenting the ball perfectly and shouting out the instructions that Joe would be shouting, in his New Zealand accent and all. We were using his buzz words and exaggerating everything, especially the accent. I can't remember who all was in the room that night but Sexton and Murray were definitely two of the comedians. Ah sure Joe was loving it, everyone was laughing their heads off. I don't think people gave him enough credit for the sense of humour he had – but he definitely did have it. He could take a slagging. It just had to be at the right time and the right place. And when you've just won a Test series in Australia, it was definitely the right time and the right place.

We only got a few hours sleep that night. The next day we headed for lunch down to the hotel's steakhouse restaurant. A bunch of us took a table, Sexton included. Myself and Johnny are massive rugby league fans. Next thing two immortals of the game walk in – Johnathan Thurston and Darren Lockyer. These fellas are gods of rugby league. Me and Johnny were as excited as two kids when we saw them.

We were wondering if we should go over to them and ask them for a picture. But we were thinking it'd be a bit embarrassing to be behaving like fan boys in front of them. We were going, will we, won't we, will we, won't we? We didn't in the end. We didn't fancy the idea of invading their privacy, they probably have to put up with it every day of their lives. So we left them to their lunch and I regret it now.

I'd love to have a photo in my memorabilia with Thurston and Lockyer. They both played their careers in the National Rugby League in Australia. I love watching the NRL. It has some of the best athletes in the world playing in it. I mean the best athletes in any sport anywhere. What they do is phenomenal. And as a game, rugby league is amazing. It's eighty minutes of non-stop play. The amount of tackles they have to make in one game would put us union lads to shame. And the way they can finish tries, they're like acrobats and gymnasts as well as rugby players. They're incredibly flamboyant.

We spent the afternoon and evening in Sydney Harbour. It was class. The sun was shining, everyone was happy, the beer and wine were flowing. We were all just sitting there going, you know what, it was all worth it, all the struggles and all the shit that you've to deal with as a player, it's all worth it for moments like this.

The try I scored against England in the Six Nations in 2021, the one that was disallowed, the somersault finish was inspired by the NRL lads. It didn't matter to the result but it would've been nice if it stood just because of the fancy finish! It was Johnny, of course, who set it up with his cross kick. He just dropped it on a postage stamp in the corner for me. The try I got against Italy in the first round didn't affect the result either. We were already thirty-one points up and the clock was in the red. The lads take the ball up to the five-metre line and suddenly Johnny whips out this pass to me off his left hand, an absolute bullet pass that takes out two Italian defenders and leaves me with a handy touchdown in the corner. You'll see me smiling on the video. It's not because I've scored. It is out of admiration for the pass. Just the speed and precision of it. I was smiling because it was so good.

Sexton is the best player I've ever played with. And I was privileged to play with some great ones. But he's the greatest for me. What he gets out of a team, what he gets out of himself, his whole understanding of the game is world class. He knows everyone else's role inside out, as well as his own. He has a rugby brain like a computer. It's like the game slows down in his head when he's making decisions. His ability to see scenarios on the run and make his decision at the last second is fascinating to watch up close. He will leave it to the last fraction of the last second. And he is a ferocious competitor. He has all the mental and physical courage. The success that Leinster and Irish rugby has had over the last decade and more, he has been a major part of it all. Look at what he has won, what he has achieved. For me he's one of the greatest Irish sportsmen of the last twenty years.

Back from Australia, we picked up where we left off the following November with a clean sweep in the autumn series. Beating the All Blacks in Dublin was another box ticked for me. It was the first time an Ireland team had ever beaten New Zealand on Irish soil. It was class being part of that performance. It was the best atmosphere I've ever played in at the Aviva, bar none. It was absolutely electric.

The crowd were singing *The Fields of Athenry* as the All Blacks launched one last attack to try and save the match. Stockdale again came up with a super individual try. Everything we had worked on in training that week came off. Including the haka. We spoke about it and planned for it. We would line up for it and when they started it we would take one step forward. It was to symbolise that we weren't going to take a backward step against them. It was saying, we're not worried about your haka. I didn't even look at it. I just picked a spot high above their heads and looked at that. Then when they'd finished the haka we would come round in a circle to symbolise our unity. O'Mahony gave an incredible performance. Several of the lads put in incredible performances. Myself and O'Mahony were having a few quiet pints in the Constitution Room in the Shelbourne Hotel that night and Pete's partner Jess had her camera phone out and just happened to press click at the perfect moment. The two of us were roaring laughing about something or other and she just caught it. It's a great picture.

That was a golden year, 2018. I turned 31 the month before the All Blacks match. I got huge satisfaction out of our achievements that year. The Grand Slam, the series win in Australia, beating New Zealand. It was very fulfilling for me having won nothing for almost ten years. You want to be lifting trophies and making your bit of history. The good days came late in my career and I enjoyed them all the more for that reason. I was still struggling a lot mentally and physically but my brain was getting better, my head wasn't as cloudy, I was able to enjoy the happy days.

England came to Dublin for the first round of the 2019 Six Nations intent on taking us down a peg or two. I had to come off at half-time with a hip pointer. Maro Itoje clattered into me from the kick-off and that's where the damage was done. I thought I might run it off but everything just shut down around the hip and it became quite swollen. Then Tom Curry hit me late after I cleared a ball and Itoje ploughed into me in the air so I was fairly well rattled.

I got an awful whack off Itoje in that second collision with him. By half-time the whole hip was swollen, it had bone bruising on it and in that case you literally seize up, you can't even walk with it. So that was that.

We won the next three games, I got a try in each of them so I was in a rich vein. Against France we had a trick play. I was standing at the front of the lineout, peeled around as pre-ordained, CJ broke off the back of the maul and popped the pass that put me clean through the gap. It worked like clockwork. We were all about consistency in 2018, backing up one good performance with another, maintaining a high standard game after game.

But it started to slip during this Six Nations. A week after beating France, Wales nearly whitewashed us in Cardiff. They were 25-0 up with the clock in the red when Jordan Larmour took the bare look off the scoreboard.

Anyway, Wales won the Grand Slam but the big show that

year was going to be the World Cup in Japan. We were supposed to be one of the favourites after our performances in 2018 so I think maybe we turned a bit of a blind eye to our dip in form in the 2019 Six Nations. Instead it would be all systems go for Japan in September/October.

And a few of us were maybe a bit too keen to get our systems going. A bunch of us players headed off for our summer holidays with our partners and children. We went to Quinta do Lago on the Algarve. The plan was to use the sports campus there for workouts. It would be kind of like a pre-season before the official pre-season training. We would leave no stone unturned for the World Cup.

I went training most days. I didn't touch much alcohol and I minded my food intake too. I was going to come back in super shape. Edel was not one bit impressed. She had gone to have a holiday, I had gone to train so I wasn't exactly in a holiday state of mind. She said we'd regret it. She said we were training too hard too soon and we'd burn out from it. And she was right. It didn't do me any favours anyway. In August I tore the patella tendon in my knee. It was touch and go for a while whether I'd make the squad at all. Fortunately the rehab went well, albeit I missed the first game of the tournament, against Scotland in Yokohama. We looked to be up and running after that performance.

Next up was Japan, the host nation. I was wary of Japan, having played against them on the 2017 tour. I was warning all week, do not underestimate these fellas, they're hardy bastards and they don't give up. If we think it's going to be a walk in the park, we're in for a rude awakening. And we got some rude awakening. They played with manic intensity. They ran us ragged. Their home crowd was going nuts. That was one bad result – very bad. One of the worst of my career. Then New Zealand went to town on us in the quarter-final. They were incredibly pumped up for it. I presume it had something to do with us beating them in Dublin the previous November. They poured everything into that match and basically we were powerless to stop them. Everything we'd practised the week before went arseways. It was just wave after wave of speed and power coming at you. Another World Cup done and dusted without us really firing a shot.

In the long post-mortems that followed, a lot of people felt that we'd peaked as a team in 2018. I didn't want to entertain that notion at all. But sometimes when you're stuck in the middle of something you don't see the wood for the trees. You don't have that perspective on things. Maybe there is some truth in it. Every team has its life cycle. There's only a certain amount of time you can sustain your best form before it starts to turn. The game itself has you on a life cycle all the time. Highs followed by lows followed by highs followed by lows.

Japan in 2019 was one of the worst of the lows. Like most of the rest of the lads, I went out on the piss in Tokyo to drown my sorrows and then we headed for home with our tail between our legs.

Rory Best called it a day after the quarter-final. I have the height of time for him as a player and a person. He was one of the best captains I've played under because he had massive respect from us as a player and leader. But he could also be one of the lads too. He'd be leading the way on the social side as well as the playing side of things. Edel and me and Rory and his wife Jodie have become good pals. Their children and ours like hanging out together too. He gave his heart and soul to the green jersey. I know that in rugby, as in any walk of life, people go their separate ways after working together but I'm hoping me and Bestie will always keep in touch and remain friends for life.

We knew the World Cup was going to be Rory's last hurrah. We knew it was going to be Joe's swansong too. For a man who never did anything by half measures, he had probably given all he could give at that stage. It was such a pity that it all ended on such a low. He deserved a happier exit than that. It had gone so well for so long.

Joe had a clear vision about what he needed to do with the Ireland team when he took over. We lacked the natural size and power of a South Africa. We didn't have the skillset of the All Blacks. So he worked around those deficiencies. He came up with ways to compensate for them. And a big part of his philosophy was about maximising our preparation for every spare inch he could find. That was why every single detail was boxed off. It was why he kept drilling good habits into us. It was why every player had to be switched on every day at training. It was why he was fanatical about our in-game discipline. And why he was obsessed with the breakdown and executing it with absolute efficiency time and again. It was why he demanded full-on concentration all the time. The "mind gym", he called it. The upshot was that most of us individuals became better performers under him. Which meant that the team was accumulating these standards too. And then our confidence started growing. The results started rolling in, so our confidence rose again. It became a virtuous circle like that.

The one complaint was that he held our hand nearly too much. That he was too overbearing. That we ended up playing to his prescriptions rather than playing the game as we saw it ourselves.

Personally I never had an issue with that. It was working. We were winning. I went into games full to the brim with confidence because of his planning and preparation. I knew what I had to do. Every single player knew what he had to do. I was known for being a broken field runner, a fella who could feed off spontaneous moments, offloads out of the tackle and stuff like that. So in theory I shouldn't have thrived under Schmidt because he didn't want broken play, he didn't like unstructured play. Arguably he took that spontaneous facet of my game away from me. But I didn't mind one bit. I found you can be creative within structured play too.

Generally we always knew what we were doing in first phase, second phase, third phase, fourth phase. It wasn't heads up rugby. It was programmed. But it created a lot of chances and it won a lot of games. It broadened our rugby education. It made us think more about what we were doing and why we were doing it. I, for one, definitely learned a huge amount from his coaching and his thinking. The biggest victories of my Ireland career came under his management. Our generation of Irish players had some of the best times of our life under Joe Schmidt. We should never forget what he did for Irish rugby. I certainly won't.

16

MALDINI

I'LL HAVE TURNED 34 BY THE TIME THIS BOOK HITS the shops. I am starting this final chapter on Monday, August 23, 2021. It's the day after the Limerick hurlers have won the All-Ireland final. It's their third All-Ireland title in four years. Back in 2018 their manager John Kiely invited me in to do a Q&A with them. They are a serious group of sportsmen. I'm not joking when I say that maybe Munster could return the compliment now and invite some of them into our camp to do a talk with us.

As a fellow sportsman, I admire everything about them. Their talent, their ambition, their total commitment, their winning mentality. As a Limerick man, I'm a little bit envious of what they've achieved. They have brought the Liam MacCarthy Cup back to the city and county three times now. I would give anything to be able to do the same with the European Cup. I would love to be able to parade that cup down O'Connell Street like those boys did in 2018 and like they would have done in 2020 and 2021 were it not for Covid. That has been my dream since I saw the Munster team of 2006 do it. I was on the open-top bus when they came home again with it in 2008, but that was their achievement, not mine. I wanted to do it having earned it on the field of play. I still want to do it that way.

It's one reason why I'm back for another season. It's for another tilt at the big one. I don't think we'll be anyone's favourites for the Champions Cup but I do believe we have a squad now that is good enough to go all the way. Obviously, the proof will be in the pudding but I'm around long enough to know a good, deep squad when I see one – and this is a good, deep Munster squad.

For this campaign, 2021/22, I had my first proper pre-season in about five years because I wasn't coming back carrying an injury and I didn't have to worry about my breathing problems anymore. I did a lot of the hard pre-season slog with the rest of the lads, including the Bronco test where I was coming in under five minutes without being flat to the boards. I was keeping an eye on my speed levels in the sprint sessions and they were in good nick too. I was next to Jonny Wren for some of them. Jonny is a young pro with wheels to burn and we were finishing neck-and-neck, which was great for me. It was proof there was life in the old dog yet. If I lost my speed I'd be devastated. It's been my friend right throughout my career.

In fairness, the fitness staff were making a few allowances for my 'elder statesman' status. They didn't go the whole hog on me. They divided the squad up into a conditioning group, a speed group and a Maldini group. I was in the Maldini group. In fact, I was the only one in it! The idea goes back to when Bryce Kavanagh was our head of fitness a decade ago. Bryce is with the Football Association in England now. He was inspired by the Italian soccer players who kept on playing at the highest level well into their late 30s. And the greatest of them all, Paolo Maldini, didn't retire until he was 41.

The basic concept is just common sense. If you value experience, look after it. And from what I can see, Italian soccer treasures experience. They are right too, in my opinion. It costs a lot of time and money to build up all that experience. You shouldn't get rid of it lightly. It is very valuable to a team. So you design a different fitness programme for them that's mostly about maintenance to keep them ticking over, rather than putting them through the grinder. You'll break down at that age if you're pushed too hard.

I feel very lucky to be getting this kind of treatment at Munster. The coaches, S&C, the physios, they look after my body really well. And to be fair to myself, I think I've looked after it pretty well too over the last ten years and more. The reward has been the longevity I'm enjoying now. So basically I'm the Maldini of Munster now! In fairness, I have a long way still to go if I want to match his longevity. Anyway, with Billy Holland retired, I'm the senior citizen now. If I'm not careful the young lads will soon enough be calling me Grandad.

I mean, one day last season I turned up at training wearing a Ronaldo jersey. The Brazilian Ronaldo. The coaches had us playing a bit of soccer just to get a break from the constant rugby and have a bit of fun. It was a retro shirt, a replica of the one he wore at the 1998 World Cup. And Craig Casey was there and I was like, do you remember this jersey, Ronaldo wore it at the 1998 World Cup? And Craig replied, "Sure I wasn't born until 1999!" Talk about time marching on.

It's amazing how things come full circle. When I was a young lad at Munster, Mossy Lawler was in the first-team squad and he was one of the older lads who looked after me. I was living in Moyross and he was living up by Edel's house close to Woodview and he used to give me lifts to Cork for our training sessions there. Craig's mother is Mossy's sister. His dad Gerry Casey is a development officer with Munster. I've known Gerry from the rugby scene in Limerick for years. So, it was an absolute pleasure to be able to present Craig with his first senior international jersey last February. He was named in the 23-man squad for the France game in the Six Nations after Conor Murray picked up a knock in training. Johnny Sexton was injured too so Iain Henderson took over as captain that week. The game was on the Sunday, Hendy asked me to do the honours for the traditional presentation of the first jersey at the team meeting on Saturday night. It was in the team room in the Shelbourne Hotel. There was a cameraman there to film it and hook it up by live video link to Craig's family in Limerick. It was a nice little ceremony. I spoke about how things had come full circle and how Mossy looked after me and I was delighted to be able to return the compliment all these years later. Not that Craig needs much looking after. He's an incredible professional with the heart of a lion who is destined for a long career.

Craig didn't make it off the bench for the France game but he got his first cap against Italy two weeks later. I got my ninety-first the same day. I finished 2020/21 on ninety-three. I never really kept count before. As everyone knows, you never look back in sport, you keep looking forward to the next target. So I never kept track. I used to have to text my father if I needed to find out how many caps I was on. But this summer past,

I'd be lying if I said I didn't think about the century as I was looking forward to the new season. I know we're not supposed to get ahead of ourselves, you can never do that in rugby when you're only one game away from a bad injury. But now that I'm in the nineties, occasionally my thoughts stray to making the hundred. That would be a nice achievement. It's not the be-all and end-all. I know that Peter Stringer finished on ninety-eight caps and you'd hear people saying that Strings must be sickened he didn't reach the ton. But how could you be sickened with ninety-eight international caps to your name?

I know I'm in bonus territory now. A century of caps would be the icing on the cake. But everything is dependent on me staying in top shape physically and in good form on the pitch, the same as it is for any other player. No coach is interested in your personal milestones. They are interested in you delivering where it matters. So if I want to stay in the Munster and Ireland teams I can't afford to let my standards slip a fraction. And I don't intend to either.

I am well aware too that when you get to my age, people are itching to move you on. One mistake and it's down to your age whereas ten years ago it'd just be a lapse in concentration or whatever. That's fuel for the fire too – proving anyone who'd doubt you wrong.

I have to admit there is one other big motivation for staying on. The nearer I'm getting to the end, the more I'm starting to fear it. And this is coming from someone who used to regularly talk about quitting. I used to say the job was six days of living the dream and eighty minutes of madness on a Saturday or Sunday. The build-up to that eighty minutes of madness sometimes dragged me down to the pits. I went through loads of phases in my career where I was seriously thinking about packing it in. The game had given me some of the best days of my life but also some of the worst days of my life. And when I was at my lowest ebb I'd be saying to myself, I just want to live a normal life. That was my mantra when I was feeling the fear. I just want to live a normal life. But now that a so-called normal life is starting to loom large in front of me, I'm starting to worry about that too.

I happened to bump into Eoin Reddan down in Kilkee during the summer and I was talking to him about it. Eoin retired in 2016 at the age of thirty-five. And his advice basically was to stay at it for as long as you can. You'll be long enough retired. As long as you're still competing to a high level, stick with it. There's nothing like it in civilian life, the buzz, the adrenaline, the craic in the dressing room, the camaraderie with the lads.

A big issue too is the routine that comes with being a professional sportsman, the structure it puts on your days. You know where you have to be every day. You are given your timetable every week. Be here, be there, do this, do that. They even tell you what gear to wear. Everything is mapped out for you so you don't have to plan anything or think about anything too much. Just turn up where you're told to turn up. Be on time and do your job. When you retire, all that is taken away. That's a bit scary. You wake up on a Monday morning, the first day of the rest of your life, and what do you do then? Okay, bring the kids to school, come home and then what? You could easily find yourself with a lot of empty days to fill, if you don't have something lined up.

I'm putting plans in place for when that day comes. I don't have the schooling or the qualifications to go into one of the professions, or into an office job. I don't have a trade. So I'm planning on going into business. I'm setting up a coffee roastery. It will be the only one in Limerick. I'm learning about the business from scratch. It's a steep learning curve. Once again, I'm putting myself way out of my comfort zone. But like a lot of rugby players I've become a bit of a coffee nerd. It's one of our treats when we're away on tour or in camp, sampling the best local coffee shops or brewing our own. When the Ireland squad went to New Zealand for the summer tour of 2012, we visited a roastery in New Plymouth one day and that planted a seed in me. A few years later I bought my own home roaster and started experimenting with various coffee beans from all over the world. I enjoy the process, it's hands on, you're working with machines and producing your own stuff.

That's for the future. Right now I'm strapped in for another season. And mentally I'm probably in the best place I've been in my whole career. I have a handle on the process now that I didn't have in the past. I know who I am, I have confidence in what I'm doing. I have confidence in my preparation, which is everything really. So the thought of that eighty minutes at the weekend doesn't spook me the way it used to. I still have my moments of panic but I'm much better at silencing the wild thoughts in my mind. I'm good at telling myself to cop on now and remind myself how lucky I have been to live this life.

And I'm not trying to be perfect anymore. I've come to understand that perfection isn't real. It doesn't exist. I wish I'd learned this sooner. It would have saved me a lot of stress. It would have saved me from punishing myself when I made mistakes. It would have saved me from taking it so seriously. I would have relaxed a lot more. I relax plenty now. In a funny sort of way, I'm probably becoming more immature, as in enjoying the whole thing more, not tensing up over what I eat and drink and how I behave. I'll have a nice glass of rosé and a good meal. There's a certain way you're supposed to behave as a Munster man in particular. You're supposed to be very serious about it all the time. But I don't sweat that sort of small stuff anymore. I try not to sweat the big stuff either. I try to switch off the week of a game, not think about it at all, enjoy my days with Edel and the kids, then switch onto the game before kick-off.

I'm nice and relaxed even walking out the tunnel before a match. I find it less draining on my energy that way. It works for me because I know who I am now. I've figured out what works for me, never mind anyone else. You have to be true to yourself instead of copying every other fella. I wish I'd figured that out too when I was younger, but better late than never I suppose.

If it sounds like I have it all figured out now, the truth is I don't. Not even close. This is an ongoing process. I still have plenty of days when the anxiety and fear, I can feel them climbing into my brain. Hank the bastard is still lurking around, always looking to become a lodger in my head again. And I know that as long as I'm playing rugby, it will open the door for him. That's the bargain I've made. Playing rugby is like leaving the doors and windows open in my brain. Hank can creep in like a burglar and really destroy the place if I let him. But I've learned how to not let him. Or at least to minimise the effect he has.

I've spent my whole career fighting off the voices in my head telling me to quit, telling me I was shit, and so on. I can say I've won that battle because I'm still in my boots at thirty-four. Rugby is where I want to be, it's what I want to do, and the willpower to stay in the game was stronger than the stranger in my head trying to ruin it for me. He popped his head in the door a few times during the summer. I got flashes of the old anger and paranoia and anxiety. And it pisses me off that it still happens because by nature I am not that sort of person at all. It's a regret of mine that my bipolar condition distorted the real me. When it was controlling me it presented a version of myself to friends and family and team mates that was different to the true me. I'm sure there are former team mates of mine who thought I was a right oddball or a strange fish or a bit of a bollocks. I probably alienated them in some way or another because of how I was acting or behaving. I'm really sorry if I did or said things that people found weird or hostile or whatever. All I can say is that my true identity was lost in the fog of this condition. The bipolar was controlling me in ways I didn't even know. I'm happy to be able to say that I am much more in control of it now.

When it afflicted me in the bad old days, it used to hang around for weeks at a time. Now it's a day or two maximum. It's never a sustained period anymore. Maybe one or two days every two months rather than six weeks of it. I am proud of that. It's a massive achievement for me, getting on top of this condition.

All the work I've done, the research and nutrition and self-improvement and understanding of the illness, it has changed my life. It has been the biggest battle of my life and I'm proud to say I've slowly but surely got on top of it. There is a journey to go, I am still taking my medication and I hope one day after I quit rugby to be able to quit that too. But in the meantime I feel like I've won this big victory for my health, for my soul, for my family.

Even being able to talk about it is a big step forward for me. At the same time, I feel very vulnerable about putting it out there. I feel exposed. I'm worried about how people will judge me. It's a big thing for me, releasing this personal secret out into the world, having kept it to myself for the guts of twenty years. On the other hand, I do feel a certain responsibility to share it with the public and show a bit of leadership in this regard. If my little bit of profile can be used for good, then I hope this will do some good. I hope it will give courage to fellow sufferers to seek help and share their burden with people who love them and people who can help them.

Joey Johns, one of the all-time greats of Australian rugby league, came out publicly with his bipolar condition years ago. He gave me a bit of courage to do the same and I'm hoping I can pass on that gift in turn.

That's it. That's my story. I'm still finding it a bit surreal that I've actually done a book. Me of all people! But I've done it now, for better or for worse. It's called *Fight or Flight* for a reason. I've done both in my time, taking flight on the field, fighting my troubles off it. There have been times when I didn't know which to do – stand and fight or run away.

On my bad days I think life is shit, life is tough, there is too much suffering and loss. On my good days I love life and all it has given me. What a privilege I have had to wear the red of Munster and the green of Ireland for so long. What luck I have had to be able to turn the sport I loved as a boy into the profession that has provided so well for my family.

Rugby has transformed my life. It has given me a fair few kickings too. But I know already it was a price worth paying. When I'm retired I will be forever grateful that I went the distance, the full twelve rounds, and that I was still standing when the whistle blew for the last time. After all, it's what the song says, the one I learned in Limerick when I was a child. Stand up and fight until you hear the bell, stand toe to toe, trade blow for blow. Keep punching till you make your punches tell, show that crowd what you know. Until you hear that bell, that final bell, stand up and fight like hell.